MW01699206

Agile Multi-Project Management

Portfolio management, Resource management and Product management

Ulla Sebestyén

Parmatur

Parmatur HB

Ängstäppevägen 6

14464 Rönninge

Sweden

parmatur.com

info@parmatur.com

This book can be used together with The Agile Pulse Model.

Translator Rebecca Lynn Foreman

Print: A-A books on demand AB, Visby 2017

Illustration: Solveig Hellmark image 1-1 and 2-16. Cover: geralt / Pixabay. Other author.

ISBN 978-91-639-2459-0

Contents

Introduction

It has been 10 years since the first edition of this book came out in Swedish in the summer of 2006. When I wrote the book, I had the feeling that we had managed to solve an age-old problem, namely how to achieve sustainable efficiency and productivity in development operations. But it is only now that I can say with certainty that our concept genuinely works. At our most recent user group meeting, companies that have now been using the Pulse concept for many years reported that they continue to achieve high efficiency in their development work. Lead times in their projects are significantly shorter, less than half of what they were previously. Project throughput has multiplied many times over for most enterprises. Before Pulse, many of the enterprises completed a project or two each year. With Pulse, it is common for them to finish one project a month, which is also associated with significantly better profitability.

How is this possible? A big part of the secret is that we have relied on what researchers have highlighted for more than 60 years: bureaucratic, closed organizations do not work. Such organizations are unoriginal, inflexible, and inefficient for all kinds of activities, making them especially unwieldy for innovative development. In the bureaucratic organization, the existing business model is associated with an organization chart, which severely limits the leeway for development work to minor product updates within existing frameworks. The cross-functional teamwork necessary for the development of pioneering new products does not exist but, at best, is limited to discussions at meetings and shared documents.

Poor productivity in development operations has not been caused primarily by a lack of ideas, though. On the contrary, too many initiatives have often been pursued at the same time. These have usually competed with one another and habitually lacked a solid footing in actual needs. The operation has become overloaded with work and fragmented in its focus, while decisions have become ever more difficult to make as uncertainty increases in the operating environment. The upshot is meager results and weaker revenue.

So what is it we do in Pulse that is so different? In fact, we do almost everything differently. First, the Pulse concept tackles the number of projects and other assignments in progress simultaneously in the operation and introduces visual barriers. With Pulse, it is no longer possible to overload the operation with work without the consequences becoming obvious. It is company management who, through their decisions, control throughput and lead times, providing a steady flow of projects and new products.

Second, the hierarchical line organization no longer plays a dominant role in decision-making. Rather, the flow of decisions is formed by a network of distinct pulse meetings at which people in various constellations meet frequently and make decisions together. The Pulse meetings are the basic elements that are linked together in permanent or temporary decision-making units. That makes the organizational structure adaptable and modular.

Third, product development is conducted at the strategic and operational levels simultaneously. The strategic work advances continuously and is focused to create advantageous conditions for the development initiatives that are started.

Finally, the fourth factor in Pulse is that we have taken decisive steps towards more effective teamwork and more cross-functional learning. Both the projects and the strategic teams have people working full-time over extended periods, while the proportion of specialists who provide short-term contributions has decreased.

The Pulse concept is based on the knowledge that organizations can be seen as non-linear systems. In other words, there are laws of nature that govern the efficiency of an organization and that explain why some approaches are more successful than others. It is not about opinions, leadership, or philosophy. The methods and the actions better equipped to succeed rest on a solid scientific foundation, something that will greatly benefit all managers in their professional undertakings in the future. This research opens up new opportunities to devise completely new organizational models. I hope I am able to contribute to the emergence of these models with this book and with Pulse.

Rönninge, Sweden, October 2016

Ulla Sebestyén

1. A first glimpse at agile multi-project management using Pulse

Pulse is an organizational model that solves problems that product development enterprises have wrestled with for a long time. These problems can be summarized in four main points. It is difficult to maintain a level workload. Methods for conducting development, which entails much uncertainty, are lacking. Too much time and energy is devoted to developing technology and too little to developing features and applications that satisfy customer needs. And there are too many mental blocks caused by prevailing organizational structures. These problems are caused by basic thought patterns that control how organizations are framed, so new ways of thinking are needed in many different areas.

In this chapter, I provide a general introduction to Pulse, so the reader can become familiar with the concepts and terminology I use. Pulse is built on an organizational model based on arenas, which is fundamentally different from how organizations have traditionally been depicted, that is, as relationships between people. This creates new degrees of freedom. In the traditional organizational structure, information and knowledge are power. In Pulse, though, power is the ability to share information and knowledge, which is important, because product development is all about the learning that occurs when people interact.

A glimpse into Agile Multi-Project Management using Pulse

When a company with products in the market refines its products and manufacturing processes, it often conducts simultaneously several projects that affect one another. The most obvious link between the projects is the competition for limited resources, but they also struggle for decisions and attention. Dependencies between projects can also be found in the technical solutions developed, which it should be possible to combine and reuse so the solutions complement one other to form an attractive product range. In addition, projects compete commercially, because over time customers have more products to choose from without necessarily wanting to buy more.

Multi-project management differs from conventional project management in several key respects.

Definition of multi-project
Conducting multiple concurrent projects that affect one another.

The Project Management Institute (PMI) has established a widespread and well-accepted formal description of the project as a working method. PMI publishes a guide containing definitions, concepts, and methods (PMBOK Guide, 2004). PMI's project philosophy can be traced back to U.S. weapon programs during the Cold War. Multiple project methodologies were developed at the same time, in the 1950s and 1960s, to accommodate these large, contract-driven defense projects. Accordingly, PMI defines "project" as "a temporary endeavor undertaken to create a unique product." This approach is common in most project-management literature.

In contrast, multi-project philosophies have largely been developed in the automotive industry since the 1950s. This origin resulted in a radically different view of projects, because the automotive industry is characterized by continuity. These projects have technical connections to one another, because automakers want to reuse objects and solutions in multiple car models. The better they can reuse their designs, the lower their costs, the shorter their lead times, and the higher their quality (Cusumano and Nobeoka, 1998; Kennedy, 2003; Wheelwright and Clark, 1992).

In agile multi-project management using Pulse, we stress the importance of coordination between projects as well as within projects. Coordination between projects helps products satisfy customer needs at the lowest possible cost in the shortest possible time. Coordination within projects helps minimize losses in the flow of information. Pulse involves continuous multi-project management. People work on a variety of cross-functional teams, for strategic direction, technical and commercial product management, and resource management—the last guiding all projects. In addition, we strengthen coordination within a project by bringing together different competencies that together can solve the tasks in the project. In product development, it is typical for people from different disciplines within the development department to have to cooperate with each other, as well as with purchasing, production technology, marketing, and service, in order to produce an optimally designed product (Cusumano and Nobeoka, 1998; Rubinstein and Firstenberg, 1999).

Definition of project
To pool resources for a large task so that together those resources can solve the task.

A bottleneck in all project work is decision-making, within as well as between projects. If work is to proceed smoothly without interruption, decisions must be made when the need arises, just-in-time (Holman et al., 2003; Cusumano and Nobeoka, 1998). Pulse includes a decision structure of pulse meetings that back up the projects with coordination and quick decisions. Within a project, Pulse solves the need for quick decisions and free information flow with teamwork by moving resources and competencies to the task. In contrast, the traditional, Taylorist approach has been to break down a task into smaller parts performed by specialists in a functional organization (Eriksson-Zetterquist, 2006:146). For example, mechanical development would be conducted by one department, electronics development by a separate one, production development by yet a third. This distances people from one another, placing problems and necessary decisions in limbo. By bringing together all the people needed to solve a specific task in the same team, the distance in time and space is reduced. This is necessary to allow information and knowledge to be shared and decisions made to move the project forward.

When a group of individuals increases their degree of organization so that they form a team, the probability that value-creating work will occur also increases (Prokopenko, Boschetti and Ryan, 2009). In practical terms, this means complex problems can only be solved by work done in self-organized teams (Alberts, 2011). A mainstay of Pulse is to increase productivity through teamwork. Everything that facilitates teamwork—such as suitable premises where the team can work together, visual methods for guiding the work, and simple rules that the team has come up with on its own—will increase productivity.

Toyota was a pioneer in working with multi-projects. In 1953, they appointed their first project manager (*shusa* in Japanese) (Cusumano and Nobeoka, 1998). In the 1960s, the rest of the Japanese automotive industry followed suit. In 1991–1992, Toyota implemented a major organizational change in its development unit. The reorganization attracted attention thanks to the competitive advantages it gave Toyota (Cusumano and Nobeoka, 1998; Kennedy, 2003). Familiar results are the Prius hybrid and the Mirai fuel cell car, as well as the Lexus and Scion brands. As a result, a growing number of automakers as well as other companies have emulated Toyota's multi-project methodology. An early adopter in Sweden was Scania, in 2003 (ProjektVärlden, 3-05: 16-17).

The gains in efficiency possible through multi-project management have been demonstrated in several different studies since the 1980s (Wheelwright and Clark, 1992; McDonough and Spital, 2003). For an operation to boost productivity, though, it must make several major adjustments. First, the number of projects and assignments running at the same time must be limited, to avoid high efficiency losses from overload (McDonough and Spital, 2003). Second, staff must be allowed to concentrate on the tasks in one project or one team at a time (Kennedy, 2003; McDonough and Spital, 2003; Hendriks et al., 1999). Third, strategy work must be carried out that specifies which customer needs will be satisfied and how the product's architecture will be designed to accomplish this (Cusumano and Nobeoka, 1998). Finally, the organization must be agile (quick to act) so it can share information and knowledge to adapt to changing conditions (Atkinson and Moffat, 2005). These measures make it possible to shorten project lead-times from years to weeks or months, to reduce costs, and to produce products that match customer needs better and thus boost profitability.

To further heighten efficiency, one can increase the capacity to reuse knowledge, which can be done in several different ways. Developing a modular system is one example. No automaker can survive today's fierce competition without reusing the same components in several car models. Running overlapping projects coordinated with multi-project management, it is also possible to share new technical solutions, to quickly spread a new technology to multiple products (Kennedy, 2003; Thomke and Fujimoto, 2000; Cusumano and Nobeoka, 1998).

Converting from a short-term focus on costs to an agile organization demands a shift from managing a development process to managing a learning enterprise engaged in development (see Teresko, 2006).

Organizing for multi-projects

Based on the discussion above, four factors determine the success and effectiveness of an organizational model for multi-project management: limiting the workload, working in teams, enhancing strategic work and separating it from operational work, and organizing to share information and knowledge. To limit the workload, we need to be able to keep track of how many projects and assignments are in progress. Above all, the workload must be made visible. Personal initiatives are good, but they should always be taken within a strategic design for a priority customer segment, project, or assignment. Personal priorities may be perceived as rational from one individual's viewpoint but are in fact counterproductive because they reduce the degree of organization and make it less likely that value-creating work will occur. In Pulse, all projects and assignments in progress are visualized in the room we call the pulse room. Each project has its own whiteboard for the project, which we call the pulse board. The assignments are gathered on an assignment pulse board. In addition to projects and assignments, multi-project management also has different pulse boards for each team. (See Figure 1-1.)

Figure 1-1. A pulse room.

For a long time, there has been talk about the importance of working in teams, but there has also been a shortage of good working methods that make that possible. Teamwork has often been synonymous with sitting in meetings. I believe the "sitting" is an inefficient way of working. Pulse methods are designed for teamwork. Many methods are based on nominal group technique and visual management. Nominal group technique ensures everyone's participation, a high level of creativity, and shared results. Visual management creates transparency in the work, which reduces uncertainty and makes it possible to level out the workload. Pulse uses teamwork at all levels; that is, nominal group technique and visual management are used by all people, whether they work with operational management, strategic issues in multi-project management, on projects, or on assignments. Visual management also makes it possible to link together the whole team in what we call an agile organization. By “agile,” we mean the organization is quick to act and can adapt to changing conditions thanks to its ability to share information and knowledge.

In a typical agile product development organization, we use the following teams and roles (see Figure 1-2). The portfolio team defines the enterprise's (business unit's, subsidiary's) strategic direction and focuses resources. The strategic direction answers the questions: "Which business models will we use?", "Which customer segments will we focus our attention on right now?", "Which development projects will we invest in?" The strategic direction is not a collection of policy documents; it emerges from the day-to-day work of the portfolio team. For example, the portfolio team starts and prioritizes projects in progress. They also guide the product team's work to make the strategic direction concrete and articulate a strategic design to realize it.

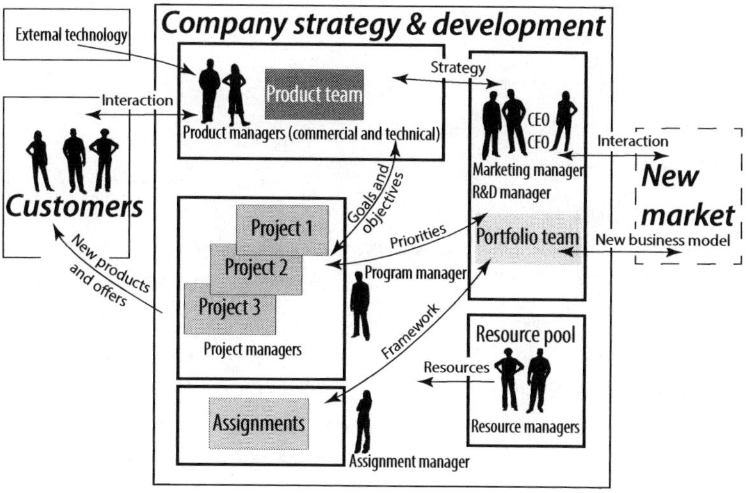

Figure 1-2. Teams and roles in Pulse.

When the product team is articulating the strategic design based on the direction set by the portfolio team, questions arise that need to be answered. What needs and opportunities are there in the market in the prioritized customer segments? How should the offers be devised? Which products should be developed? Where should they be developed? In which steps should this be done? How should the launch be done? What technologies should be used? Where should production take place? Where should assembly take place? How should the logistics be structured? What variants of the product should be available? In what price segments? Should the product be designed as a reusable modular system? How should products fit together in terms of technology? How should the architecture be designed? The product team will work continuously to formulate informed responses to these commercial and technical questions, which will provide information for the portfolio team's decisions to start selected projects.

Projects are temporary teams, or groups of teams, that are brought together to implement a step in the strategic design. Good preparatory work by the product team can help keep each project relatively short, preferably less than one year.

Assignments are even shorter efforts, often related to product maintenance. Each may comprise anywhere from a few hours of work to a few hundred hours.

In addition to the CEO (or general manager) who has ultimate responsibility for the operation, we have four fixed roles in Pulse: program manager, product managers, assignment manager, and resource managers. The program manager maintains contact with the projects and makes overall technical decisions. The product managers, with their backgrounds and their contacts, must be able to define a picture of customer needs in the future, what opportunities are available in the market, and the economic potential for these opportunities. The assignment manager manages the assignment operation and is responsible for building a system that handles and prioritizes assignments. Because the assignments are often about adjusting existing products, the assignment manager often becomes knowledgeable about the current strengths and weaknesses of the products. The program manager, product managers, and assignment manager are all part of the product team. I recommend that neither the program manager, product managers, nor assignment manager be responsible for human resources. The advantage is that they can concentrate on strategic work and avoid getting locked into the old structure. In Pulse, resource managers are responsible for human resources and often also for equipment and working methods. The resource managers provide projects and assignments with resources based on the priorities set by the portfolio team.

Pulse meetings for visualization and decisions

Visualization is central to an operation that works with Pulse. The boards relay to everyone what is going on. We call these boards "pulse boards," and the meetings held while everyone stands in front of the boards are called "pulse meetings." Pulse meetings are the arenas that serve as a foundation for the agile multi-project organization. Pulse meetings are where strategic direction, strategic design, resources, projects, and assignments are managed.

All teams need just-in-time decisions, and the pulse meetings are the mechanism that ensures they are made. All pulse boards have logs for decisions made. The decisions are written up on the spot. When the team leaves its pulse meeting, everything has been documented and settled.

Projects and assignments

A project working with Pulse has short stand-up meetings at its pulse board every day or even more frequently. At these pulse meetings, the project team checks the situation and decides what results are needed to move forward. It is always the need that determines what they will work on. Figure 1-3 shows an example of a pulse board for a project. The pulse boards for portfolio teams, product teams, and assignments are similar. The project pulse board shows the goal scenario that describes what the project should deliver. The goal scenario is produced by the product team and the project group together and builds on the preparatory work done by the product team when they drafted their strategic design.

The project group should be self-organizing, so they themselves create a structure for the work using a synchronization plan. In this plan, the project has been divided into subresults that are needed to reach the goal. The subresults are grouped into work packages based on their mutual dependencies. Each work package is implemented by a cross-functional team assembled to solve its task. Handover points between the teams are scheduled. The pulse board also visualizes all unexpected events and the handling of these via the inbox.

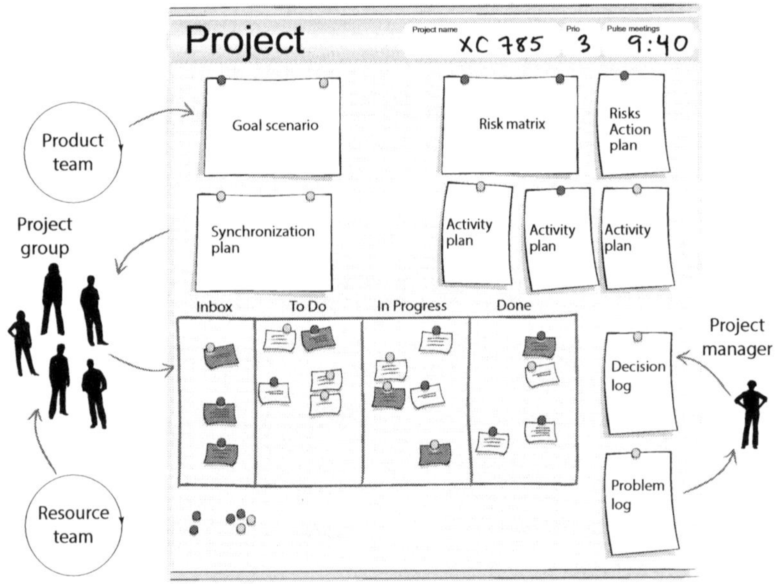

Figure 1-3. Pulse Board for projects.

Unexpected events such as problems and interruptions are immediately brought up at pulse meetings, where decisions are made on how to handle them. If enough information is available, a decision is made immediately. Otherwise someone is tasked with preparing information for making a decision by the next pulse meeting, or else the problem is escalated. The projects have weekly program pulse meetings together with the program manager where they can escalate problem cases to the next level, to be dealt with at the product pulse meeting or resource pulse meeting. If the case cannot be resolved at any of these pulse meetings, it is escalated to the portfolio team. Otherwise, a rapid response workshop is called with the appropriate people (from the portfolio team, product team, and perhaps the project) who will work out a solution.

Pulse involves all the concerned parties in the planning of a project. In traditional project literature, planning has been the task of the project manager. In Pulse, we strive for the project team to create a common understanding of what is to be achieved and how the work will be carried out. The planning of projects is kept on an overall level, while activity lists for each subresult are drawn up by that particular team when work starts.

Specifications of requirements are not used to control the project's outcomes. Instead a goal scenario is used as a tool to sustain dialogue within the project and with the product team about what is to be achieved. The project group is responsible for finding solutions that fulfill the goals in the scenario in the best way. Product development is learning, and learning occurs through dialogue. The operation becomes knowledge-oriented, with a constant desire to build up and reuse the organization's collective expertise. The work is structured so that projects are front-loaded, which means that people actively seek out problems. This makes it possible to reduce the number of changes towards the end of the project. By asking questions and seeking out problems, one begins with creativity, open to different solutions, and ends with order and structure (Rubinstein and Firstenberg, 1999).

The product team

The work of drawing up a strategic design for a prioritized customer segment or focus area makes great demands on broad expertise. It requires an understanding of customer needs, the customer's applications, how the market works, what features provide benefits for the customer, what new technologies can be used, in what areas the enterprise has a head start, the opportunities and limits in the production—to name a few factors. In simplified terms, one might say that a strategic design describes how the product portfolio, consisting of existing and new, not yet developed products and their production processes, will create value for the customer and simultaneously create sustainable profitability for the enterprise.

The work on the projects and assignments will then solve technical challenges to achieve the sought after features in the new products.

In this book, I will write about the product team in the singular, but in large corporations, there may be several teams with different emphases. There is also always a resource pool from which persons may be allocated to work on strategic assignments for limited periods. Some of our Pulse clients have virtually no technology development of their own and conduct no projects. Instead, all work is about function and architecture. In those cases, technology development is done by their subcontractors.

The product team is collectively responsible for the operation's product portfolio being profitable in the short and long run. They forecast revenues and costs for various products and draw up long-term plans for how to develop their products and their most important market segments (Gorchels, 2005). They review production capacity, production processes, logistics, quality, and production costs to maintain margins better than their competitors'.

The product team defines the requirements to be satisfied or the effects they wish to achieve with the results of the project's development work. There are two main types of needs: customer needs and operational needs. Even if it should always be possible to trace operational needs back to a customer need, it is easier to keep them separate. Customer needs govern the development of new products or new variants of a product. An operational need governs improvements in the production process to boost capacity, improve quality, reduce costs, simplify work, reduce environmental impact, or in some other way indirectly improve the product. The product team is responsible for preparing business goals and program plans that can satisfy customer needs and operational needs.

To manage the day-to-day contacts between the product team and the projects, there is a program manager, responsible for a group of projects that are technically interdependent. The program manager leads the weekly program pulse meetings and has the authority to make decisions. To cope with this task, the program manager must have a high level of technical expertise and authority.

The program manager's tasks require physical presence, while the product managers have to travel often to meet with customers. In some enterprises, the product managers are stationed close to the market, which can be far from the development center. To be able to combine travel and individual work with teamwork, the work needs to be structured and assistive technologies acquired so that both types of work can be done.

The portfolio team

The portfolio team determines the enterprise's strategic direction and also develops new business models that will ensure the enterprise's long-term survival when existing markets have been displaced by new competing innovations. The portfolio team are proxies for the owners and thus determine how the resources will be invested. Consequently, they decide which projects will be implemented and when, based on the current resource situation. If they start too many projects in relation to the capacity available, lead times for projects will increase, and profitability will suffer.

The portfolio team also guides and prioritizes the work of the product team. At the intersection of the portfolio team's top-down perspective, formulated as a strategic direction, and the product team's strategic design, based on meetings with customers and an understanding of the opportunities in new technologies, we find an interesting and creative tension.

The portfolio team can be seen as owners and caretakers of the structures built up with Pulse. They are responsible for monitoring how well the structures work and initiating changes when necessary.

The portfolio team is often part of the management team and consists of the CEO (or general manager), marketing director, R&D director, production director, and CFO.

Work in teams with a variety of competencies

Working on a team is something completely different from sitting in meetings together a couple of hours at irregular intervals. Working on a team means a group of individuals is assigned a common task to produce one or more results by a specific date. The individuals on the team depend on one another and must work together efficiently to solve the assignment. A team is composed of people with complementary expertise, so that together they can solve a coherent task.

Working on a team is really like playing a team sport. To win, one has to do more than sit around a conference table. You have to get out on the field and struggle, and hopefully you will have fun and learn something at the same time. Teamwork entails handing off lots of information, helping colleagues with problems, shouting encouragement when the going gets tough, and celebrating when you have achieved something good together. For this to be possible, you have to work closely with each other. The players cannot play in the same game if they are not on the same playing field. It can be difficult enough just to sit on different floors of the same building. A team can get together as frequently or infrequently as a few days a month, and be spread out. That may work, but it will make greater demands on assistive technologies like video-conferencing, perseverance in learning how to use them, and focus once you do meet.

A team reaps major benefits if it can sit together some of the time the members are working on their tasks. The bigger the challenge is, the more time needed together. Getting a team to work well also requires common rules, which include goals and plans for the work to be done as well as rules for social interaction. Individuals must be able to collaborate informally or ask questions of their colleagues on the team, while at the same time everyone must be able to concentrate on their tasks. The conflict between the need to get information quickly and to work undisturbed can be solved. With simple rules for social interaction that the team itself agrees on, the average workday can be a balanced mix of creative information exchange and problem solving, on the one hand, and concentrated work, on the other.

One practical problem is often the lack of suitable premises. After all, the team is uniquely composed of the competencies needed to solve a unique assignment. They normally do not have their workplaces next to each other. Flexible premises are needed to be able to create areas where temporary teams can work together for longer or shorter periods.

The path to Pulse

Working in the form of projects has been in fashion for several decades. Professional training companies have enjoyed a golden age educating people in project management and project work. One would expect a stream of glowing reports. And, yes, many reports and books have been written about projects, of which this book is another one on the stack. Yet positive things are rarely written about projects. Instead, all the problems dominate. Recurring themes are long lead times and constant delays, high costs and significant cost overruns, and major or minor defects in the quality of the results delivered.

Either the advantages of working in the project format have been greatly exaggerated, or the format is being used incorrectly. Projects have been used for several decades, so it is possible to evaluate the benefits. If all the publicity promoting projects is true, then innovation—as well as productivity—should have increased. But a growing body of research indicates the opposite. In a comprehensive study, Sjöö (2014) shows that innovations in Sweden have decreased and productivity has halved since the 1980s. (See Figure 1-4.) Edmund Phelps wrote in *the New York Review of Books* ("What Is Wrong with the West's Economies?", August 13, 2015) that innovation in the United States began to decline in the 1960s and that Europe followed two decades later. In other words, something is fundamentally wrong. I believe that something basic is missing, specifically agile multi-project management. Projects are not islands. On the contrary, they are interactive parts of a whole.

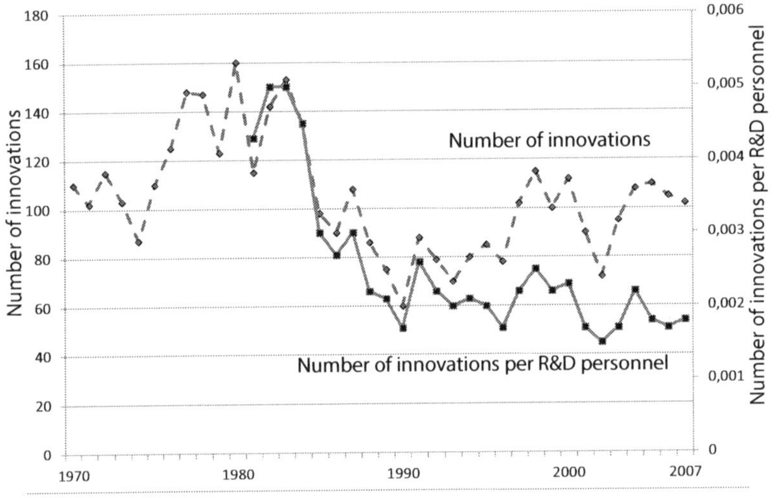

Figure 1-4. Innovations decreased in Swedish industry at the same time as productivity declined by half (Sjöö, 2014).

To efficiently work in projects in an enterprise demands a series of thorough changes. It is not enough for employees to work in teams and increase the pace in projects and assignments. Managers and executives must change their way of working, otherwise they will become bottlenecks that limit the speed at which projects can advance. The introduction of projects has often been seen as the domain of the research and development (R&D) department, something that does not concern the rest of the enterprise. And even in R&D, changes have often been minimal when the way of working switched to projects. They have appointed people to be project managers and made sure these people produced project plans (De Maio et al., 1994). Projects have often come to be associated with their plans. Many people have even come to perceive project management as work with tools for project planning and follow-up (Packendorff, 1993). I believe this is part of the problem. A project plan, as usually depicted, has been a comprehensive detailed plan often drawn as a Gantt chart. In lean practice, this is called "push planning". In the automotive industry, they learned early on that this was an ineffective way of planning that led to huge uncertainty and waste (Ohno, 1988; Womack et al., 1991; Hope and Spearman, 2008). In push planning, one attempts to forecast the future, which is impossible for a non-linear system (Mitchell, 2009). Planning and management must be done in real time, as one looks a few hours into the future, so that uncertainty can be kept at a reasonable level. (See Figure 1-5.) In lean, this is called "pull", or "visual management". I also use the concept "real-time management." The current situation, the immediate need, controls what needs to be done next. In production, kanban is used, in Pulse, regular and frequent pulse meetings.

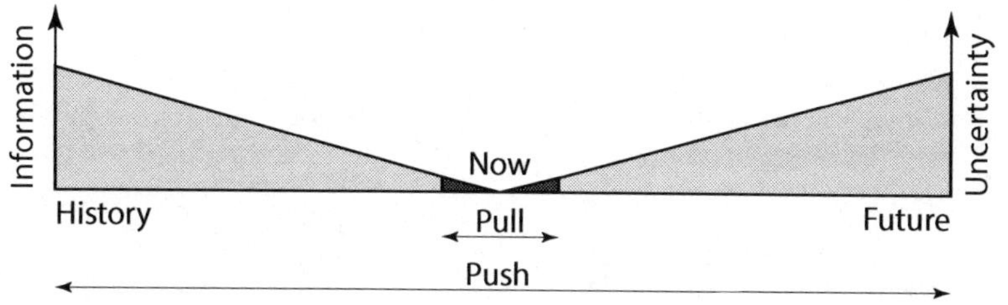

Figure 1-5. The uncertainty of traditional project management (push) versus Pulse (pull).

Another reason that many companies have had problems working in the project format may be that the description of "project" is often based on one-off projects in a contract-driven enterprise. That was how industrial projects were born in the arms industry during the Cold War. Defense departments placed orders in the form of big contracts that the suppliers then fulfilled. When the project format became more common and spread to other industries, projects got smaller, changing the prerequisites, but the descriptions and working methods did not change at the same pace. The focus remained entirely on the events in a project, and projects were described so that they came to be seen as autonomous from their surrounding enterprise. But that is not how it works in a multi-project operation, where a project is a way to realize a strategy by focusing the work and moving the expertise and resources to different tasks. The strategic work of defining a feature, coordinating resources and technology, and assessing the quality of results is up to the operation's executives and management. To take advantage of the opportunities that focused work offers—with shorter lead times, lower development costs, and higher quality results—the ability to make decisions and act just-in-time at the strategic level must be accommodated. In plain language this means that teams composed of cross-functional managers must meet daily to deal with problems, make decisions, and drive the strategic work forward at the same pace as the projects.

If you are inspired by this book and want to introduce Pulse in your business, I highly recommend that as a first step you and your colleagues visit an enterprise that has already implemented an agile organization. It seems necessary to soak up the atmosphere if one is to subsequently carry out the necessary cultural changes with success.

Summary of the tour

In this chapter, I have tried to give an idea of what the structure of an operation working with Pulse looks like. I have also summarized key concepts and ways of thinking.

With Pulse, you can get to grips with overloading and fragmentation, increase your ability to develop innovations through teamwork, shift from technology-driven development to customer-driven and feature-driven, and get away from the gridlock that happens in functional organizations where information is power.

"Multi-project" means that an operation runs several projects simultaneously that affect each other commercially as well as in terms of resources and technology.

Visualization using pulse boards and work in teams is central to Pulse. The pulse boards are used to advance, through short and frequent pulse meetings, all work in the development organization, which includes strategic work, product management, resource management, projects, and short assignments. At these pulse meetings, the team checks the situation, makes decisions, and determines what results are needed to move forward. They can also quickly pass problems and the need for decisions to the next decision level.

Pulse involves everyone concerned in planning. One strives to create a common understanding of what is to be achieved and how the work will be carried out. Planning is kept at an overall level, while detailed activity plans are drafted by the teams as work progresses. Control occurs in real time via pulse meetings.

Specifications of requirements are not used to control the project's outcomes. Rather, a goal scenario is formulated that is used to continuously define at various levels what the project should achieve and check that against the outcomes that the team produces.

The product team is tasked with finding potential new projects, which are thoroughly prepared with commercial and technical background data. They should also back up projects in progress with the decisions necessary so they can maintain a rapid pace forward and fulfill their goals. To manage the day-to-day contacts between the product team and the projects, there is a program manager. The project's recurring demands for decisions mean the product team must be able to act quickly, which is ensured through their pulse meetings.

Decisions about which projects to start and when they will start are made by the portfolio team. The team takes into account economic and strategic assessments as well as the resources available. The information supporting these decisions is prepared by the product team. The portfolio team also has regular pulse meetings.

Work in teams means a group of individuals is assigned a common task to produce one or more results. The individuals in the group have complementary competencies and must cooperate effectively to solve a compact task. A team reaps major benefits by sitting together some of the time they are working on their tasks. This applies generally to teams, whether they are working on a project, assignment, product management, market development, or strategic direction.

2. Multi-project and agile product development

In this chapter, I will define the problems with current methods for working on strategy and development. Based on those problems, I will then set out guidelines for a solution based on Pulse. The four basic problems are overloading and fragmentation, slow learning as a result of the high proportion of work done alone, lack of understanding of customer needs, and an organizational structure that impedes change. The solution is multi-project management that works inside an agile organization structure where work is performed by interacting teams.

Halve the lead time in projects

"Halve the lead time in our projects? Impossible! It's hard enough for us to meet the deadlines we have now. How could we cut that time by half?"

When I wrote the first edition of this book in 2006, many people regarded cutting project lead times in half as utopian. But even then, I had already shown that it was possible with Pulse. Ten years later, as I prepared the second edition of this book, I knew that it was possible to carry out certain projects in a few weeks. A development project always consists of work, problem solving, and decision-making. The parts dominated by problem solving and decision-making can be carried out in much less time than before. Achieving these short lead times demands that there is multi-project management (Jerbrant, 2009) with what I call in Pulse a portfolio team, a product team, and a resource team working in an agile organizational structure where decisions can be made at a fast pace. Also, working in teams must not only be possible but be supported.

Much time in projects evaporates in waiting and uncertainty. According to McManus (2005), between 60% and 90% of all working hours in a development operation disappear into activities that do not add value for the customer. The low proportion of value-adding work is apparent in unnecessarily long lead times, high costs, and deficient quality. What deficiencies and faulty practices are behind such excessive losses in efficiency? We can divide the deficiencies into seven types of waste that frequently occur in multi-project operations. This division is patterned after the description of efficiency potentials in production systems (see Ohno, 1988).

Wrong products – Projects producing the wrong results. Too much time is spent on features that customers do not want or are not prepared to pay for. The projects lack goals related to customer needs and profitability. As a result, the projects develop the wrong products, at too high a cost, and take a long time. One reason for this, according to Adam, Day, and Dougherty (1998), is that companies find it difficult to absorb information about customer needs and market needs that differ from the products they previously made. To develop the right results, the operation needs to create an understanding of market needs through a team- and workshop-based approach that involves everyone—from managers to developers (ibid).

Unnecessary mental shifts – Employees split among many projects and other assignments. They are constantly forced to move between tasks without completing any. The long-term work must often yield to new emergencies. Employees are pressured to solve simple tasks they can do fast, instead of dealing with the difficult tasks that require focused, undisturbed teamwork. Researchers such as Wheelwright and Clark (1992) have pointed out how important it is to limit the number of ongoing projects and assignments to assure their success.

Long distances in time and space – Too little collaboration with few or no contacts at all with people working on closely related tasks. The tasks have been divided into small parts and spread out in a functional organization. Staff working on the projects are scattered, sometimes geographically far from each other. Much time is devoted to meetings where staff try to coordinate work between departments. Nothing indicates that these meetings and exchanges of documents actually help the projects (Kahn, 1996). There are numerous sittings (meetings), which steals valuable working time but does not result in effective coordination or collaboration. As a result, the same problem is solved in multiple locations, and the results produced do not fit together. McDonough and Spital (2003) point out that product development is learning in an unknown area. For learning to take place, there needs to be a sufficiently large core team (ibid). Takeuchi and Nonaka (1986) use the same reasoning and conclude that information and knowledge are shared openly only when people work together. Only teams can solve complex problems (Alberts, 2011). When work is chopped into little pieces, and each piece assigned to an "expert," no learning occurs. And if no learning occurs, then there is no product development, either.

Waiting time – Time spent waiting unnecessarily on decisions to be made or searching for information and documentation that have not been passed on. The overall decisions on coordination between projects are made at long intervals. At the same time, the project group does not have the authority to make decisions itself. A lack of decisions leads to rising uncertainty, which manifests as stress and a poor work environment. To minimize uncertainty, decisions must be made as needed, just-in-time (Holman, Kaas, and Keeling, 2003). This requires an organizational structure that makes frequent and flexible decision-making possible at all levels.

Faulty practices – Knowledge, components, and technical knowledge from previous development work are not made use of. Each project develops its own technical solutions. As a result, projects often start from square one, making the projects unnecessarily complicated and expensive (Thomke and Fujimoto, 2000). This results from the project participants not working together. The tasks are divided into smaller parts carried out by "experts." It is like a relay race in which developer A does a job then passes the baton to B (see Takeuchi and Nonaka, 1986). This division makes it difficult, if not impossible, to explore and understand complex problems, which is crucial in creative development (McDonough and Spital, 2003; Alberts, 2011).

Overproduction and overdocumentation – Unnecessary work to produce supporting documents and subresults that are not needed for the final product. This includes detailed project plans that do not say anything about the future. It also includes features and solutions that the customer is not prepared to pay for.

Unnecessary inventory and unnecessary lead time – Each individual project has little activity, because staff are simultaneously working on other projects and assignments. One effect is that the results from the projects lie around most of the time waiting. Too few value-adding work hours are devoted to the projects, especially at the start. Even management's commitment to these projects is low at the start (Wheelwright and Clark, 1992). Only when a project approaches its final deadline does the demand for subresults and decisions appear. Then they discover, too late, that some results contain errors or are completely missing.

Linear systems and non-linear systems

Researchers in organizational theory have long discussed the differences between mechanical and organic organizations (Burns and Stalker, 1994) or between closed and open systems (Thompson 1967). What researchers have found in innumerable studies is that companies with a system they refer to as mechanical, Taylorist, bureaucratic, or closed perform significantly worse than companies that are the opposite (organic or open systems) (see Burns and

Stalker, 1994; Woodward, 1980; Takeuchi and Nonaka, 1986; Blomberg, 2013). But organizational researchers have been unable to explain why this is so or to demonstrate any connection between management principles and employee productivity (Czarniawska, 2005).

Research findings in recent years, though, have provided insight into what "mechanical" and "organic" really mean for systems. A milestone on this journey (Gleick, 1988) was research by the mathematician and meteorologist Edward Lorenz in the 1960s. Lorenz tried to build a computer model to forecast the weather far in advance. His thesis was that, with a good model, a powerful computer, and enough data, it would be possible to forecast months and years into the future. After many simulations on the computer, he realized it was impossible. Weather is an unstable system that is highly sensitive to small variations. It is possible to make a decent forecast based on current conditions for the next few hours or perhaps days, but forecasts further out have much greater uncertainty (see Figure 1-5). Weather is what nowadays is called a "non-linear system". All systems with feedback loops are non-linear (ibid). Machines, however, are linear. A machine and an automated production line are examples of linear systems that produce predictable results. In contrast, an organization of people, with all their feedback loops, is a non-linear system.

Early research on non-linear systems was captivated by chaotic systems. A system in chaos may at first glance appear extremely complex, but researchers found that they are actually simple to describe (Mitchell, 2009). The definition of a chaotic system is that it is non-linear and "simple," that is, it has a limited repertoire. However, there is another group of non-linear systems that are difficult to describe and predict (require a longer description). These have been named "complex systems" (Mitchell, 2009).

A complex system occurs when a number of agents interact with one another in a non-trivial manner. Researchers such as Prokopenko, Boschetti, and Ryan (2009) define a complex system as a group of agents that are so well synchronized that they can be regarded as a

Product development
Learning that happens when people collaborate.

system, so the group exhibits new characteristics that the agents do not have as individuals. It is as if the agents organize themselves, and out of this self-organization arises, or emerges, a pattern (ibid). The pattern that emerges from the interaction between people in a development organization is what we commonly refer to as "learning" or "product development."

A machine or production line is a linear, "mechanical," system in which linear laws apply. We can take a reductionist approach to it, divide the system into parts, and engineer the parts separately. When the parts are put together, the system becomes the sum of its parts.

If we use the same mechanical approach for an organization, which is a non-linear system consisting of interacting people, we run the risk of creating a chaotic system. And that is precisely what researchers such as Burns and Stalker (1994), Woodward (1980), and Blomberg (2013) found in their research. Mechanical (Taylorist, bureaucratic) approaches lead to chaotic, underperforming companies. Companies that take an organic approach are successful (ibid). These companies, such as Swedish Handelsbanken, avoid organization charts, budgetary control, and other "top-down" practices (Wallander, 2003).

So why do so few companies apply an organic approach like Handelsbanken and so many choose the mechanical approach? I think part of the answer is that managers use the tools they have available. Handelsbanken did not use a ready-made toolkit to build the company. They used trial and error for decades. Few have the opportunity and patience to work so long-term when decision makers are constantly shifting position. In other words, an organic approach requires a toolkit that can be used to transform the company in a short period of time. Pulse is such a toolkit.

In this book, I will present methods that make it possible to create an organic organizational structure, establish learning through teamwork, keep the workload under control, and develop an understanding of customer needs through various activities within and outside the company.

Building blocks for agile multi-project management using Pulse

Agile multi-project management using Pulse provides the prerequisites and tools so companies can avoid "the seven wastes." But Pulse also presumes that the operation incorporates key building blocks and principles for an organic organizational structure. Those building blocks and principles will guide the operation's culture, decisions, and choice of working methods.

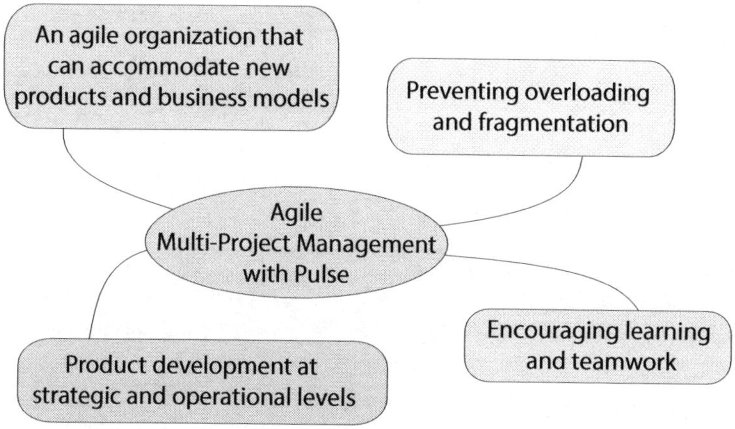

Figure 2-1. Key building blocks for agile multi-project management using Pulse.

The seven wastes, which I borrowed from lean practice (Ohno, 1988), can be summarized in four fundamental problems. In the analyses I do before introducing Pulse in a company, three problem areas consistently appear: overloading and fragmentation, "relay race" thinking, and a lack of strategic work. Another problem also emerges in more detailed research (Adams et al., 1998; Christensen, 1997): the organizational structure sets limits to what products can be developed. Today's organizational structure—the hierarchical line organization—reflects today's business model, which in turn is based on today's products (ibid).

A hierarchical line organization reflects a company's current business model and products, thereby limiting the possibility of developing new products and business models.

For the problems presented above, I propose a solution consisting of a system that prevents overloading and fragmentation, with methods and other conditions that encourage teamwork, following practices that make it possible to simultaneously work strategically and operationally, and an organizational model that is detached from the current products and business model.

Preventing overloading and fragmentation

Many years ago, when I first asked a management team how many projects were going on in their company, I was surprised that they could not answer. By now, I've asked so many management teams that I can be pretty sure that they do not know how many projects are in progress. This may surprise the reader but it is entirely consistent with the findings of researchers such as Wheelwright and Clark (1992). The situation has worsened with the introduction of projects (Cusumano and Nobeoka, 1998). That is why multi-project management is needed that controls the number of ongoing tasks, whether they are called projects or routine work. I will call all operational work that is not a project an "assignment." Projects are larger interrelated tasks, while assignments are everything else and thus smaller.

With coordinated management inside and between projects, we can avoid splitting up the staff over several projects and assignments and at the same time create the prerequisites for teamwork. Fewer projects will also speed up decisions, because a limited number of projects makes it easier for multi-project managers to focus their time and make quick decisions. The result I want to achieve is faster communication within projects through work in teams, as well as an operation that can make decisions frequently and flexibly.

Developing new products and processes is a demanding task. It requires knowledge and experience, something that most development operations have readily available. In contrast, they have less scope for thinking, testing, and discussing in teams. Work has a tendency to get chopped up by customer requests, production problems, departmental meetings, and urgent e-mail. If no priorities have been set for the separate tasks, each person will try to evaluate the priority individually. As a result, the manager who yells loudest gets his/her tasks completed. Having a lot of cases lying around with no set priority is stressful. Even the most disciplined employees often feel too much pressure when they get stuck on an assignment. Instead of spending even more time and energy to solve the problem, they change to easier tasks. This further increases the number of assignments in progress at the same time, which greatly prolongs the lead time for all the assignments. Those individuals may well feel efficient, having so many irons in the fire, but the results are not achieved for the operation as a whole.

To correct this, the number of projects that the operation runs must be reduced, at the same time as other short assignments are dealt with to reduce interruptions. When the operation is no longer overloaded, people can concentrate on one task at a time, solve complex problems, and work on one team at a time. I will discuss lead times in more detail in the next chapter, Lead times and feedback.

The two channels, projects and assignments, must be controlled so that the operation handles no more tasks than staff can deal with. Projects are started and prioritized in Pulse by the portfolio team, while the assignments are started and prioritized by the assignment manager.

The portfolio team ensures that the projects are started only when they do not collide with each other in terms of resources. The task of the portfolio team is to start no more projects than the operation is capable of running. This means that the portfolio team must pick projects they consider important and possible to run while allowing other projects to wait their turn. The projects are prioritized based on a few select parameters that affect the operation's profitability in the short and long term. In the Portfolio management chapter, I will describe this work in more detail.

The assignments are handled similarly. The difference is that every decision is simpler, but there are many more assignments.

Encouraging teamwork

Lack of effective communication within projects is a common problem, according to the analyses I have done. This may manifest itself among managers and employees as a lack of information or commitment to tasks. Working on a team means much more than getting together and talking at a sitting. A team has joint responsibility to deliver the subresults requested. The individuals are tied to a team in that they plan their work together and work physically close to one another. Ideally, they work in the same room at least a few hours each day. If continuous communication is encouraged, information will be shared in the course of work, thus reducing the risk of faulty or deficient results.

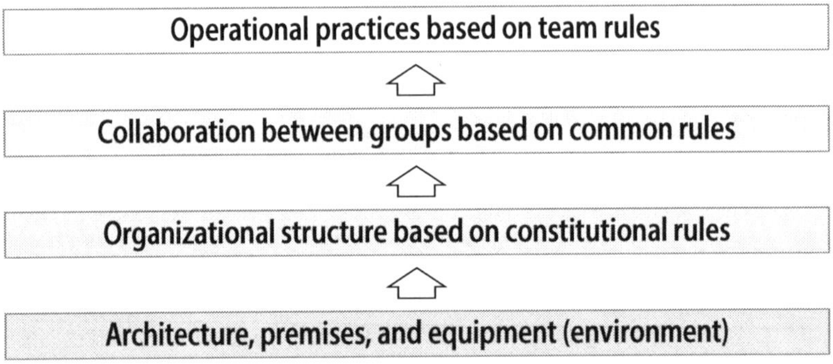

Figure 2-2. Layers of rules. The figure underscores the importance of the configuration of the workplace and other physical conditions.

Two conditions are critical for team work to be possible. First, a structure of simple rules is needed (Ostrom, 2009). If there are no rules, the participants risk getting stuck in a game where, over time, everyone loses (ibid). In Pulse, I have chosen to develop rules on three levels: constitutional, common, and team. (See Figure 2-2.) The constitutional level is determined by company management in the form of an agile organizational structure consisting of interacting pulse meetings (see Figure 2-4). Rules at the common level are defined by managers and employees together as simple routines for interaction between teams. These routines describe, for example, how pulse meetings are held, what information is on the pulse boards, and how to design interaction between pulse meetings. Team rules are defined by each team or project. Rules for a project consist of the goals and plans the project team have jointly determined, by which they have agreed on what is to be achieved and how work will be carried out, as well as the rules for social interaction.

The second prerequisite for teamwork is that the workplace is designed so that teamwork can take place. That is rarely the case today. Today's workplaces are usually designed for solo work where each person is alone in his/her office. It might be nice not to be bothered, but it is not efficient. Or else employees may sit in an open-plan office that is also intended for solo work, though communal. In Pulse, we start with a Pulse room in which teams can interact at pulse meetings. In addition, we need flexible activity rooms and team rooms where teams and working groups can work together for longer or shorter periods, for example to plan a project or conduct a fast-track study.

Product development at the strategic and operational levels

By "product development at the strategic level," I am referring to work to understand which opportunities the market holds, which customer needs have not yet been satisfied, how important the needs are to the customer in their application, and how these needs can be satisfied with technical features that describe how the product will work to solve the customer's needs. Thinking in terms of customer features is difficult for development engineers, because they are divided into technical disciplines. This division is part of the company's organizational structure (design engineers in one department, production engineers in another) as well as a result of education. It leads to mental blocks in the perception of the product. The organization chart will affect what the new product looks like, which risks producing a solution that the customer is not at all interested in (see Adams et al., 1998). That is why I have a product team in

Pulse that continually works on product management, inspired by Cusumano and Nobeoka (1998) and their description of how, among other things, Toyota conducts product development at the strategic level. As I understand it, it was the introduction of multi-project management at Toyota in 1991–1992 that led to the company's success in recent decades. In other words, it was not lean production, which did help Toyota succeed much earlier in the 1970s and 1980s.

Developing the right product

Efficient product development demands that the only products developed are those with characteristics the customer is prepared to pay for. According to Cusumano and Nobeoka (1998), Toyota applies a strategy in which product management reduces the number of features in a car to the 20% that result in 80% of sales. The rest are too expensive to add on (ibid).

The goals of development projects are based on knowledge of market opportunities and customer needs. In traditionally structured companies, product managers obtain and communicate knowledge about the market (Gorchels, 2005). In Pulse, product managers are an important part of the product team that works with product management. The product team works on analyses intended to collect knowledge of customer needs as well as on definitions of the architecture (such as a modular system or new technologies) for the products. The product team also needs to sustain an internal dialogue within the company where customer needs and architecture are made known and comprehensible (see Adams et al., 1998). Specifically, I use methods such as workshops, teamwork, demonstrations, and pulse meetings.

A product's profitability depends, on the one hand, on the costs of development and production and, on the other hand, volume and what customers are willing to pay for the product. Time and the cost of development and manufacturing can be compressed by planning to reuse articles and solutions in multiple products. Revenues can be increased by making products that can satisfy customer needs better than competitors' products do.

In Pulse, customer needs are expressed as effect goals when the projects' goal scenario is articulated. These are linked to product goals for the projects that describe what features the projects should deliver on an overall level. Pulse does not use detailed specifications of requirements. It is the task of the projects to develop new knowledge and find solutions that fulfill the product goals. A specification of requirements would only be an obstacle to producing the best solution (Kennedy, 2003). A creative approach requires intense dialogue, within each project as well as between projects and the product team.

In the Product management chapter, I will discuss this in more detail.

Building technical knowledge

By systematically building and recycling knowledge, we avoid constantly reinventing the wheel. The effect we want to achieve is to provide prioritized market segments with attractive products, but at the same time reuse good solutions, for example through modular systems, to be able to keep costs down and quality up.

By developing a modular system for their products, companies can save much time when developing individual products or unique solutions for different customers. Automakers have long developed platforms on which they can produce different car models for different market segments. The Scion, Lexus, and Toyota brands are aimed at completely different market segments through their car models, but the various brands' model programs are all built on several common platforms and components.

The reuse of components and modules can work in many products, but an analysis has to be done in each case to evaluate profit, volumes, and product structure. Using modules can save lots of time and money, produce better products, and at the same time enable the development of the exact products that customers demand. The result of a smoothly functioning modular approach is not the same product under different brands. The result should be products that are better adapted to each customer group.

The reuse of modules and components is a strategic task (see Cusumano and Nobeoka, 1998), so in Pulse it is part of the product team's job.

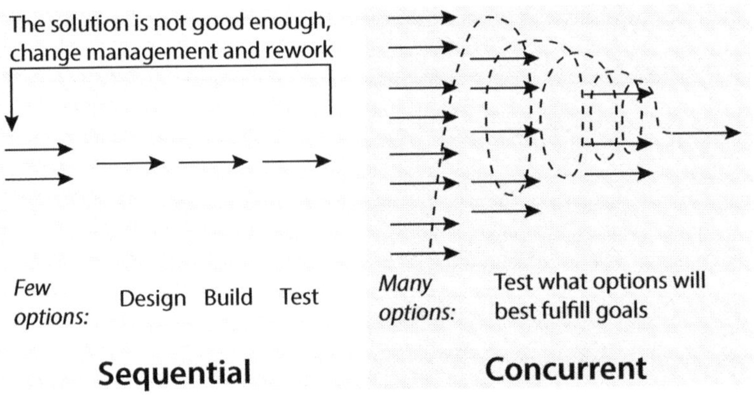

Figure 2-3. Front-loaded project with concurrent design process. In development work, it is likely that several iterations are needed before a satisfactory solution is found. The more unknown an area one tackles, the more iterations. In a concurrent (set-based) design process, several alternative solutions are conceived at the start, and those that best fulfill the goals are successively selected and combined. The number of solutions is gradually reduced until one has the final solution (Kennedy, 2003).

When lead time is key to profitability, a good strategy could be to work out several possible solutions early in the project, as shown in Figure 2-3. This is a hedge against the risk that a concept being worked on may not meet expectations. This approach takes into consideration the uncertainties always present in product development. One avoids ending up in a succession of late and time-consuming reworking, which might otherwise result from concentrating on a single solution (Wheelwright and Clark, 1992; Kennedy, 2003). Successful product development is not about eliminating uncertainty and risk in project work but about managing uncertainty (McDonough and Spital, 2003). Using concurrent design is one way of managing uncertainty.

Successful product development is not about eliminating uncertainty and risk in project work but about managing uncertainty.

For a single project, the cost can be higher, but it is not at all certain that profitability will be lower for the company as a whole. Solutions that are not used in a project may very well become key knowledge for another. The operation slowly builds up knowledge about various technologies and how they can be used in the product. This can also shorten development time, thus increasing revenues. Working with a set of solutions is one way to make projects more front-loaded. The main advantage of the concurrent design process is that learning increases, making product development better.

Concurrent design is run at the strategic level by the product team but realized at the operational level by initiating multiple projects and feasibility studies. To be able to implement the concurrent design process, the company must first have agile multi-project management in place. Otherwise, the uncertainty, work load, and fragmentation will increase so much that the benefits will be lost.

I will discuss this in more detail in the chapter titled Building knowledge.

An agile organization that can accommodate new products and business models

In the now classic book *The Innovator's Dilemma: When New Technologies Cause Great Firms to Fail* (1997), Clayton Christensen tells how new technologies create enormous problems for existing companies. Christensen studied the dynamic computer industry, but other research has come to the same conclusions (see Adams et al., 1998).

Unlike what most people seem to believe, it is not a lack of new ideas or an inability to develop new technologies in an old company that is the problem. Christensen shows that companies that went under when start-ups took over their market with new technology had already developed that new technology in their own development department. But they did not succeed in getting it to market. The reason was their organizational structure. The old product and business model was etched into the enterprise through its organization chart (Christensen, 1997; Adams et al., 1998). An organization chart creates an inertia that slows down change because it is associated with people's positions (Wallander, 2003). A hierarchical organizational structure has feudal characteristics in that a subordinate inherits the power and position of his/her boss (Burns and Stalker, 1994). Power derives from position to an excessive extent. This makes information

Figure 2-4. This is one example of how strategy and development can be designed with an agile organization based on pulse meetings. The strategic direction is devised by the portfolio team and coordinated at the portfolio pulse meetings (yellow in the figure), strategic product management is run by the product team who make their decisions at the product pulse meetings (red), operational development is managed by projects (all of which have project pulse meetings) and is coordinated at the program pulse meetings (blue), assignments are coordinated at the assignment pulse meetings (green), and resource allocation is managed at the resource pulse meetings (orange).

and knowledge a tool for gaining and maintaining power. And that prevents learning, because learning is based on the sharing of information and knowledge (Atkinson and Moffat, 2005).

In Pulse, I solved this by introducing a new way to describe organizations. A hierarchical line organization is built around individuals and positions, which are nodes in a network. In Pulse, the pulse meetings serve as the nodes; they are forums where information and knowledge are shared and decisions are made. The organizational structure of Pulse is created by defining which pulse meetings there will be, who will participate in these pulse meetings, and the links between the various pulse meetings. (See Figure 2-4.) There are fixed positions in Pulse (product manager, program manager, assignment manager, and resource manager), but they are few. The agile organization in Pulse is based on the work being conducted in teams that are composed of different expertise to solve specific tasks. Some of the teams are permanent, such as the portfolio and product teams, while others are temporary, such as projects,

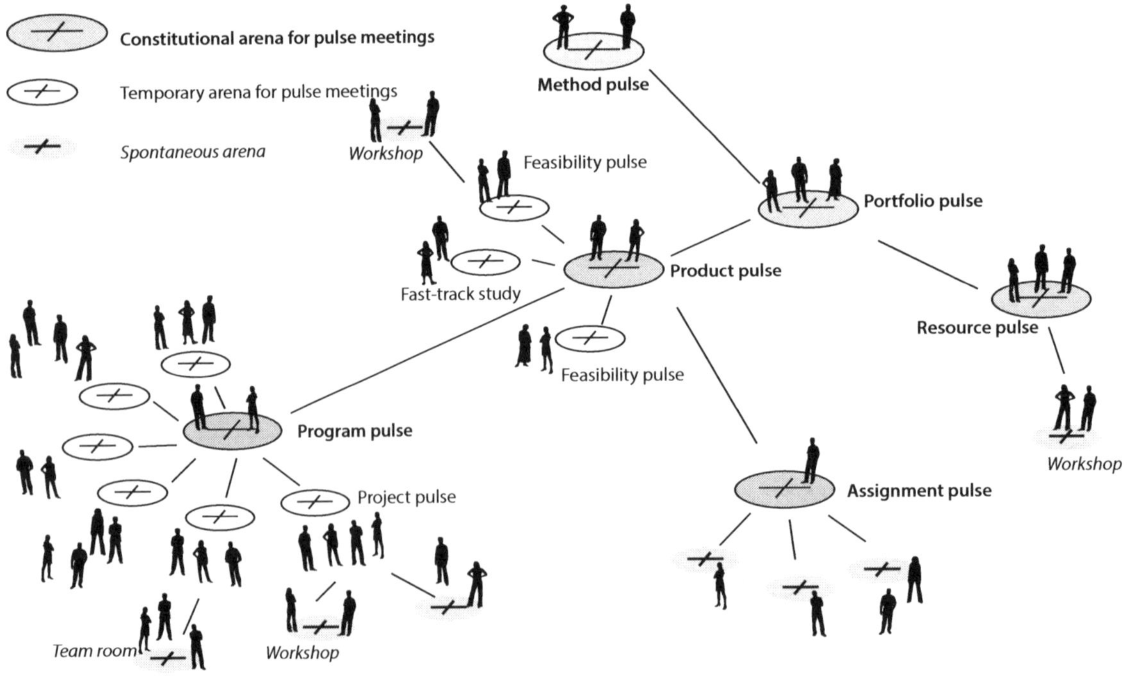

feasibility studies, and assignments. Positions and power in Pulse are strengthened by the individual being able to contribute knowledge and social skills so that together the team can produce the results required. Each team has pulse meetings with a pulse board for real-time management, sometimes also called visual or daily management. Who is contributing to the work is evident in the transparency that visualization creates.

Visual management—Planning and managing in real-time

The basis for real-time management comes from the two principles formulated by Taiichi Ohno (1988), the originator of lean practice. The first principle is to replace detailed long-term plans with just-in-time planning based on the current situation. Production uses tools such as kanban, a signal that tells a production cell that materials further downstream have been used up and need to be replenished. In Pulse, the signals are relayed by sticky notes on the pulse board, in what I call the activity window, as shown in Figure 2-5.

Figure 2-5. Activity window on a pulse board.

The "To do" panel in Figure 2-5 contains sticky notes with activities that would take anywhere from an hour's work to a day or two to complete. The person at the pulse meeting who has the time and opportunity now to do the work takes the note and puts it in "In progress." At the next pulse meeting, or the following one, when the person has done the task, he/she moves the note to "Done." (For more details, see Agile Pulse Model.)

The pulse board contains more information than an activity window. Being able to work efficiently on a team requires condensed information that everyone has access to and shares a mutual understanding of. This applies to goals and plans, for example, that are put up on the pulse board and communicated visually.

Ohno's second principle is to deal with problems directly when and where they appear. In production, this can be implemented by turning on a red light and calling in a "rapid response team." In Pulse, unexpected events are flagged in the Inbox on the pulse board. Most unexpected events can be handled by the team via pulse meetings, but some events require raising the issue to the next decision level or calling representatives from the product team and portfolio team to a "rapid response workshop."

Visual communication

Using visual communication, we can create pulse in our work (move forward at a steady pace). Large amounts of information can be visualized and condensed into a few images. These images transform abstract information into concrete communication between people. People can actually see the current situation of their team, creating effective coordination between them, which picks up the pace of work. The amount of information and the frequency of decisions are adjusted to the need, so that everyone has the information they need for work to move forward. Thus we avoid producing unnecessary documentation.

With pulse meetings, you can encourage interaction and cooperation in the team, creating a mutual understanding of the task to be solved. Here the effect is also a faster pace of work. Pulse boards visualize information about goals, the current situation, the problems detected, and the plans for further work. Everything can be condensed into a few pictures and matrices.

The pulse meetings are short, 5–30 minutes. The more often pulse meetings are held, the shorter they become and the faster the work proceeds. The fact that pulse meetings are held standing picks up the pace, too, because the group dynamics increase when there are no fixed seats. In addition, participants feel more open and trust each other more when they stand close to one another.

PMI's project philosophy, and all project models based on Taylorism, is based on detailed planning. The idea is that a project manager can plan in detail the results to be produced, the activities required, when the work will be performed, and by whom. However, as I have already mentioned, the future cannot be predicted—it goes against the laws of nature for complex systems such as projects. In a system for planning in detail, it is popular to use "gates" as checkpoints for quality and overall control. The idea is for all the pieces to be in place so the project can be allowed past the gate. In practice, having a few large gates does not work. Often the project is allowed to continue, although it is impossible to monitor or control the quality. In contrast, a pulse project may have 50–100 small gates. These serve as handshakes within the project or between the project and the product team. In Pulse, such gates are called "subresults" and "handover points," respectively. The handshake is done using demonstrations that show how the project group has verified that the result is correct. By having many demonstrations, we get feedback to flow within the project and between the project and the product team. This feedback is the very heart of learning and thus product development.

Coordination within and between projects

In hierarchical organizations, the product manager is seen as having sole responsibility for a product or product family (see Gorchels, 2005). Sometimes the product manager is also the sponsor of the projects' results.

In Pulse, the product team develops technical architecture for products and product families and also prepares the commercial and technical supporting information required to start a project.

Having a unique steering committee for each project is not an appropriate organizational form for multi-projects, because it misses out on coordination between the projects. Instead, I use a product team whose ongoing work results in a strategic design that shows which technologies and performance are required to meet customer needs.

The product team defines what effects the project will achieve, which features the project will deliver, and on what basis the project is deemed profitable. This requires coordinating the technical issues between projects, because the solutions in the projects affect one another. The technical dependencies arise partly as a result of the desire to reuse good solutions and partly because, to some extent, the projects compete for the same customers.

Projects are decision-intensive, repeatedly reaching crossroads and problems that demand decisions. Each time work is congested for the lack of a decision, efficiency and commitment are lost. Decisions need to be made as needed, just-in-time. Thus, for their work to progress smoothly, projects need a well-oiled and rapid decision process. The speed of decision-making must be adjusted to the needs of a multi-project organization (Holmen et al., 2003). Speed and flexibility are built up through the network of pulse meetings and the frequency of the pulse meetings. Consequently, if the product team and portfolio team hold more frequent pulse meetings, the projects can be run faster.

Coordination within a project is accomplished through parallel workflows and work in teams (Millard, 2001). Often one can work simultaneously in different distinct parts of the project with no problem. By doing several parts of the project simultaneously, lead times can be significantly shortened, while in the course of work project members can communicate and take into account demands from other sections. The ingrained habits of thinking serially and dividing up work based on a functional organization can be broken by working out the overall plans as a group and organizing the project as a team.

Pulse meetings

In Pulse, planning is based on real-time management, sometimes called "visual management" (pull), as opposed to "detail-oriented management" (push). Everyone working with product development belongs to some team, and each team has its pulse meetings (see Figure 2-6). The participants communicate their observations from work they have done since the preceding pulse meeting and simultaneously see on the pulse board what results are missing and what problems need to be solved for the work to progress. Real-time management helps create a steady flow, a pulse, in the work. Mistakes are detected faster, and the team can remedy errors and deficiencies together.

Figure 2-6. Pulse meeting for visual management.

By working with a few things at the same time, the team can concentrate on each step and strive to get a more even flow with fewer interruptions. In development work, there is a constant need for decisions and information. It is vital to minimize all waiting time—the time that individuals wait for information and decisions as well as subresults waiting to be used. When unfinished products and results get held up for a long time in between steps, lead times lengthen, and the cost of tied-up capital and rework increases.

Decision-making in multi-project organizations

In a multi-project organization, several projects that depend on one another are in progress at the same time. Typically the projects compete for the same resources. They can also be affected by common technical solutions and interfaces. Thus in a multi-project model, attention focuses on the managers above the projects, referred to here as the multi-project management. Projects are temporary: they are started, carried out, and concluded. The multi-project management, however, is permanent, as are, to some extent, the channels that provide information to the various parts of the organization.

The multi-project management handle several different types of decision. I have chosen to divide the decision-making structure for strategy and development into several parts: product management, portfolio management, resource management, assignment management, and project management. Each of these parts is handled by a team that coordinates their work via pulse meetings.

The first part, called product management, handles the product's design, quality, and customer value. Background information, needs, problems, and ideas are processed by the product team (see Figure 2-7). The work should focus development efforts on the product characteristics that create new opportunities in the market and can be charged for. The product team prepares prospective projects, while the portfolio team chooses and starts projects that the operation has the capacity to carry out. The "core team" in the product team consists of commercial product managers, the technical program manager, and the assignment manager. In addition to these, the team can include more people to bolster its expertise in logistics, purchasing, or production technology. There is also always a resource pool that can be used for product management work, alongside projects and assignments. Work on the product team is organized as workshops, feasibility studies, and fast-track studies. Switching up the staffing for these is one way to encourage learning.

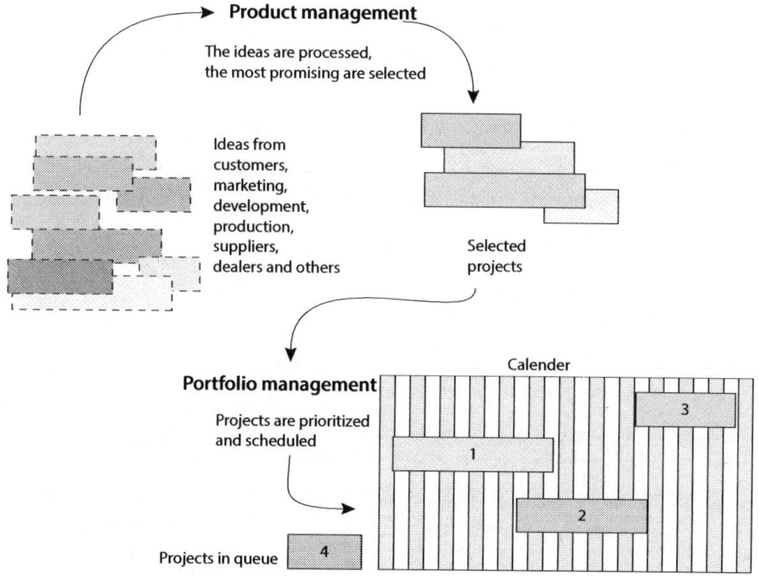

Figure 2-7. Overview of idea handling and project start-up in an agile multi-project organization. Product management is handled by the product team, while portfolio management is handled by the portfolio team.

The second part is called "portfolio management" and concerns the organization's strategic direction and thus questions about the product team's and projects' directions, profitability, and relative priority. Supporting information for the projects will come partly from the product team and be coordinated by the portfolio team in the project portfolio. The portfolio team directs the operation's resources to the customer segments and projects where they are deemed to produce the best benefits. This work requires ongoing analysis of profitability and potential for projects that are new, in progress, and completed. Each project is assigned a priority that affects its allocation of resources. Projects that lack resources are queued. Portfolio management is a job for all or part of the management team.

The third part consists of the practical work of supplying product management, projects, and assignments with resources in the form of individuals and equipment, and those duties are resource management's. All available resources for development work are included in a resource pool. Resource managers allocate people to the feasibility studies, projects, and assignments based on the current needs, the projects' resource plans, and the priority set by the portfolio team. At the same time, they ensure that staff are not spread thin, by allocating each individual to no more than two projects at a time.

The project manager's tasks in Pulse

- **Use the methods of pulse meetings, workshops, and demonstrations that realize the principles of visual management.**
- **Ensure that the members of the project can focus on performing value-adding work by identifying and eliminating interruptions.**
- **Attend to the entirety of the project, in terms of technology, time, and financing.**
- **Represent the project to the outside world and escalate problems and decisions as needed.**

Assignment management is the fourth part: to prioritize, queue, and coordinate the work on assignments. Responsibility for assignment management is concentrated in one person, the assignment manager, to avoid the suboptimization that occurs in a functional organization. The portfolio team sets a framework for handling assignments by specifying the average share of resources that may go to assignments and approving the rules that will be used to prioritize assignments. Assignments vary in size and may take from a few hours to several hundred hours of work. The assignment manager typically has 10%–30% of the resource pool at his/her disposal. Rarely can all desired assignments be carried out, so the assignment manager will have to set limits and reject certain requests. To carry out the assignments, there are resources that often constitute a loosely composed team.

Product management, portfolio management, and resource management are prerequisites for every project manager being able to succeed with the task of managing a single project. To carry out the work, there are one or more project teams, which will vary in staffing during the course of the project. As I described earlier, traditional project management has been planning work, which I have "streamlined away" using visual management. Project management in Pulse is done to a large extent at pulse meetings, demonstrations, and workshops. At the pulse meetings, the participants manage the project together as a team on a daily basis. The project manager's task is to ensure that the system works, for example that project participants come to pulse meetings, that communication between participants flows, and that the pulse board is kept up-to-date. In addition, the project manager shall attend to the entirety of the project—its technological, temporal, and financial aspects—and call for help when decisions need to be taken or problems cannot be solved in the project. The project manager also represents the project externally, such as at program pulse meetings and with customers.

Summary of multi-project management

In this chapter, I have discussed the problems that create waste in organizations with a bureaucratic structure. Examples of waste are the wrong results, unnecessary mental shifts, long distances in time and space, waiting times, faulty practices, overproduction and overdocumentation, and unnecessary inventory and lead time. These kinds of waste are typical effects of a Taylorist approach.

Taylorism is based on reductionism and seeing the organization as a linear system. But an organization is a nonlinear, complex system. In linear systems, the whole is the sum of its component parts. A complex system, on the other hand, emerges from the interactions between its parts, which means the system is quite different from the sum of its parts. One example is learning as product development, which arises from interaction between different agents.

As a solution to current problems, I propose a system that prevents overloading and fragmentation, with methods and other conditions that encourage teamwork, following practices that make it possible to simultaneously work strategically and operationally, and an organizational model that is detached from the current products and business model.

A pulse organization consists of arenas where people in various teams meet to share information and knowledge. The structure of arenas, designed as pulse meetings for each team, has no connection to the current products and business model. Thus, new products and business models can be developed. A pulse organization for strategy and development typically consists of portfolio pulse meetings, product pulse meetings, resource pulse meetings, project and program pulse meetings, and assignment pulse meetings. Collectively these pulse meetings form the agile multi-project organization.

The portfolio team consists of part of the operation's top management team. They define the strategic direction, prioritize the product team's work, set a framework for the assignment manager, and decide which projects will be implemented and when, based on available resources.

The product team works with the operation's strategic design: for which customer needs could a solution be economically viable and what should the technical architecture look like for the product to be profitable. The product management translates the strategy into action by proposing projects and assignments.

The resource team consists of managers with staff responsibility for the employees working on strategy and development. They allocate resources to feasibility studies, projects, and assignments.

The assignment team handles all assignments, that is, all operational work that is not defined as a project. The assignments are to be prepared, prioritized, and queued by the assignment manager and then carried out when the capacity is available.

Project management in Pulse is done at pulse meetings, demonstrations, and workshops. At pulse meetings, the participants manage the project together on a daily basis. The project manager's task is to ensure that the system works and interruptions are dealt with, to attend to the entirety of the project, to escalate problems that cannot be solved in the project, and to represent the project to the outside world.

In this chapter, I have provided an overview of Pulse. In the next few chapters, I intend to discuss the various areas in more detail.

3. Lead times and feedback

In this chapter, I will discuss the benefits of short lead times and how to achieve rapid throughput. Having shorter lead times in strategy and development than the competition's gives a company an advantage in information, because it provides feedback faster. And feedback from customers is fundamental to developing profitable products. Lead times depend on the number of projects and assignments the enterprise has in progress at the same time. Lead times also depend on what percentage of the hours worked constitutes value-adding work, which in turn depends on the enterprise's capacity for teamwork and work on strategy. This chapter shows how the portfolio team can take control of the number of projects and thereby lay the foundation for short lead times and teamwork.

Efficient product development

The management of a company invests resources in product development to achieve various results. They might want to attain a market position that blocks competitors and sets the standard for that product area. Usually they also want to be able to efficiently utilize the resources and investments already made. This means, among other things, that it should be possible to convert previous research and development into products that can be taken to market, to use new and better technologies in the products, and to overcome past problems. Above all, they want the efforts to generate profitability for the company through increased sales volume, improved margins, and lower costs. Over time, the investments should guarantee the company's survival and growth.

Today many companies are pushed to develop their products faster, to introduce new products more often, and to better satisfy customer needs. This pressure is evident in the fast-moving market for consumer electronics. But the pressure is also evident in industries with traditionally long development cycles. The changes required to meet the demands for faster and more efficient product development are revolutionary for many companies.

Around the turn of the century, many companies introduced the project as a way of working, using standardized project models. Some also introduced IT support for in-depth detailed planning. In the project models, a development process was established that fixes the detailed requirements in specifications early on, which resulted in extensive bureaucracy. The project models have also demanded extensive project documentation, steering groups, and fixed decision gates, as well as the clear delineation of responsibilities between project managers, line managers, and sponsors. All of this limits the room for action by individuals who are supposed to initiate and run the projects. The idea behind bureaucratic models is essentially to limit and standardize, with the aim of achieving productivity this way. But research shows that, on the contrary, bureaucratic approaches lead to low productivity (Burns and Stalker, 1961; Woodward, 1980; Takeuchi and Nonaka, 1986; Cusumano and Nobeoka, 1997; Blomberg, 2013).

To lift performance in product development to new levels requires a new approach. Effective product development involves being able to rapidly meet new or changing customer needs, which requires a short development cycle and high productivity, that is, doing the right things and being able to use resources well. This has become a competitive advantage as a result of increased international competition, an increasingly fragmented and demanding market, and many new technologies that are quickly being developed. Industries have matured, but so have their markets and customers. The obstacles on the path to efficient product development are the problems I stated in previous chapters: overloading and fragmentation, minimal cooperation and hence minimal learning, that too little energy is devoted to understanding customer needs, and being stuck in the old products through the organizational structure.

Through development work, an operation strives to shape its future. Many promising paths can be chosen, but new circumstances or unforeseen problems can quickly alter the basic assumptions. Effectiveness ("doing the right things") and productivity ("doing things the right way") in an operation's product development depend on multiple interacting factors, such as culture, knowledge, organizational structure, management policies, strategies, and methods. It is difficult to improve effectiveness and productivity, but that is also why change gives such strong competitive advantages.

It is not enough to be the best at coming up with ideas, best at designing plastic widgets, or best at lean production. The entire system must work and interact with its parts, that is, design, production, logistics, and interaction with customers. And not just for one project at a time, but for all projects and parts of the operation as a whole. As technical complexity and cost pressures have increased, interactions between projects have multiplied greatly and they contribute to increased complexity. Projects share the same components, same suppliers, and the same architecture. It must be possible to systematically connect the results. The product has to fit into an existing production system and be sellable as a key part of a complete range of products. Gradually, new elements will be developed that fit in and function as part of the whole. To lead successful development work, one must learn to manage the interactions between different parts of the operation, technologies, markets, and projects.

The change facing product development can be summed up as a drastic shortening of the development cycle. However, this is not about working harder but about organizing work in a better way. You have to work differently. And management's work in particular will be designed differently, so the managers face the biggest changes.

The advantages of shorter lead times

So why are lead times so interesting? There are many different reasons, but I think the biggest advantage of short lead times is more opportunity for feedback and learning. Feedback from customers is what drives the enterprise forward. Innovations are developed in interaction with customers and the market (Klofsten, 2005). Launching new products often gives rise to recurring feedback from the market. And it is this feedback that provides the impetus for development work (ibid). An enterprise that has short development cycles will also have a strong competitive advantage and can keep its products in the market longer. For most products, this results in more sales volume over the product's lifecycle, which can lead to more loyal customers, higher peak sales, and better conditions for becoming market leader and thus the price setter. All in all, shorter lead times mean the possibility of earning more money.

The increased flexibility that results from shorter development cycles can allow access to more recent information on customers, which makes it easier to match products to the expectations and needs of customers. Then it becomes possible to act quickly on new information about customers, markets, suppliers, and the products' performance, and thus retain scope for action late in development work. Decisions should be made just-in-time when sufficiently good information is available, not as a result of a scheduled meeting. The upshot is better decisions and fewer bottlenecks, information gaps, redos, and interruptions.

Whether you want to be first with a new product in the market or aim to be a fast imitator, you profit from a shorter development cycle. In both cases, you can wait longer to make the critical decisions. You are also forced to maintain your focus on customers, because you cannot watch your competitors to copy them (Smith and Reinertsen, 1998).

The path to shorter lead times

The development cycle can be shortened dramatically in all multi-project operations. To achieve that, you must take initiatives in many different areas that deal with the fundamental problems.

First, overloading and fragmentation can be remedied only if the operation can concentrate its efforts on just a few areas at a time (Wheelwright and Clark, 1992). The strategic work needs to be a priority for the portfolio team, so that the operation works on a few customer segments or focus areas at a time. For these segments or areas, the product team prepares business goals and program plans that describe what the operation wants to achieve in the next few years and what development steps are planned. The operation must also limit the number of projects it works on so as not to get overloaded. Employees should be able to complete their tasks one at a time without being tempted to switch to other assignments that might be easier. With more alert control of the number of projects and assignments, overload can be avoided and the number of interruptions reduced. Employees can work undisturbed, concentrate on their work, and also have what they need to be able to work together. A project that starts should also cross the finish line. A completed project provides feedback, and being able to cross the finish line gives employees and managers extra energy.

The second problem is the lack of learning. Getting away from work done alone by "experts" with the resulting minimal learning requires multiple initiatives. Innovative development requires teamwork (Alberts, 2011), hence the need for workplaces and methods that allow it. Teamwork is also key to shorter lead times in development projects, as it boosts organization (Prokopenko et al., 2008). The enterprise also needs to improve its ability to pick up feedback from its environment through various channels (Grinyer and Norburn, 1975) and to interpret and draw conclusions from that information. A team is far more capable of solving complex problems and challenges than a group of individuals who work independently are (Alberts, 2011). For teamwork to truly work, team members must have access to a space where they can work together and methods.

The methods I refer to here are primarily pulse meetings, workshops, and fast-track studies. Workshop methods are based on the nominal group technique, which ensures everyone's participation and maximizes creativity. Fast-track studies involve intensive work in small working groups during several consecutive short periods of 1–2 hours. Between each period, the results are demonstrated for all participants and the next period is planned.

The third fundamental problem is decision making. It should be possible to make decisions just-in-time (Holman et al., 2003), but that demands more frequent decision-making meetings and that decision-makers are more in synch. More efficient product development requires a new way of making decisions. The key is to prepare only that information about the product, market, and process that is required for each decision. Such supporting information has a short shelf life, so no documentation should be prepared too early. On the other hand, no decision can be made if information is lacking. At the same time, it is important to improve the quality of the information made available and to continually fit the pieces together for a more complete picture. This approach requires more flexibility and more frequent communication. The decision-making structure has to be much more fast-acting (agile).

Fourth is the lack of strategic thinking. Understanding of customer and market needs can be enhanced with more work at the strategic multi-project level (Cusumano and Nobeoka, 1998). Development work must be formulated around a strategic design. In the traditional project literature, everything revolves around the projects. With this way of thinking, the background documentation for projects becomes a feasibility study, or a pilot project, that is initiated because the projects need them. That is not how I see development work. A project is a way to accomplish a step in a strategy, where the strategy work is central to success. Analyses and studies are carried out within the scope of the strategic work to produce better strategies, not to be documentation for projects. In Pulse, the unifying force for strategic work is provided by the product team. They should have a helicopter view based on what is best for the enterprise. When there is a thoroughly prepared strategy that describes customer needs and opportunities and how the enterprise intends to realize them, the projects and assignments that are initiated to implement that strategy will have great potential to be carried out in a short time.

The fifth and final obstacle, mental blocks created by today's organizational structure, absolutely must be eliminated. A hierarchical line organization is built around individuals, their positions, and attachments to the existing business model. This obstructs, perhaps even prevents, the development of new innovative products. Instead we need a nimble, agile structure. In Pulse, the organizational structure is based on an assembly point for people: pulse meetings. This provides completely new degrees of freedom, while the importance of position in the hierarchical line organization is toned down.

Shorten the development cycle with decisions and knowledge before the projects start

Decisions should be made when options have been considered, neither earlier nor later. Background information needed for the decisions should be requested. No documentation is produced and no analyses are done unless someone needs them for their work. If decisions are to be taken at the right time, decision-making meetings need to be held frequently, which is accomplished with short and frequent pulse meetings.

In product development, it is primarily knowledge and information about the product, market, and processes that are being developed. When all the pieces are in place, the finished product can be marketed, sold, and produced. Until such time as the new product is ready and, to a large extent, also afterwards, it will be necessary to collect information and data that can be compiled into new knowledge. This knowledge is used to make trade-offs, solve problems, and make decisions.

When a new idea for a product is presented, there are often many questions. How big is the market? Which customers would buy this product? What customer needs will the product primarily satisfy?

What price can we charge? Are there any competitors? Even later, when you have reviewed the conditions in the market and decided to work out an architecture for the product, a lot of knowledge is still missing. What should the product look like? What attributes should the product have? What technical solutions should be chosen? Will the different parts fit together and work well together? What will it cost to manufacture? Every question like this—and there are many more—requires information to be answered. Sometimes gathering the right information, analyzing the information, and drawing conclusions that can build new knowledge represent an exhaustive process. Market research may be necessary, as well as interviews with customers or analyses of discussions in online communities. This can be augmented by building prototypes to test different technical solutions. With new knowledge, one can incrementally make the decisions that set the course for the strategy and the design of the product.

So much of the information that describes the finished product is missing at the outset, it is impossible to initially specify the product in detail. Such early specifications become a theoretical exercise, which will never work in the real world, something that the operation finds out when the projects' results do not turn out as imagined. Costly rework and changes in requirements then become necessary, at the same time as pressure mounts to get the product to market. Specifications and manufacturing documentation can be written only after the design of the product and the manufacturing processes are complete. Instead of specifying a particular solution from the start, you should work broadly with multiple technical options at the same time. Multiple parallel solutions reduce the risk that development efforts will fail. This risk includes the risk that the product will not achieve the correct technical performance and hence will fail to fulfill customer needs and to meet the launch deadline.

Shorten the development cycle with dedicated staff

Although employees in many project organizations feel they have a lot of work going on and sometimes also feel a lot of stress from tight schedules and tough demands, surprisingly little of the work done is value-adding. According to data from the United States, on average engineers devote 10%–40% of their working hours to adding value and building necessary knowledge. Managers of engineers generally devote even less time to adding value for customers. This can be compared to Toyota, a successful company where engineers and managers utilize 80% of their working hours (Kennedy, 2003).

Value-adding work includes design, testing, decisions, and technical problem solving, which lead to the design of the product progressively being determined. Non-value-adding time is spent on coordination, seeking information and waiting for decisions, travel and moves, correcting errors, inconclusive meetings, and preparing reports and documents that no one uses for decisions. If you want to shorten lead times, you must master this waste of time—time at work and calendar time.

There are several reasons for poor efficiency. One reason could be the weak commitment and lack of concentration of each employee, which is a result of too many projects going on at the same time and a low degree of teamwork. Product development is a learning experience, where a team explores an unknown area together. If developers act like "seagulls," which fly in, do their thing, then fly away, there is no learning, and consequently no product development, either.

Dedicated and co-located staff shorten lead times as the degree of organization increases. Many companies find it difficult to organize their work this way, although it is a profitable way. Perhaps a dedicated staff is seen as utopian. Managers are concerned that staff will not be able to keep themselves fully occupied. Far-reaching specialization leads to individuals making sporadic efforts for virtually every project and assignment. To fill downtime with useful work, at least two projects, often many more, are assigned to each employee. When a person has a little time to spare, he/she can work on the next project, which increases the load per person. But this fragments work on the projects, and great distances in space and time open up between people in the operation, which leads to cases falling through the cracks. It is unlikely that individuals will be working on the same project at the same time, so teamwork becomes impossible. The degree of organization in the operation declines, which makes it less probable that value-adding work will be done (Prokopenko et al., 2008). If the enterprise's priority is to shorten lead times for projects, then they should ensure that each individual can focus on one project at a time. The enterprise gains faster throughput thanks to teamwork and an increased degree of organization. And with short lead times, no individual gets tied up in a project for a long time (see Figure 3-1).

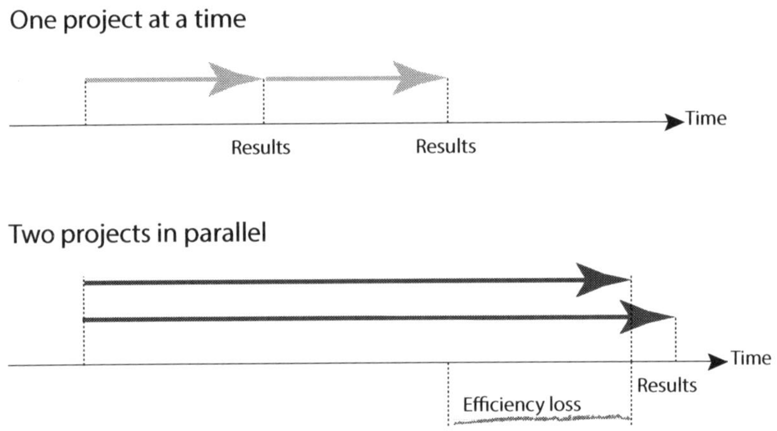

Figure 3-1. Effect of dedicated staff. The difference between a group of people carrying out one project at a time and the same group carrying out two projects at once can be seen in the lead time.

The combination of increased throughput and fewer projects and assignments in progress leads to a reduction in lead times, according to Little's law. Little's law states that there is a relationship between these three quantities such that the number of works in progress equals the throughput multiplied by the lead time. This means that the lead time for a project is the ratio of the number of projects in progress to the throughput. The more projects in progress, the longer their lead times.

$$\text{Lead time} = \frac{\text{Work in Progress}}{\text{Throughput}}$$

In many operations, it is difficult to work with dedicated staff on projects. That can be a result of many short projects where the contributions from each person are relatively limited. The solution I use is to differentiate between projects, which are major efforts, and assignments. All short tasks are channeled through the assignment manager, who has resources at his/her disposal to perform the work. This will give the projects breathing space to work undisturbed.

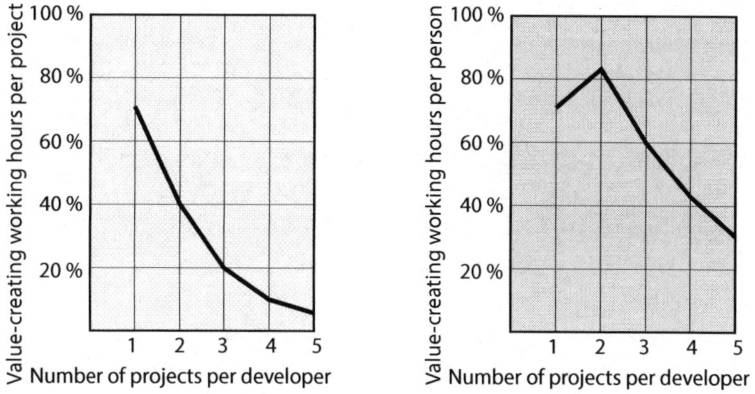

Figure 3-2. Proportion of value-adding working hours. The graph on the right shows how much value-adding work a project participant can perform when involved in multiple projects. The overall proportion of value-adding hours increases from one project to two but then drops sharply. If participating in five projects, the person spends about 25% of total working hours adding value. The graph on the left uses the same data to show how much of the value-adding working hours each project can benefit from (adapted from Wheelwright and Clark, 1992).

There is no point in producing subresults and materials far in advance. On the contrary, that is a losing proposition, which manifests itself in reduced productivity and poorer quality. When all subresults produced are immediately transferred to a recipient, any errors or defects in the material quickly become evident. Correcting an error right away is much easier than having to go back to something worked on several months ago.

Material that has been prepared has a short shelf life. Results from development work waiting to be used lose their value very quickly. This is because the technologies used are constantly evolving and staff constantly learn to better understand customer needs and also learn new ways to solve the technical problems. Designs produced a few months ago feel hopelessly out-of-date today.

Shorten the development cycle by avoiding overload

How many projects is each person in your operation working on at the same time? How many projects are completed in relation to the number started? It is common to have several low-activity projects that will never be finished. They rob the organization of energy. How long does it take from a decision to start a project until it actually gets going? Do the staff have time to deal with new projects? Are there projects in which activity is very low, for which the staff only work a few hours each week? The impact of overload appears obvious if you ask a team to plan a new project. How long does it take for a team of five people to complete a project that is budgeted for 1,000 work hours? Theoretically, it could be done in six weeks, but often the answer is six months. When someone asks why, the response is often, "I know how it works. So many other things always get in the way." In successful enterprises, the management team makes sure that nothing else gets in the way, according to McDonough and Spital (2003).

Remember, in successful enterprises, the management team makes sure that nothing else gets in the way of completing the projects.

If the operation gets overloaded, the cycle time—the time it takes to complete a project—grows much longer (Smith and Reinertsen,

1998). Staff get split among projects, and the efficiency plummets, while lead times soar. If results are not produced in a project, then no work is done, either. To get an idea of how much lead time is actually lost in the operation, you can compare the projects' budgeted working hours with the theoretical working hours during the calendar time scheduled.

In the example above, 1,000 hours were budgeted, and five persons were appointed to the project team. Suppose each person can work a maximum of 32 hours per week, which corresponds to 80% effective working hours. During those six months (equivalent to 26 weeks) that the project is planned to last with five people, the theoretical working hours are thus 26 weeks * 32 h/week * 5 people = 4,160 hours. The efficiency in terms of lead time would then be 1,000/4,160 = 24%. The rest of the time, material lies around waiting. "But the employees are working on other important projects during that time," someone might object. Yes, that is precisely the problem. Why don't they work so that this project is completed quickly instead and starts generating revenue?

Many projects have long lead times built in at the planning stage. One can calculate a key ratio that I call "speed" that indicates how many people on average are working on a project. Speed is calculated by dividing the number of budgeted hours of work by the number of hours the project is planned to last. In the example above, the project is planned to last for 26 weeks. The time the project is underway would then be 32 hours multiplied by 26 weeks, or 832 hours. Dividing the budgeted time of 1,000 hours by 832 gives 1.2. Thus, the plan is to have an average of 1.2 people work on the project. A speed of 1.2 is common for the projects I see. It is a woefully low level. How can teamwork be possible with 1.2 people on the team? And even more interesting, what are the 3.8 persons doing who are not working on the project?

How can something that should be doable in a few weeks turn into a six-month project? General reasons given are delivery times for materials and test runs. Delivery times ranging from five weeks and up are common. Why? The enterprises that have Pulse and that have questioned these times have been able to drastically reduce them. It is possible that you will have to pay a little more, but being able to complete a development project in a few months instead of years is worth a lot.

The 1,000-hour estimate is based on conspicuous relay race thinking, where one person at a time works without any dialogue with the other participants. Productivity is low, and innovation nonexistent. What an enterprise can earn money on is coming up with new innovative products, and that requires collaboration within the enterprise and with customers. It may require many more hours to achieve a good product. An alternative setup for the aforementioned six-month project is to put together a team of 10 people in a team room and give them four weeks to get the job done. That equates to a speed of 10, a total of 1,280 work hours, and a reasonable chance of producing an innovative product.

If the employees are to work while focusing on one project at a time, management cannot start an unlimited number of projects. Too many initiatives under way at the same time in an operation prolongs lead times at the same time as efficiency and quality decline. The project portfolio is a tool that gives the portfolio team an opportunity to prioritize which projects will be started and in which order. Without overall control, overload becomes inevitable. Several mechanisms drive the number of projects in an operation. Product managers are often rewarded for the number of initiatives they start, which adds to the number of projects. With several product managers, competition between them emerges, too, further increasing the load. Line managers have their own initiatives for improvement. Salespeople earn commissions and sometimes sell products that do not actually exist, which demands quick reworks that steal development resources.

By running two projects one after the other instead of overloading the operation with both projects simultaneously, several advantages are won, according to Smith and Reinertsen (1998). First, you reach the market in less than half the time for the first project, and project number two also gets into the market more quickly. Second, you get more flexibility and can schedule crucial decisions for later. When it is time for project number two to start, you can choose to start an entirely different project instead. In addition, decisions can be based on up-to-date information about the market and customers. With late decisions, you will be closer to the market. Last but not least, the staff will go through the entire development cycle faster, which means that they will learn faster (ibid).

The task of the portfolio team is to limit the number of projects allowed to start and to assess which of the proposed initiatives has the best prerequisites to become profitable. The project portfolio contains an overview of which projects are in progress and their priority with respect to one another. With assignment priorities and assignment lists, the assignment manager also makes sure to limit the number of short assignments in progress simultaneously. Short assignments often become acute and without effective control will be perceived as interruptions.

There should be only one priority in the enterprise. Thus, the project portfolio must be visible to everyone in the pulse room, so everyone can see which projects are in progress, which are queuing, and what unique priority each project has. The same applies to the assignment priorities and the assignment list.

The effect of faster development cycles

What happens to the competitive situation when one of the players radically shortens its development cycle? To illustrate this, we can paint a scenario from a mature market, as shown in Figure 3-3. Suppose that at the start there are two large and relatively equal companies, Alpha and Beta, that compete in the market. With development cycles a little longer than 18 months from project start to finish, for the technologies they work with, both companies have so far launched new product generations every other year. In between, they have introduced multiple model upgrades at reduced prices, as the cost of production declined because of increased volume. Until now, the two companies have been close in terms of costs and prices.

Then company Alpha decides to take the plunge and introduce Pulse. They manage to shorten the development cycle by six months and can launch their next generation (G3) six months before their competitor. With a more advanced product, Alpha can now charge a higher price. Half a year later, Beta comes out with its next generation (G3) as planned but does not manage to retake its traditional market share. The consequence for Beta is that their volume rises more slowly than normal, so production costs stop declining.

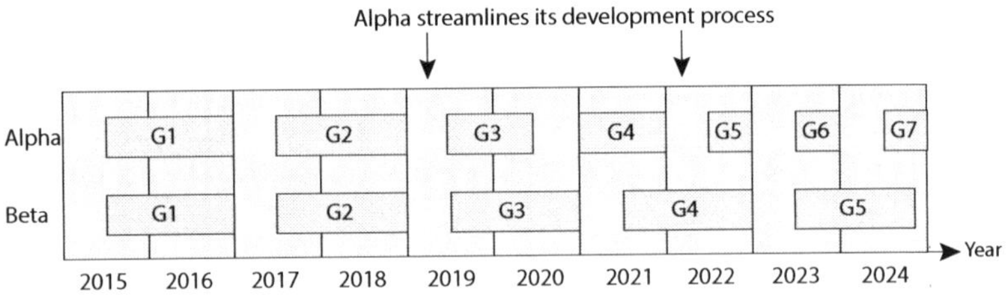

Figure 3-3 Competitive advantage of a shorter development cycle. Alpha's and Beta's product development projects and their launches of new product generations.

Then Alpha launches its next generation (G4) after 12 months. Again, they could charge a higher price but choose to win market share instead. Now Beta is not only trailing its competition technically speaking but has also ended up in a difficult position as a result of Alpha's aggressive pricing. Although Beta in turn fights back with lower prices and aggressive marketing, the company cannot prevent its market position from steadily weakening. Beta has now found itself in an even tougher cost situation.

With its next product generation (G4), Beta tries to retake the technical advantage seized by Alpha. They push hard to produce a more innovative product. Unfortunately, the launch is not successful. Alpha has further raised the bar in its development by shortening lead times for purchasing and testing during the development project. Now they can launch their next generation (G5) in six months, at the same time as Beta is launching its G4. Now Beta is a whole generation after Alpha.

Beta now has no choice but to accelerate the development of its next generation. But they lack the principles and methods required to accomplish that. Instead, pressure is rising in the company, and Beta is losing control of costs. At the same time, they have problems with their previous product generation (G4). Some of the resources needed for the development of G5 must be redirected to address problems with products in the market. The new product (G5) is expensive, and the company fails to fully achieve a development cycle of one year, which they had hoped for. At the same time, Alpha has once again developed its next generation (G6) in six months and is first to market again.

Beta loses more market share, and margins contract further. Beta's new product generation has many quality flaws as a result of the tight development schedule and is a financial flop.

Alpha's ability to bring new product generations to market much faster than its main competitor has, in less than five years, radically changed conditions in the industry. Beta has been forced to play a game that it was not ready for. Beta is now on the brink of collapse.

The shorter development cycle has given Alpha three decisive competitive advantages. First, Alpha can start development closer to the date of introduction, which means it has more recent information on customers and technology and can match customers' needs better. Second, they can take advantage of the latest technologies and bring them to market faster, leaving the competition behind and strengthening their market position. Over time, that difference will grow even more. Third, the advantage means they can choose either to raise the price to improve margins or to gain market share in order to increase volumes and lower costs. Alpha can also successively take advantage of faster knowledge creation that opens a gap between the company and its competitor at an accelerating pace, also making it possible for them to reduce their costs ever more quickly.

What does lead time cost?

Calendar time can be perceived as free. Tomorrow is a new day. Working hours, on the other hand, require compensation in the form of wages and thus are valuable. Can this be true? No. In fact, calendar time is often worth far more than the working hours put into a market-driven development project. The reason is that calendar time is linked to revenue, which depends on the number of units a company sells and at what price. Both the number of units and the price decline over time as a result of increased competition, as shown in Figure 3-4.

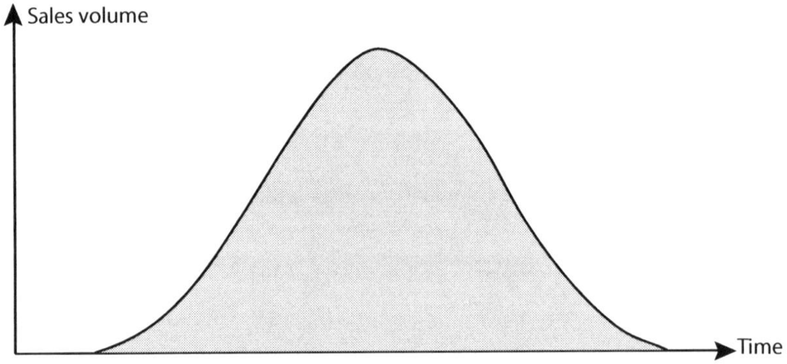

Figure 3-4 The bell curve. The sales volume of a product over time often follows a classic bell curve.

The sale of successful products follows a bell curve. Sales are weak initially, but then they take off and rise sharply, before plateauing and then falling back. How quickly sales get started and how long they are sustained is related to the market and the product being sold. A forecast of sales growth for a specific product must be based on lessons learned from similar products and take into account changes in the competitive situation.

With background data and knowledge from other similar products, as well as assumptions based on experience, it is possible to calculate what lead time is worth by performing a profitability analysis, as shown in Figures 3-5 and 3-6. The profitability analysis contains a section for revenues and one for costs. Revenue comes from the sale of the product. For how many years will it be possible to sell the new product? How many units will be sold each year? To calculate the sales volume, it is necessary to estimate the size of the overall market and its growth over time as well as the company's own market share.

	Basic assumptions	Year					
		0	1	2	3	4	5
Sales volume [units]			200	800	1000	800	800
Annual price reduction [%]	10%						
Sales price [€]	€1,400		1,400	1,260	1,134	1,021	919
Revenue per year [€k]			280	1,008	1,134	816	734
Cumulative revenue [€k]			280	1,288	2,422	3,238	3,973
Product development and support [€k]		450	50	50	50	50	50
Reduction of production cost per year [%]	5%						
Cost of production per unit [€]	€400		400	380	361	343	326
Cost of production per year [€k]			80	304	361	274	260
Marketing (percentage of sales) [€k]	12%		33	120	136	97	88
Overhead (percentage of sales) [€k]	4%		11	40	45	32	29
Total costs per year [€k]		450	174	515	592	454	428
Cumulative costs [€k]		450	624	1,140	1,732	2,187	2,615
Annual return on investment [€k]		- 450	105	492	541	361	306
Cumulative return on investment [€k]		- 450	- 344	147	689	1,050	1,357

Figure 3-5. Profitability analysis for a planned new product.

The selling price will drop over time, as a result of increased competition. How quickly the price drops depends greatly on the product being sold. Here, too, a value must be assigned based on experience from other similar products. The total revenue per year can now be determined based on the volume multiplied by the selling price, adjusted for the price reduction. The cumulative revenue can also be calculated. The cost of developing the product consists entirely or partly of the cost of implementing the development project. Details about that cost can be found in the project's estimate or budget. After the launch, support and product care are required. An estimate of what they cost may be based on key ratios. The cost of manufacturing the product consists of the cost of raw materials and inputs and the cost of processing. The cost of production declines over time as a result of efficiency gains in the processes and pressure on input prices. The rate at which costs decline depends on the type of products manufactured, how large the volumes are, and how effective the company's own production is at continuous improvement. Generally the cost of production tends to decline more slowly than the selling price. How much can it cost to market the product? Here one often uses key ratios, critical values expressed as a percentage of sales revenue. How much will other overhead cost? Here, too, one uses key ratios expressed in relation to sales.

The total costs are now determined based on the sales volume and the assumptions made. When revenues and costs are combined, they give an overall picture of profitability.

What happens to profitability if the product launch is delayed six months? The effect of a delay impacts different types of products differently. There are three main types.

For stable products, total sales are not affected (Scenario A, Figure 3-6). This assumes loyal customers who patiently wait for the product. The competition is weak, and the next technology shift that will replace the recently developed new product is influenced to a large extent by the launch date of this particular product. Profitability is affected marginally by the reduction in the selling price over time.

For other products, the point at which sales peak is determined by the market (Scenario B). With a later date of introduction, there is less time before the peak is reached. This means that a delay does not affect the rate of increase in sales. Sales will peak at the same time as in the original scenario, but at a lower level. The result is lower sales throughout the product's life cycle.

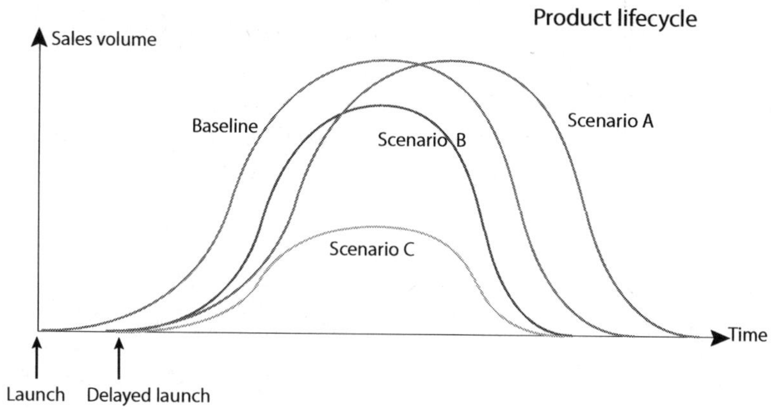

Figure 3-6. Different sales scenarios. Forecasts of sales growth for different products as a result of a delayed launch compared to a baseline. Scenario A: Sales curve for a stable product is shifted forward in time. Scenario B: Sales curve where the time that sales peak is determined by the market. Scenario C: Sales curve with greatly reduced sales.

For some products, sales growth declines sharply, and sales never take off in the same way (Scenario C). Sales peak at the same time as in the original scenario, but at a significantly lower level. The result is a much smaller market share throughout the product's life cycle. Instead, some competitor has become the market leader.

In the example in Figure 3-7, total profitability is estimated to fall by more than 40% as a result of a six-month delay in the product launch.

Six-month delay	Basic assumptions	Year					
		0	1	2	3	4	5
Sales volume [units]			50	600	800	600	600
Annual price reduction [%]	10%						
Sales price [€]	€1,400		1,400	1,260	1,134	1,020	919
Revenue per year [€k]			70	756	907	612	551
Cumulative revenue [€k]			70	826	1,733	2,345	2,897
Product development and support [€k]		450	50	50	50	50	50
Reduction of production cost per year [%]	5%						
Cost of production per unit [€]	€400		400	380	361	343	326
Cost of production per year [€k]			20	228	289	206	195
Marketing (percentage of sales) [€k]	12%		8	91	109	73	66
Overhead (percentage of sales) [€k]	4%		2.8	30	36	24	22
Total costs per year [€k]		450	81	399	484	354	334
Cumulative costs [€k]		450	521	930	1,414	1,767	2,101
Annual return on investment [€k]		- 450	- 11	357	423	259	217
Cumulative return on investment [€k]		- 450	- 461	- 104	319	578	795
Difference from the baseline scenario	loss of €562k	- 41 %					

Figure 3-7. Analysis of a delay. Calculation of the impact that a six-month delay in the launch has on profitability. Sales growth is not affected, and sales peak at the same time as in the original scenario in Figure 3-5 but at a lower level.

What impact does a 50% increase in development costs have on profitability? If we assume that the costs of carrying out the project rise, as do the costs of support and product care as a result of a more complex design, the original cost of EUR 70,000 will increase 50%. The cumulative profit falls a total of EUR 35,000, which corresponds to more than 25% compared to the original scenario.

There are rules of thumb used to quickly show how much profit is affected by time-to-market for a new product generation. By comparison, a company uses the profit accruing if it launches its product at the same time as the competition does. A delay of six months compared to the competition means that the company only breaks even. If they can instead bring their launch forward, six months ahead of the competition, they can triple their profit. Getting to market even earlier is not necessarily as beneficial. If customers are not ready for the technology shift, the company will invest much money in marketing before sales take off.

Time, cost, and performance trade-offs

Shortening lead times is profitable, especially if costs simultaneously decline. But the decisions an operation faces often involve trade-offs between the launch date, development costs, production costs, and product performance. Should the launch date stay fixed, although the project has failed to reduce production costs as much as the project goals specify? Or is it better to invest more time in development to solve the problem? Should the project be allowed to add extra features to the product at the expense of the delivery date? Should the project bring in consultants to meet the delivery date? The profitability analysis described above can be used to make financially correct decisions weighing various options. (See Figure 3-8.)

To do these calculations for every decision would be laborious. Instead, calculate key ratios for the product that can be used in every decision that requires a trade-off.

How much does a one-month delay of the launch cost? For the calculation to be accurate, one should estimate a bigger delay, otherwise there is a risk that the revenue loss will be underestimated. In the example above, a six-month delay would cost EUR 56,000. That means a one-month delay would cost EUR 9,300.

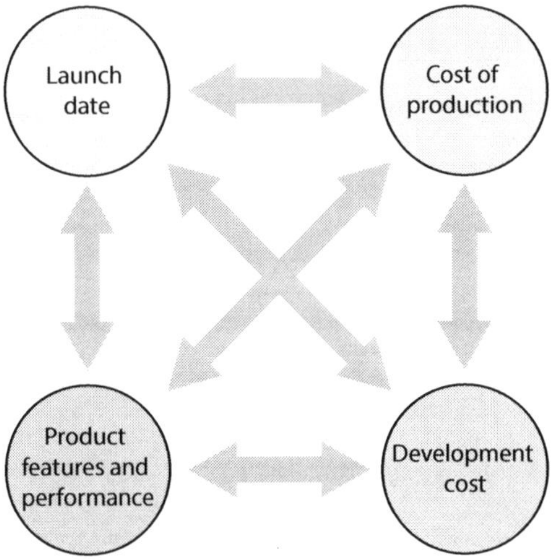

Figure 3-8. Decisions with trade-offs. Trade-offs must be made here to maximize the profitability of the product. With four different areas that affect profitability, there are six possible trade-offs.

In the example above, a 10% increase in the development costs of the project and support would cost EUR 7,000. Likewise, you can calculate what a 10% increase in the cost of production would cost. Note that the cost of production decreases over time. An excessively high cost of production initially will be compensated in a year or two by extra development efforts to solve the problem.

The last key ratio is linked to changes in sales. What is the value of a 10% increase or decrease in sales? The question is linked to changes in product performance. If the project fails to develop vital attributes in the product, sales will decline. The alternative is to offset this by charging a lower price. On the other hand, the introduction of new features might increase sales or support a higher selling price. How much must sales increase to compensate for a delayed launch and increased development costs? Maybe it is better to launch the product as planned and add the extra parts in the next model? The key ratios derived can be compiled in a table, as shown in Figure 3-9.

10% increase in development costs	- €70,000
10% increase in manufacturing costs	- €140,000
10% increase or decrease in sales volume	+/- €210,000
One month's delay in the launch	- €93,000

Figure 3-9 Key ratios. A few simple key ratios facilitate the decisions that require trade-offs when developing a new product.

Based on the key ratios in the example, we can see that a two-month delay due to enhanced performance of the product must be compensated by 9% additional sales. Also that a 20% increase in development costs is cheaper than a 12% increase in the cost of production, and that a 13% increase in development costs is preferable to a delay of one month.

The accuracy of the profitability analysis depends above all on the quality of the input data. So simple calculations are sufficient. Instead, focus efforts on obtaining better background information and making good assessments. Often, the biggest challenge is estimating sales volume, which can easily be off by a power of 10. The problem lies in being able to correctly predict both market size and market share.

By using simple methods, the calculations can be understood by everyone. Then the profitability analysis can be worked out by people from marketing, production, development, and accounting together. The advantage of working together is that the group simultaneously acquires a common understanding of the product and the project's prerequisites, something that will prove valuable later when difficult decisions must be taken under time constraints. Doing the calculations is only meaningful if economic arguments are used to back up decisions and that is done consistently. For the product team, the financial ratios facilitate decision-making. It is not necessarily the case that the launch date is holy, or that production costs must be reduced at any price. It depends (Smith and Reinertsen, 1998).

Summary of lead times

This chapter has demonstrated the benefits of shortening development cycles and the steps required to achieve shorter lead times.

With shorter lead times, the products enter the market earlier, which results in revenue sooner and extends the product's lifetime in the market. You can use newer technologies and make decisions about the final design of the product later, which gives you a technical edge over competitors. In addition, employees will learn faster, and problems will be highlighted that previously might have been ignored. The overall effect is increased profitability for the products.

Short lead times require a focused operation that concentrates its collective energy on a few things at a time, which in turn requires management to decide which projects to start and to give them a unique priority. You have to be able to make decisions just-in-time, which means that decisions are often made with greater flexibility and more frequent communication.

To shorten project times, the foundations of the projects must be thoroughly researched. The product team must prepare background information that illustrates customer needs linked to important product attributes and technical architecture. Knowledge of the design of the finished product is then built up incrementally during the course of development work and is finally documented in a specification.

Short lead times also require that staff are co-located and work focused in cross-functional teams with one or two projects at the same time so as not to be spread thin.

Using a profitability estimate, it is possible to calculate what the lead time costs. A rule of thumb is that a launch that is six months earlier triples revenue. With key ratios, one can accurately assess the economic trade-offs between the launch date, production costs, development costs, and the attributes of the product.

4. Product management

Product management is a way of creating understanding of customer needs and architecture using a holistic approach. In this chapter, I describe how a product team can work to achieve this holistic approach.

Focus on the customer: Product management

In the process of developing products that will be sold to a wider market, obviously the project team cannot work directly with all the customers who will buy the finished product. Rather, the product managers work with technical managers to set goals for projects and new products, based on an analysis of the market and customer needs within a market segment. So the product manager can be seen as the customer's advocate in the operation and vis-à-vis the projects.

Product team
The product team translates customers' needs and the operation's capabilities into business goals, operational goals, and program plans that describe development efforts into the future. The product team initiates projects and is the recipient of their results. The product team will ensure that the technologies in the results of the projects harmonize in the long run, build up the operation's long-term expertise, and ensure that the operation's products are profitable in the short and long run.

On the product team, the product manager contributes knowledge of customer needs, customer applications, and profitability by assessing the customer base, the competitive situation, and what the customer is willing to pay. The program manager, who is also on the product team, will contribute how the strategic plans can be accomplished by developing the overall product architecture, estimating costs, and initiating and coordinating projects.

The product team's work cycle

The product team is what powers the development operation and triggers all development efforts. Work on the product team is wide-ranging and can easily become fragmented. That is why the team plans its work in periods, as shown in Figure 4-1. Each period starts with setting priorities, defining what is to be achieved, and planning. Priorities and what is to be achieved are defined in dialogue with the portfolio team. The period ends with a demonstration for the portfolio team of the results that were defined at the start of the period.

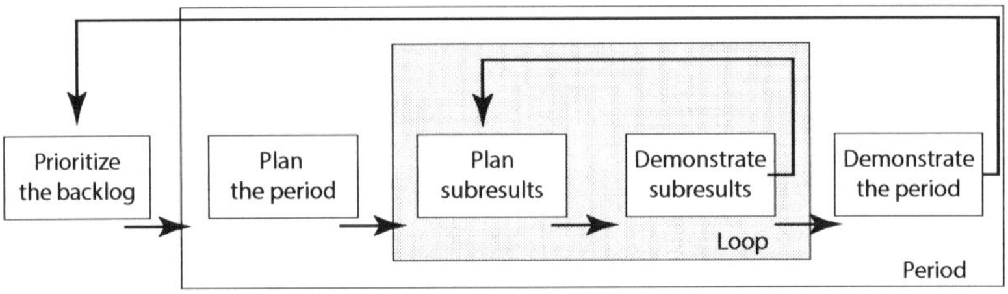

Figure 4-1. The product team's work cycle.

The product team fills its backlog itself with larger tasks that must be done, but priorities are set together with the portfolio team, which means that together they select which results should be achieved during the coming period and document these in the period log. At the same time, they discuss the desired results, so everyone agrees on the scope and goals. In Figure 4-2, the backlog and period log are at the bottom of the product pulse board.

The length of a period is optional and can be changed between periods but is usually 1–2 months. This allows enough time to achieve results while simultaneously keeping up a brisk pace.

The product team should attempt to concentrate its work on just a few areas at a time. They can do this by segmenting the market and simultaneously focusing their efforts on only one or a few segments (or by setting higher priorities on focus areas if working with operational development). In Figure 4-2, two segments each have their own business goals and program plan. How long the product team chooses to work on a segment varies, but to make an impact it should reasonably be at least six months. All the same, they should be able to change direction over time and evaluate the potential of other segments. That means that after a year or two at least one segment has been changed. How many segments can be worked on depends on how big the operation is and, above all, how many people work on product management.

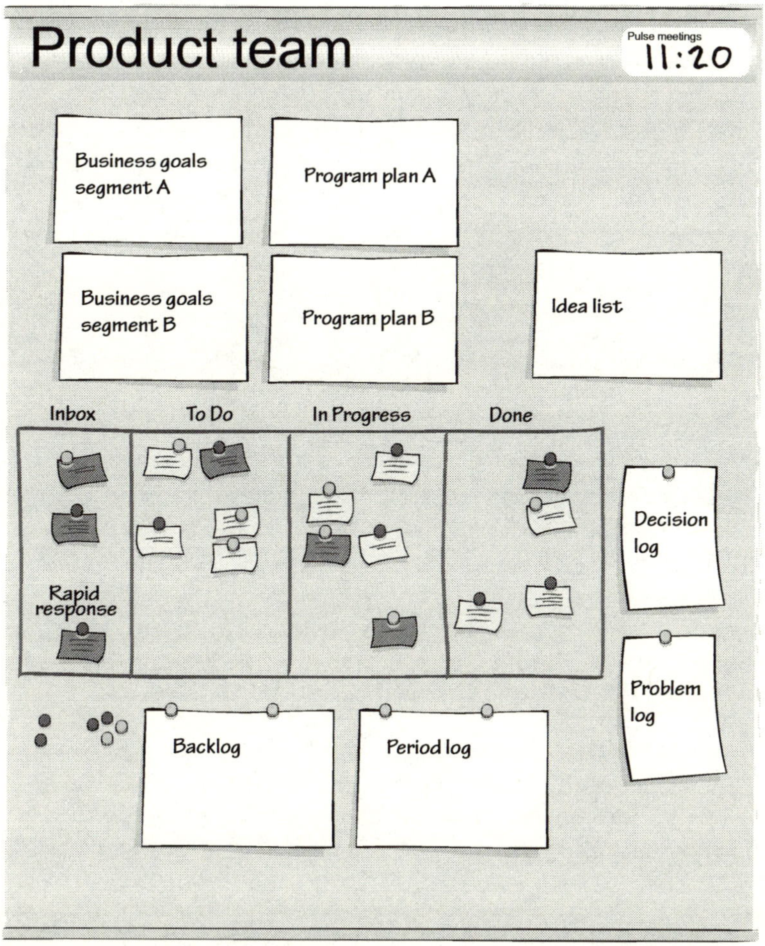

Figure 4-2. Product pulse board.

The business goals show what the product team wants to achieve and believes is possible in terms of increased revenue for the business during a period of a few years. The program plan describes in general the steps that the operation intends to take to achieve the business goals, in the form of market studies, feasibility studies, projects, launch activities, and the like. (See Figure 4-12 for an example of a business goal and Figure 4-13 for an example of a program plan.)

Some of the tasks and results in the backlog come from activities defined by the program plans. But there will also be a flow of unplanned tasks that need to be handled. This means that the product team cannot plan their working hours in detail using the period log. There must be time to deal with unforeseen, significant, and sometimes urgent events. Some of these relate to decision-making support for projects in progress, others to existing products in the market.

A product team that has most of its members gathered in one place has daily pulse meetings. If team members are geographically dispersed, the product team can hold pulse meetings via videoconference once a week or more often. When team participants do get together, the goal is to make efficient use of time for intense teamwork through workshops and fast-track studies. Between pulse meetings, members work on tasks agreed to at the most recent pulse meeting, individually or in groups and often in collaboration with people who are not on the product team.

Control the development of new products

When Wheelwright and Clark (1992) researched management involvement in development projects, they found remarkable phenomena. In the early stages, when managers had ample opportunity to control which results the projects would deliver, involvement was negligible. It was only when projects had developed a prototype, were approaching the launch, or were about to start delivering to customers that the managers got involved in the work. But once a project has gone that far, it is too late to influence anything other than the details of the results. The upshot is that managers devote most of their time to putting out the fires started by poorly selected solutions and the lack of decisions early in the projects. For managers to be able to control the company's development of new products, they must fix a strategic design for product development. They must also focus the development resources and their own time on activities that add value in the long run for the company and its customers. But above all, management must get involved earlier and to a much greater extent, to be present when the real choices have to be made.

For a company to succeed in getting a winning product into the market, it is not enough for the design engineers in the development unit to have done a good job; many more departments must get involved throughout the development process. First and foremost, the product team has to analyze market conditions—everything from customer needs to what competitors are doing—to find attractive areas to invest in. They also need to sketch plans for the initiatives and create a technical architecture that can be cost-effective at the same time as the products' features satisfy key customer needs. When the development project finally kicks off, production engineers should develop a production process that is cheap and fast and turns out products with a minimum of defects. Development engineers should engineer a robust product with the attributes that customers ask for that is also easy and inexpensive to manufacture. Other parts of the operation also need to be involved, such as the purchasing department engaging suppliers, the logistics department building up distribution channels, and the marketing department launching the product. But it is not enough that each of these departments makes brilliant efforts individually. For the product to be a success, all of these departments must work together, all the way from idea to launch (Wheelwright and Clark, 1992). The need for coordination requires one or more product teams that can work on product management and can point the direction work should take and can make decisions when conflicting demands force trade-offs.

The overwhelming majority of enterprises are technology-driven, or perhaps one should say product- and sales-driven. An integrated approach as to how to win and retain profitable customers is rare. A lack of customer focus has strongly affected development projects. In many cases, the goals of these projects have been unclear, out of control, or based on detailed technical specifications rather than genuine customer needs. As a result, many investments in new products have been unprofitable. For example, McKenna (1991) reports that of the 1,300 products launched in the United States in 1990, 70%–80% failed, largely because the development of the products was not market-driven.

One reason that development work is driven by technology—rather than the needs that customers actually have—could be the lack of market analysis. Yet many enterprises conduct analyses and have a variety of channels to their customers and the market. Adams et al. (1998) demonstrate in their research that development engineers take in market data related to technology but not data related to customer needs. What developers can influence is those things that exist within their own department or their own field of technology (ibid). An enterprise's organizational structure strictly limits which products can be developed (Adams et al., 1998; Christensen, 1997). I believe there are two fundamental problems. First, to some extent many developers have tunnel vision in their field of technology, that is, have difficulty seeing the big picture. Second, the organizational structure restricts their latitude for action. An existing business model has formed the organizational structure, so power and influence are rooted in the old products. Projects that could lead to new products and that challenge the existing order are actively opposed.

I think it is only natural that developers find it hard to see the big picture. It is difficult to work at different levels, with in-depth specialist knowledge and with an overview. That demands people who work with what I call strategic product development. To satisfy the need for strategic expertise, many companies have employed product managers (Gorchels, 2006). According to Cagan (2002), a company must be able to identify opportunities for new products, understand customer needs, and transform those needs into technical demands on the product as well as to effectively integrate marketing, development, and production. These tasks can be gathered under the responsibility of a product manager. But the real reasons that companies have employed product managers have varied, as have their duties (Gorchels, 2006). Many product managers have ended up in the role of problem-solver, technical product specialist, and provider of sales support, rather than long-term strategist for product road maps and prioritized market segments. For a company to survive long-term in a rapidly changing environment with tough competition, it must be able to satisfy customer needs, find profitable niches, and stay ahead of the competition. In this process, purposeful efforts in strategic product development are critical to success.

Organize for product management

The title of "Product Manager" is common in the literature (see Gorchels, 2006), but in reality there are several different titles for more or less the same position. The "Product Manager" designation is often used in companies that sell to a large number of customers, whether consumers or businesses. The titles "Product Development Manager," "New Product Manager," "Market Manager," "Business Area Manager," and "Segment Manager" also occur. Companies that have a few large customers with different unique needs often use the title "Key Account Manager," especially companies that work with contract-driven development assignments. In both market-driven and contract-driven companies, the planning of how to reach out with cost-effective products to customers with purchasing power is a key task that lays the foundation for developing successful products.

In attempts to define the role of a product manager, the list of tasks can become fairly extensive. A product manager should understand customer needs today and, perhaps even more importantly, be able to anticipate needs several years hence. The product manager should be able to see which of these customer needs can be transformed into profitable products. The product manager should understand the possibilities and limitations of the company's production, product development, and sales. And, based on his/her understanding of customer needs and the company's capabilities, the product manager should formulate goals and establish long-term plans that communicate the focus to the rest of the company. Success in this role demands broad as well as in-depth expertise, which is difficult to find in a single individual. So the product manager should be seen instead as one person on a product team that is composed of individuals with expertise from the market, production, and development. This product team will jointly work out a strategic design with business goals and program plans. It is best if the members of the product team can work full-time on these issues. They should produce the long-term plans and results currently lacking in many operations, where instead the product manager puts out fires and initiates short-term, low-yield projects.

In large operations, there may be multiple teams and resources working on strategic design. In an enterprise with 1,500 development engineers, 150–200 people may be needed for strategic work on everything, from platforms and technical architectures, to market analyses. I see a trend toward an increasing proportion of resources working with strategy. For example, some companies have chosen to outsource all development work at the technology level and deal only with strategic development in-house.

Without effective product management, market risks cannot be taken into account. Management may then choose to ignore such risks and focus instead on project risks. Consequently, they react sharply to projects that go over budget or do not reach a goal of lowering production costs. Yet it is not considered nearly as serious when the new product does not reach its revenue targets. Rather, when sales do not take off, it is seen as "bad luck" and nothing anyone could have predicted. If you have resources that can work strategically, you will find that a lot of the conditions that affect market risk can be anticipated and also influenced. The product team has the vital task of getting everyone to think in terms of the profitability of the products and demonstrating which factors affect this profitability. This means they have to pay attention to both revenues and costs. There is no point in developing a product within budget if it is not going to sell. To assess profitability, above all you must take the time to prepare data that shows the potential for revenue and which factors will influence revenue. How large is the potential market? What percentage of the market is estimated for the new product? How much will customers be prepared to pay to satisfy their needs? What problem of the customer's does the product solve and how much is it worth to the customer? What attributes must the product have so it can meet customer needs? Does the customer have a strong negotiating position? Will there be competition?

The product team is the link between the market and the company's operations. The product manager has the role of driving these efforts and, above all, should prepare the background data that illuminates customer needs and conditions in the market. The background data is used for decisions on long-term strategies for technologies and markets, which must be expressed clearly in the business goals and program plans. Based on these goals and plans, then, programs, projects, and assignments will be initiated as the means to achieve the business goals.

Projects often suffer from a lack of decisions, especially decisions about goals and product performance. During the course of a project, trade-offs are necessary between, on the one hand, more time to achieve specific features (performance) and, on the other, meeting deadlines and holding costs at a level that keeps the investment profitable. A well-functioning product team is a cornerstone in an effective development operation, for shortening development times as well as lowering costs, and also for developing profitable products. The product team will approve the results produced by a project during the course of the project and make decisions that influence the profitability of the product. Are the results good enough? Does the product satisfy the customer's priority need? Should the project work more on reducing production costs? Should a new technology be rolled into this product at the risk of the project being delayed? Should old technology be reused? Should modules be replaced? Can shortcomings in the product's quality be accepted or should the project be given more time to resolve them? With the product team, the operation achieves the continuity and integrity it needs on issues relating to customer needs, technology, quality, costs, and product profitability to successfully develop profitable products.

In this book, the main theme is product development, so you might think primarily of projects that develop new products or new models of existing products. But a project can also be a marketing project. It is just as important to be able to market new products and make potential customers aware of the needs that can now be satisfied as it is to bring out the product that the market is asking for. Projects can also consist of market research, carried out in the form of a project, aimed at generating the background data needed for the long-term decisions. It could also be a quality project or a capacity project to ensure that existing products and processes better satisfy market demands and reduce costs, or internal improvement projects could develop IT support for the operation's processes. All projects and longer investigative assignments can, in one way or another, be traced back to the ambition of better satisfying future customer needs. These projects should fit into the operation's long-term strategy for technology and the market. That is why all projects should be initiated via the program plans that the product team works out.

Market-driven product management

The work to create a strategic design for the development of products and offers should lead to goals for what the enterprise wants to achieve and a plan for how to reach those goals. I call these goals "business goals" or "operational goals." I call the plans for how to reach the goals "product road maps" and "program plans." With a pulse board, it is possible to visualize strategic goals and plans as well as the assessments and analyses on which they are based. The visualization will form patterns revealing new insights to the product team and will also communicate the strategic design to the rest of the operation.

The goals and plans that the product team produces should be based on analyses of customer and market needs. It is not enough to go out and meet customers. What is required are systematic tools for obtaining good supporting data. One possible source of errors is that customers are not necessarily able to articulate their needs. It is likely that their responses reflect their current problems and organizational structure. Good analysis methods should be able to see through that.

Business goals, product road maps, and program plans are not ends in themselves. They are tools that the product team uses for its work. The portfolio team prioritizes the segments that the product team should focus their efforts on. If they try to cover all products and market segments at once, there is a danger they will get in over their heads, according to Moore (1998). Concentrating on product development in a few market segments is relevant chiefly for new products that will open new markets but also for old products where one wants to carve out a position in relation to the competition. For products with strong sales growth, one must instead plan to increase production capacity and to ensure that the operation can deliver (ibid).

Initial product development is a relatively small part of a product's life cycle but often a risky and dramatic part. If the product survives the development stage and manages to gain a foothold in the market, subsequent stages will consist primarily of maintenance and updates.

Most product development takes place within an existing product family or is aimed at existing customers. Entering completely new markets is risky and laborious, as is developing completely new innovative products. But risk is also synonymous with opportunity. By "product development," I am referring to new or improved products within an existing product type. For example, Atlas Copco or Caterpillar might develop a new drilling rig. However, developing a completely new product for a completely new market or a fundamentally new technology that changes the conditions in a market is considerably more difficult, and I call the latter "market development" or "innovation." That is genuine entrepreneurship and a relatively uncommon occurrence. One example is when Apple developed the iPhone, which led to customers changing their behavior.

Market development is a big risk but also a great opportunity to make money. To not develop is also a risk. As soon as the Apple iPhone and Android smartphones were launched, other companies manufacturing mobile phones faced big problems. A portfolio of projects needs to strike a balance, between development projects within the framework of existing products and markets, and market development and research that can create innovations. Not all market development will succeed. Not even the supremely innovative Apple is always successful. The Apple Newton and the Apple Pippin were never hits.

The product team will work with strategic product development. However, strategic market development must be driven by the portfolio team or the board of directors, because such initiatives must survive the stranglehold that the existing business model and organizational structure take on new, innovative ideas.

The product team compiles important information about products and market segments in a product portfolio. This includes information about sales volume, sales revenue, market share, market growth, quality trends, costs, and sales forecasts. The product portfolio can be divided into several different sections to cover new product ideas, products being developed, and existing products in the market.

The product team should analyze the conditions that serve as the basis for prioritizing which products will receive resources, to be developed or strengthened, and which products will eventually be taken off the market. A recurring task is to evaluate ideas for new products. Some of these ideas will turn out to be so attractive that development of the product will start. The product team should also evaluate existing products to maximize their life cycles and profitability through various actions. Continuous improvement in production is one way to achieve better margins on high-volume manufactures. New marketing campaigns can highlight attributes not emphasized previously and result in the product winning new market share or starting to be bought by new customer groups. The product can be augmented with new features that make it attractive to new market segments. For products with strong market growth, one must start to expand capacity in time. All initiatives from the product team that lead to project proposals, however, must be submitted to portfolio management to be prioritized and assured of resources before they can start.

Strategy for technology and the market

Strategies guide a business in the right direction in the long run. They delimit and provide a framework for decisions made with a shorter time horizon.

A strategy for technology should indicate which technologies the company must adopt, develop, and use in its products to gain competitive advantage. In these areas, the company should strive to be the global leader. The strategy should also indicate whether the knowledge should be built up entirely in-house, using the enterprise's own resources, or by collaborating with universities, linking up with partners, purchasing technology, or buying out other companies. Finally, it is important to determine whether to be first with new technology and how often to introduce it to the market in new products. Should the company introduce small technological improvements often, providing continuous quality improvement through many small development projects? Or should it marshal the operation's efforts for major technological breakthroughs, which occur less frequently, with big development projects? A balanced project portfolio should contain both varieties (Wheelwright and Clark, 1992). Through feasibility studies, projects, and assignments, an enterprise incrementally builds up its technology and market expertise based on feedback received from customers.

A product road map can be used to show how the enterprise should realize the strategy through a series of launches. Advanced technology development and any buyouts must fit into the timeframe for developing new product models and new modular systems. To avoid the risk of delaying product development projects, research and development on pioneering new technologies are organized in their own projects. Only when the new technology is proven to work is it implanted in new product models. This means there must be multiple technical options on the shelf from which to choose, to avoid being forced to rely on the results of risky research projects. In most cases, one should also develop production technology in parallel with the design. Consequently the product road map includes the long-term research projects, the medium-term projects developing advanced production technologies and new modular systems, and the short-term commercial projects that bring the next generation of products to market.

The market strategy should answer the questions, "What products will we offer?", "What customers should we target?", "How should we distribute the products?", and "What values should we highlight that set our products apart from our competitors' offerings?" To be able to link the market strategy with the individual development projects, it is necessary to define how many articles there should be in the modular system and product program as well as how often and when they should be updated. The answer comes partly from the speed at which technology is advancing. When new technology is available, it can be implanted in the next product generation. In part, competition will put pressure on how long an existing product program can be used and the rate at which new technologies have to be launched. The size of the investment in relation to the product's sales margins is also significant, because it affects the sales volume needed to reach profitability. Access to resources will limit how many module and platform projects can be carried out during a limited period.

The flow of product development projects will be influenced by the number of platforms or components in the modular system, the number of product families to be supplied, the number of individual products, and the frequency with which new products will be launched. Some companies choose to have relatively few articles in their modular system that are updated rather infrequently but can be freely combined, varied, and adapted as customers request. Other companies choose to have a limited number of core products but offer many product variants that are updated frequently. In young industries, each development project tends to become a new platform, broadening the market and correcting the mistakes made in the launch of the preceding product.

How often new product generations, modular systems, and platforms are developed will affect the product offering, of course, but also affect the development operation. While projects for new product generations, modular systems, and platforms require significant development resources, the development of variants based on existing products and components will require relatively brief efforts. That is why the development and introduction of a new modular system must be coordinated with the development of product models, customer solutions, and quality improvements. The extent to which one should sell products that either are entirely based on the modular system or allow additions to satisfy the specific needs of a particular customer segment and to maintain a market position while waiting for the next product generation are trade-offs that make up a strategy for technology and the market.

Strategies for technologies and markets will strongly influence product road maps and ultimately what projects are conducted, what products are launched, and the company's future profitability.

Modular systems and platforms

Modular systems and platforms are a tried and true concept in certain businesses, such as the automotive industry. But this way of thinking can be applied to other industries as well. This section should be read as an example of how the product team can work with a technical architecture for the products.

A platform is a basic version of a product. Components can be added to and even removed from this basic framework to develop product models and produce unique customer solutions.

A modular system contains several possible articles for each distinct component, which can be combined to make a finished product. Even with a small number of different articles for each component, the number of possible combinations and product variants can become very large. The modular system enables a wide variety of products to be customized for customers. With ready-made, off-the-shelf components to start with, much design work can be devoted to combining these in a good way and to developing the parts one wants to improve. This reduces the complexity in individual projects, because so many components and dimensions are predetermined. At the same time, the aim of development work will shift, from perfecting separate products, to building up a common technical expertise, where all the parts will fit together into a whole.

Modular systems and platforms are effective ways to reuse technical knowledge. The effects of introducing a modular system are improved quality, lower costs, and shorter development cycles. However, defining a modular system is no simple task. It is difficult for a company to reorient itself, from being an innovative start-up with a few unique products, to developing modular systems that reduce costs and offer many product variants, all of which are positioned to compete in the market. On the one hand, there are advantages in being able to offer multiple well-defined products that customers can easily distinguish in the market. On the other hand, there are advantages in design and manufacturing, in that the products share the same components.

Balancing between the extremes of differentiation and standardization can be difficult, and it is the product team's task. What parts of the product should be standardized? Might it be better to standardize the production technology instead? How few modules can there be in a modular system without the products losing their individuality? How many modules are needed to satisfy customer needs in different markets? Should the platform be a basic product, that can be added on to with different features to make many product variants? Or should the platform be a full-featured product with many expensive attributes that can later be pared down to make cheaper product variants?

According to Ulrich and Eppinger (2003), to help make these decisions, one must clarify how the products will be differentiated from one another. What key attributes of the product does one want customers to notice? These attributes should speak to customers' different needs in the respective market segments. This results in a wish list of products that are far too expensive to develop. The next step will be to pinpoint the various components that already exist or could be developed. Finally, one must determine how the platforms and modules will be shared among the products to achieve reasonable costs and profitability, without forsaking the distinctive values one wants each product to have (ibid).

Once a modular system is in place, it requires maintenance. When is it time to upgrade a module? That may be when a new module has demonstrably better cost and performance characteristics than the old one. When is it better to update the modular system instead of making unique customizations? To what extent should the customer pay for the adaptations that must be made when the modular system is not updated? When is it time to increase the number of modules? To be able to make the proper tradeoffs between differentiation and standardization, it is best to use profitability calculations. These calculations measure development costs and increased production costs as a result of more articles against the increase in sales expected to result from a better match with customer needs.

When modular systems or platforms are introduced, the amount of technical interaction between products and projects increases. This means the need for effective product management increases greatly. The projects are no longer completely free to seek their own solutions. Every solution will influence all the other projects and also influence the costs of production and sales. Another effect of introducing a modular system is that different types of projects will be conducted—both projects to develop new modular systems and model projects. Projects that develop modular systems produce components that satisfy fundamental customer needs and can be combined with all other modules. Each modular system builds up an entire product generation with multiple different product models. In contrast, model projects select modules and add or remove features to develop a unique model or put together a customer-specific product. Development projects that produce new modular systems require creativity, initiative, openness to new solutions, and cross-functional problem-solving. The development of product models, on the other hand, requires much shorter projects in which the number of changes and additions are few and relatively easy to pinpoint, because they are largely delimited by the modular system. The technical risks associated with these projects are therefore small.

With continuous basic research or basic development, an operation can try out new technologies and lay a solid technical foundation for new modular systems. The new technologies might very well be used in several modular systems. Over time, each modular system will give rise to a growing number of product variants or models. Some of these will be developed at the same time as the modular system, others will be developed in separate projects in an effort to prolong the life cycle of the product and cut costs.

A modular system that generates many models during a run of years keeps costs down, as Cusumano and Nobeoka (1998) have shown in their research. In the automotive industry, this is a matter of survival. However, the risk is great that customers will ultimately be dissatisfied as the design becomes increasingly old-fashioned. On the other hand, it takes a long time to develop a unique design for each product. Certainly, one could customize products for each customer group, but designs are not reused. Many independent models become expensive in the long run. Transferring technology between modular systems, even to those not yet finished (concurrent technology transfer), opens up new possibilities for updating the products faster. New models can be launched faster while costs decline faster (ibid).

Communicate driving forces and shared knowledge

Competition in an industry is defined by the forces that drive the development of the market, designs, and manufacturing. Such forces might include changes in distribution channels as the share of e-commerce grows, the development of new materials that can reduce weight, or reduced manufacturing costs in a highly competitive market. Graphs can be used to illustrate these driving forces.

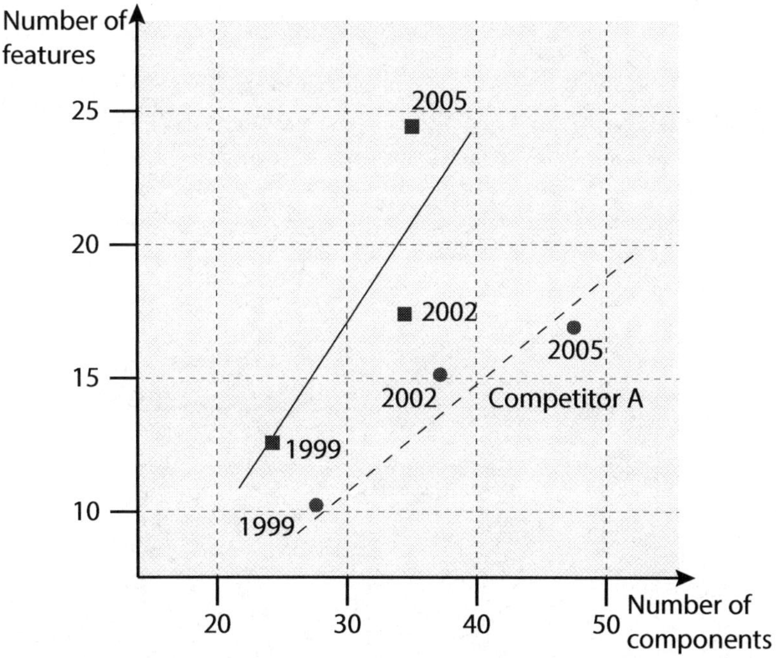

Figure 4-3. Critical interacting parameters. This graph plots the number of features against the number of components, two critical parameters of the product that interact. The company's product is also compared to a competitor's.

The primary task of such graphs is to facilitate communication and develop a common understanding in the company. (See Figures 4-3, 4-4, and 4-5.)

The graphs should show the development of driving forces over time for the company's own products. The trends provide a basis for decisions on strategic design. By including competitors' products, one can study differences in competitiveness. Some companies may have a wide range of products, while others have focused on a few profitable segments that they now dominate. The graphs can provide valuable information and knowledge that clearly shows the choices being faced. Which market segments do we focus on? Which products and processes should we develop? What production units should we use for different products? The graphs can also ensure that everyone in the company shares the same perception, so individual projects effectively contribute to the common strategy. Which graphs to prepare depends on the conditions in the industry. However, it is possible to identify some fairly general combinations that illustrate different aspects of market position, design lead, and manufacturing efficiency.

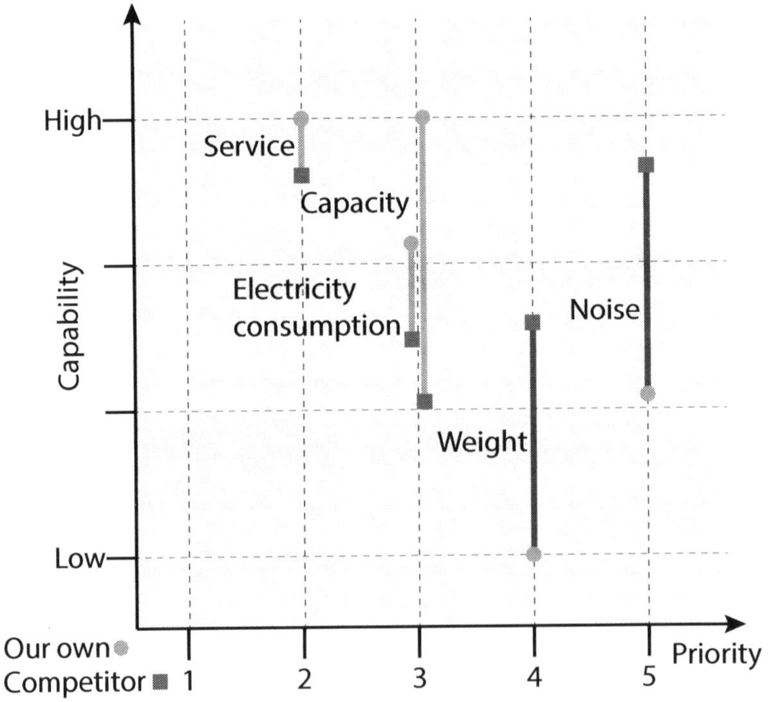

Figure 4-4. Comparison of key attributes in one of the company's products compared to a competitor's product.

By graphing changes in critical interacting parameters of the product, one can illustrate technological change over time and compare it with the main competitors' capabilities. This is one way to reveal technological competitive advantages.

The product profile for a market segment shows the development of key attributes of the product over time and can relate them to how the customer's focus has simultaneously changed. By adding the chief competitor, one can see the areas in which one has fallen behind.

To illustrate the cost situation for a product in different market segments, one can plot manufacturing costs against the complexity of the products as measured by the number of components they contain. Here one can see trends over time. Adding the competition makes it possible to compare how well one has fared. An unfavorable development calls for additional research, which may lead to graphs showing the number of manufacturing facilities, degree of automation, and volume.

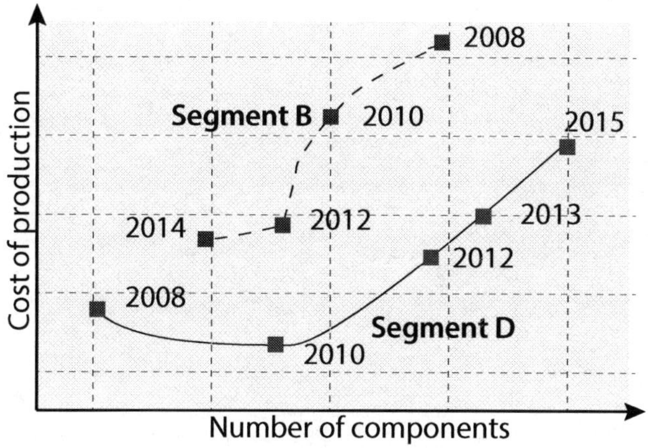

Figure 4-5. Trends in costs and product complexity. The graph shows the development of two different market segments during 10 years.

Together the graphs form a common understanding of strengths and weaknesses and how they have developed over time. The graphs provide a starting point for discussions about the vision, goals, strategies, and focus of projects (Wheelwright and Clark, 1992).

Product portfolio

Products already in the market are compiled in the product portfolio. One could also include new products under development. Using the product portfolio, the product team can follow how the products develop in the market and gain the overview needed to be able to plan the development of new products. The product portfolio also provides background information vital for prioritizing improvements, such as quality and capacity projects, as well as initiating marketing efforts.

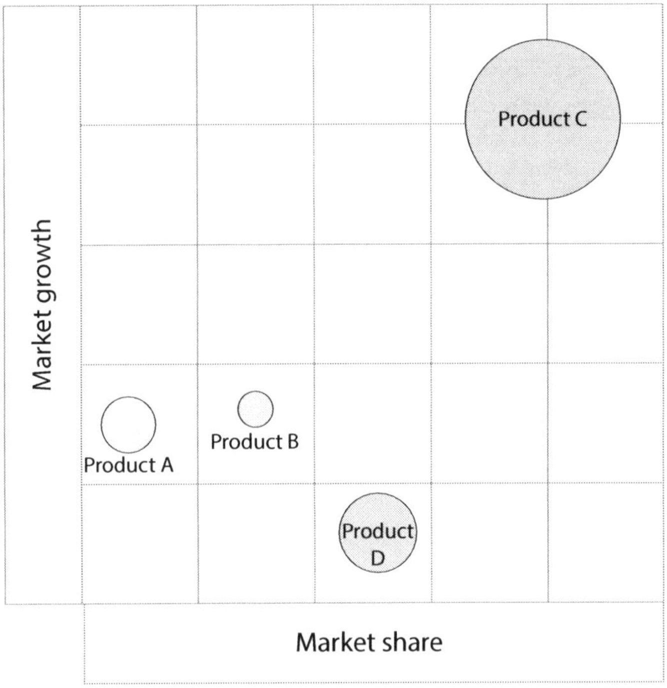

Figure 4-6. Bubble chart for a product portfolio. The chart shows the products in the portfolio. The products in the most important market segments have been plotted based on market share and market growth. Sales revenue is signified by the size of each circle.

The product portfolio summarizes information that shows the existing products' market positions and profitability. By compiling a few key parameters for the products, one can analyze the product portfolio and direct initiatives to the areas that will increase the profitability of the products in the long run. The product portfolio can also be presented in a chart, such as Figure 4-6. The chart simplifies comparisons between different products and market segments, which facilitate the emergence of a coherent strategy for all products. Here one can draw conclusions about which products require focused segmentation, investments in product development, and more aggressive marketing.

By compiling information about the products' revenues and costs, the product team can identify initiatives that can improve the margins on existing products. Figure 4-7 shows examples of parameters in the form of production cost, warranty cost, and production capacity. If different market segments have different costs, the table should be split up to show each part separately. The table helps identify products that have high production or warranty costs. Quality projects to cut costs can be initiated based on these analyses. Here one can also locate future capacity issues, which might trigger investment projects for new production equipment.

Product	Market	Cost of production	Warranty cost	Production capacity	Forecast—sales in 3 years
600 series	U.S.	€50 per unit	€7 per unit	195,000 units per year	300,000 units per year
	Others	€30 per unit	€5 per unit	25,000 units per year	60,000 units per year
900 series	Total	€95 per unit	€10 per unit	45,000 units per year	37,000 units per year

Figure 4-7. Product portfolio. This table contains information on the costs and production capacity for each product. As an alternative to production cost, one can measure production lead time or a quality index. Instead of warranty cost, one can measure the support time.

The product portfolio can be augmented by tables showing the revenue potential and market for products under development, as well as information on new product ideas that have not yet commenced development.

The product portfolio assumes that reliable sales statistics and production statistics are available for the products. Inadequate data on costs or market position need to be addressed first, before well-substantiated decisions can be made to develop new products, improve processes, or expand production capacity. Market share, in particular, is difficult to estimate. The value will depend largely on how narrowly the market is defined. The market size and the market share, in turn, will determine how much revenue can be expected from the product and thus how profitable it might be to develop new products.

The product team's task

The product team is tasked with maximizing the profitability of the company's products in the long run. They should act to improve the margins on existing products and initiate the development of new products that will become successful a few years hence. The product team should scan the customers, market, and competitors to acquire information on how best to develop the products. They should also look in-house to build up technology, knowledge, processes, and products long-term that match customer needs. The results of their analyses must also be communicated within the company, so that everyone can share a common understanding of problems, opportunities, and the path chosen.

Product road map

The products in the product portfolio need to be positioned vis-à-vis the competition and one another so they do not cannibalize sales. The products will be updated little by little with new models that satisfy new customer needs. To keep costs down, the products in a product family should be based on common components that are reused in various models and products. It takes planning if the development of new products and product variants is to actually lead to a strengthening of the company's market position in the long run. In what order should new models be launched? What new technology should be incorporated in each model? What customer segments should the new products target? The answers to these questions are provided by the product team and can be visualized through the product road map (as well as other means), as shown in Figure 4-8.

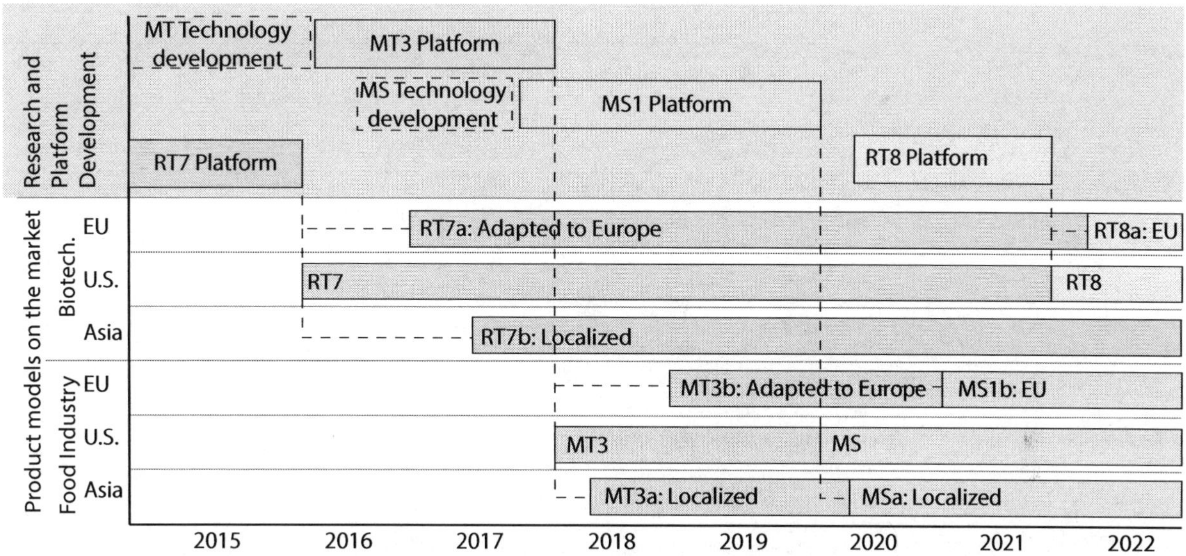

Figure 4-8. Product road map. Each modular system generates several products for different market segments. The operation in this example has the capacity to develop one modular system at a time.

The product road map is a strategic plan that builds on the decisions taken on the operation's strategy for technologies and markets. The product road map looks like a family tree and is a map for each product family forward in time. The road map covers long-term and advanced technology development, development of new production technologies and new modular systems, new product generations, and planned model launches.

A strategic plan, such as a product road map or a program plan, may be seen as a current description of the product team's ambitions. Over time, these plans will change as the team learns more about the market, their own potential, and possible technologies. That does not mean, though, that the plan is unnecessary. On the contrary, a visualized plan makes change possible, because it can be reconciled with new knowledge and initiate discussions that otherwise would not have happened.

Ideas for new products

Unfulfilled customer needs represent potential products that can be developed and sold. However, not all unfulfilled customer needs are profitable. Some are limited by too few customers or customers with too little purchasing power, others by inadequate or costly technology. Technology shifts can open up new opportunities to develop products and processes that fulfill previously unfulfilled customer needs.

Weighting of market segments for Tetra product line			
Market segments	**Preferred customer needs**	**Our ability to meet the customer needs**	**Weight**
Large multinational food companies	Service worldwide Compatible systems	Lacking service Not fully compatible with other brands	4
Medium-sized food enterprises in the EU	Local support Standard system Easy maintenance	Good conditions	5
Pharmaceutical industry	Fast deliveries GMP classification	No GMP classification.	2
Medium-sized biotech companies in the U.S.	Long-term cooperation	Good conditions	5
Contract laboratories	Local support Fast deliveries	Good conditions in the EU och the U.S.	5
Research laboratories	Assist with troubleshooting	Knowledge is lacking locally	3

Figure 4-9. Weighting of market segments. This example summarizes information about customer needs in different market segments for one product line. The table is used to weight the attractiveness of segments based on the product line's ability to satisfy customer needs, providing a basis for the decision about which segments to focus on.

To find ideas for new products, different analyses may be used. One way is to survey the market, customer needs, and how well the company's own products as well as competitors' products can satisfy those customer needs. Such an analysis may reveal several potential market segments where existing products can fit in after more or less extensive product development. The information in Figures 4-9 and 4-10 can be summarized in a matrix, as shown in Figure 4-11. The background data is used to decide which market segments are most attractive.

Financial attractiveness of market segments for Tetra product line					
Market segments	**Sales volume (units/year)**	**Sales revenue (€ mn/year)**	**Market share (%)**	**Market growth**	**Weight**
Large multinational food companies	7,000	6	5	→	2
Medium-sized food enterprises in the EU	12,000	12	30	↑	4
Pharmaceutical industry	6,000	10	10	↑	3
Medium-sized biotech companies in the U.S.	50,000	100	80	↑	5
Contract laboratories	150	0.15	-	→	1
Research laboratories	30	0.05	-	→	1
Others	20	0.05	-	→	-

Figure 4-10. The financial attractiveness of market segments. Table of market data for various market segments. The table is used to weight the attractiveness of the segments, providing a basis for the decision about which segments to focus on.

To be able to effect technology shift and introduce completely new products (innovations), one must find market segments where one can attain a dominant position. In those selected market segments, one must then strive to find customers who are interested in trying something new. These customers become "pilots" for the new products. The initiative must be focused and sustained to succeed.

If a company is active in a mature market, though, there is already strong competition (Moore, 1998). If the company is not the biggest player, to be successful it must find niches for its products. By satisfying unique needs in narrow market segments, a company can command a better price. In a mature market, targeted customer surveys may be used, because small additions to the product can be tested directly in the market and provide quick feedback from customers (ibid).

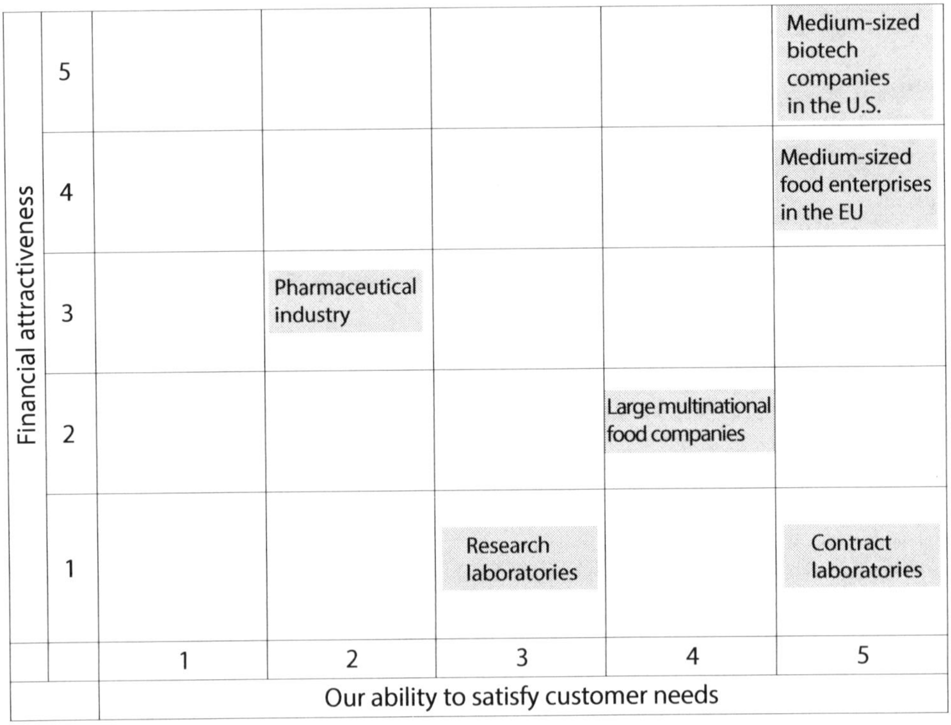

Figure 4-11. The attractiveness of each segment based on the ability to satisfy customer needs (from Figure 4-9) and the financial attractiveness (from Figure 4-10). The matrix is used to prioritize the segments, providing a basis for the decision about which segments to focus on.

To find ideas for new products, one can also rely on the creativity of employees and partners. Salespeople get ideas when they have discussions with their customers. Engineers get ideas for new technologies and new ways of designing products. Suppliers demonstrate new technologies that open up new possibilities. Ideas can be collected in the form of tips. They can also be refined during a joint workshop, for example at a sales conference, to achieve greater sophistication in a fairly short time.

Even if one relies on creativity, each idea must be worked through systematically to evaluate the economic viability of the new product. Is the idea in line with the company's strategy? How large could the market become? How big of a market share can we count on? What price can we charge? What is the competition like? How many years will we be able to sell the new product? What basic technical designs will be used? How does the product fit into the existing product road maps? Do we have the necessary expertise? What will it cost to develop the product and invest in new production equipment, if needed? When can we launch, at the earliest? How profitable will it be?

With an effective process for sorting out new ideas, one will soon find oneself with many more ideas for new products than can ever be realized. The product team's task is to decide which ideas are most promising and to weed out the rest. The results of the screening process are a few very promising new ideas whose plans can be elaborated.

It is a good idea to save all the ideas in an idea bank—even the ideas rejected at an early stage. In the future, one might find a plum in the idea bank that over time has become ripe for realization. Supporting data quickly becomes obsolete as the market changes and technologies evolve, so the value of saving background documentation declines sharply over time.

Set business goals

To set business goals, one defines the economic growth that a customer segment is expected to achieve, in terms of increased revenue, higher prices, or greater sales volume, within a limited period of one or a few years, based on strong customer needs not yet satisfied. To achieve these business goals, one must invest in marketing activities, product development, or process improvements. Or a combination of all three might be needed. To define how the company intends to achieve its business goals, customer needs are broken down into development goals, which will later lead to the initiation of one or more projects that will be kept together in one program. These projects will all contribute to fulfilling the overall business goals for the segment. Using business goals, the product team controls the direction of development work for the next year. Business goals also make it easier to see the context for the work being done and how the various projects jointly contribute to profitability. Examples of business goals may be to reach a specific rate of sales growth in a given market, to defend one's market position, or to increase the margin per product sold. (See Figure 4-12.)

The business goals shall state clearly the revenue expected to be generated if the development effort is carried through. The size of the revenue will determine whether the investment in product and process development will be profitable. With business goals, it becomes clear what the operation can achieve in the next few years, but the goals are not merely wishful thinking. The product team decides on reasonable goals based on the information they have and will later be evaluated based on how well the goals were reached.

The number of business goals must be small to enable focus, in a small operation no more than two or three. In preparing the background data, more could be considered if ample resources were available for product management. At the decision-making stage, the portfolio team will then determine the most attractive options.

Figure 4-12. Business goals for a customer segment. To achieve business goals, the product team in this example envisages developing the product as well as improving the process.

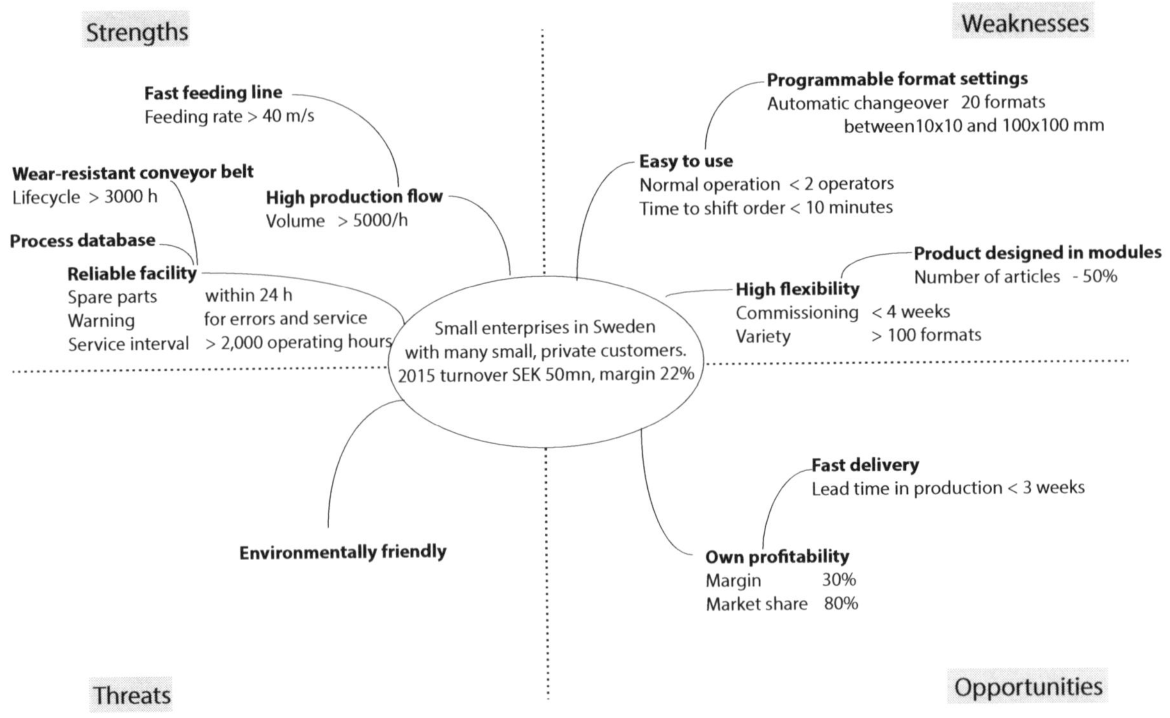

Plan new products

The business goals that have passed through a coarse screening and been deemed promising require additional planning before development work can begin. The product team draws up a program plan that shows the labor required to achieve the business goal. The program plan includes efforts the product team itself must do as well as the work to be performed as projects and assignments. The program plan in Figure 4-13 starts with a feasibility study. Three partially parallel projects follow, to develop the product and production process. Last is the market launch.

In the program plan, development work is divided up into several projects, each of which will focus on different aspects of the new product. One project can develop the design and production technology. Another project can prepare the market launch. A third project can work with investment in new production equipment. All of these projects are run in the same program. There will be strong links between the projects in terms of timing, results, and technology. But the advantage of organizing programs of multiple projects is that it makes it easier to staff each project with the right expertise and to focus on results. Coordination between the projects is handled during the course of the project primarily by a program manager, who is part of the product team.

Implement the development project

Once work has started in the project, product management must not let go. On the contrary, that is when extra attention is needed,

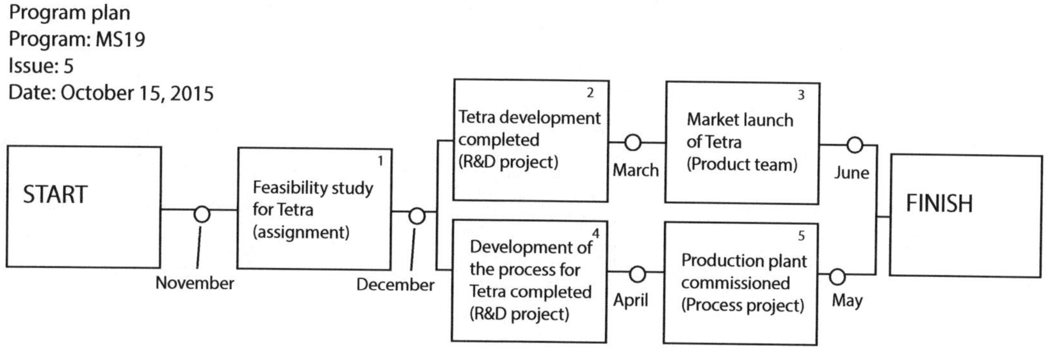

Figure 4-13. Program plan. A program plan is drawn as a network. Later the various projects will be prioritized and scheduled in the project portfolio.

as the ideas are being realized and goals achieved. In the course of their work, people will run into problems in the projects. The majority of the problems can be solved within the project or with the support of the program manager. Other problems may affect the ability of the product to satisfy customer needs or may strain cost or time restraints, which ultimately influence the profitability of the product. In addition, the products in a product family are based on common technology, so some problems will affect multiple projects and multiple products. The decisions required to solve those problems cannot be made within a single project but must be escalated to the product team. Questions that arise may include whether the project has achieved sufficiently good performance, whether more resources should be added or the project allowed to be delayed, what trade-offs are needed in the solution to reach conflicting targets, and how the design can be adapted to fit multiple products.

The product team must be available to make decisions about problems that the projects cannot solve themselves. Because work in a project has a tendency to stall while waiting for such crucial decisions, it is important that decisions can be made frequently, at least every week. The program pulse meeting is one way to handle problems. All project managers take part, and the meeting is led by the program manager. The program pulse meeting is held every week at a fixed time. The problems flagged there are either solved right away by the program manager or passed on as a problem to the inbox on the product or resource pulse board.

The projects will also complete subresults. Using a synchronization plan, one can lump together several subresults in a work package and identify handover points in between. When a project reaches a handover point, the project participants demonstrate the results for the program manager. At the same time, they discuss expectations and requirements for the next handover point. Through demonstrations, the program manager can keep projects focused on challenges and problems that have an impact on the customer's perceptions of the new product. The program manager will be well briefed on the projects' progress, which is a prerequisite for conducting technical planning at the strategic level. At the same time, the projects get the feedback they need to continue working on the right things and solving technical interdependencies with other parts of the operation.

Evaluate existing products

The product team has responsibility for the products throughout their lifecycles. Launching a new product is just the beginning of a long process. Until a product is being phased out, continuous efforts are needed to improve the quality, complement it with new models, or increase capacity. All these efforts require resources, to develop new products as well as to care for existing ones. The product team's task is to produce the background data that will enable the portfolio team to decide which initiatives to take for existing products in order to keep the product family profitable long-term while balancing these against the development of new products and modular systems.

Product	Market	Cost of production	Warranty cost	Production capacity	Forecast—sales in 3 years
Tetra	U.S.	€850 per unit	€70 per unit	150,000 units per year	200,000 units per year
	Others	€630 per unit	€50 per unit	25,000 units per year	18,000 units per year
Delta	Total	€545 per unit	€10 per unit	40,000 units per year	37,000 units per year

Figure 4-14. Product portfolio with production capacity. This product portfolio summarizes the existing products' costs and production capacity. Here one can see the need for initiatives to reduce the warranty and production costs for Tetra in the U.S. market and to expand production capacity.

Quality improvements in products and processes are often carried out in relatively short projects with a short payback period. These savings make it possible to cut production costs and improve margins. With an improvement project, for example, one can remedy design flaws and reduce costly warranty commitments. Expansion of capacity will also be necessary over time to be able to supply the market with successful products and maintain market position.

In the product portfolio, information on existing products is compiled that can help identify initiatives to boost the products' quality and capacity. Parameters suitable for such a compilation are warranty cost, production cost, capacity, and forecast of future sales volume.

The information is combined with data on sales volume, revenue, and market share in different market segments. New markets that the company wants to focus on can be added to the product portfolio afterwards. Here one can monitor whether sales evolve as envisioned. Perhaps there are additional initiatives that should be taken to further increase sales and market share in a particular market.

To form an image of what customers think of the products and the processes that supply the products, customer surveys can be conducted. These can be focused surveys carried out with some regularity. They can also be built into the sales process, such as by having customers answer questions in connection with an order. Irritation and obstacles in the process can cause a customer to not purchase the product, though it fits the customer's needs. In customer surveys, one can find ideas for improvements that increase revenues while reducing costs.

Unfulfilled customer needs represent potential for additional sales. To genuinely understand how customers perceive and use the products, one often needs to conduct in-depth studies with individual customers to map out problems and time-consuming steps. It is an advantage if engineers and product managers can experience using the products themselves in their proper context. However, it is not certain that employees will be able to fully understand the customer's situation. For example, young people may find it difficult to understand problems confronting the elderly.

Set operational goals

Setting operational goals means defining how much margins on existing products could be improved by shortening lead times, reducing costs, and increasing capacity. Operational goals aim inwards, at the company's own operations. The main idea behind streamlining processes and improving products is to save money, at the same time as one satisfies customer needs for fast delivery and reliable, eco-friendly products. This differentiates operational goals from business goals, which instead strive to increase revenue through new products or markets. In smaller operations, though, it is often appropriate to describe business goals and operational goals in the same graph.

For example, operational goals can be defined as sales margin, production volume, lead time, environmental impact, or scrap ratio. Achieving operational goals requires initiatives in the form of product development or process improvements. Or one might need a combination of the two. Product development may involve modifying the product so that it is easier to manufacture, assemble, and service. Process improvements can be changes or investments in machinery and equipment. They can also be changes in logistics. To find out which initiatives are needed to achieve the operational goals, they are broken down into development initiatives, which will later lead to the initiation of one or more projects, kept together in one program.

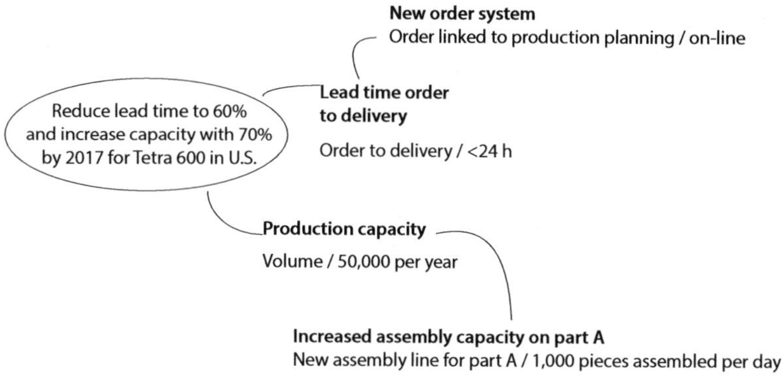

Figure 4-15. Operational goals. The goals set should in this case be achieved through a combination of product development and process development.

When working out ideas for operational goals, one can focus on one product group at a time, working out possibilities for improving that group alone. For prioritized production sections, it is also possible to work on all product groups simultaneously, to find synergies and set priorities on the initiatives to be taken.

Workflow for the product team

Projects in progress need constant attention. Problems that emerge need to be solved, and the projects need to be given direction so they stay on track. Most problems that a project encounters and needs help with can be handled at the weekly program pulse meetings. But if a problem is urgent, the project must be able to quickly get help from the program manager. Urgent problems may need to be handled by a wider group, a mix of the portfolio team and product team. This can be done in the form of a rapid response workshop, called when needed.

Work evaluating new ideas is under way more or less constantly. As the market changes and new technologies appear, new opportunities also arise. These must be evaluated quickly so as not to miss the window of opportunity in the market for any plum ideas. When candidates for new projects emerge, they are allowed to undergo a screening process. Do the ideas fly or should they be filed away right then?

Existing products in the product portfolio can be evaluated on a regular basis at relatively long intervals, perhaps quarterly. Changes are not likely to be as fast, and the initiatives for improvement already in progress must be completed before the effects of such initiatives can be assessed. The same applies to planning new initiatives that pass the screening process. The projects currently under way take up all available capacity in the development operation. Only when a project nears completion or is discontinued prematurely will it be time to select one or more new projects for the project portfolio. Because each project's delivery date is known, there is an inherent rhythm to the product team's work on business goals, program plans, and feasibility studies, as well as to the portfolio team's decisions to start and shut down projects.

Should the product team prepare more than one candidate for a new project in the project portfolio? Hopefully, there will be several promising candidates. To avoid the product team getting trapped in internal conflicts or decision anxiety, it is better to thoroughly prepare several proposals. The portfolio team will then assess their profitability, strategic importance, and business risk, as well as which resources are available, which will finally determine which projects are started first. Thanks to the work of the product team, the background for these decisions will be more complete and the decisions more widely accepted.

The participants in the product team need to be experienced people with deep and broad knowledge of the products, customers, and technologies. The work on the product team is in no way administrative. Here they work out the strategic design that determines the direction of the enterprise and its future profitability. To produce a sufficiently good strategic design, they must have done their homework, that is, the team has to have gathered the requisite background data relating to customers, competitors, earning potential, profitability, and technical solutions. This data is produced by the members of the product team together with other resources in feasibility studies, workshops, or fast-track studies.

Staffing the product team

In the product team, information about customers and technology converge and is then transformed into decisions that control the company's development work. To be able to transform information into knowledge and make thoroughly deliberated decisions requires broad and deep expertise in both areas. Thus more than one person is needed to bear the burden of product management. For example, the product manager is likely to have a strong market focus but may lack technical expertise. For the program manager, the opposite is often true. The smallest product teams consist of a product manager, a program manager, and an assignment manager. Larger teams may also have senior expertise that supports work on production technology, logistics, purchasing, or product architecture, depending on the nature of the operation.

Researchers have found (Jacobsen and Thorsvik, 2008:462) that members of the product team's core team should not hold positions in line management, because they will not have time to do the strategic work. I see this is true when I follow up with enterprises working with Pulse. The people who are on the product team and also do a line manager's job have little time for strategic tasks. That is why I recommend that the number of managers in the line organization is kept to a minimum, so that the company can make the most of senior expertise in strategic work instead. The work of line management and the work of product management are both important and require a high level of expertise and focus.

Program manager

The program manager plans and organizes multiple projects that have technical links to one another. Thus the program manager is responsible for holding together the work and the results that the projects generate. Program manager is a full-time position. In large companies, there may be several program managers, each of whom holds together all the projects that, as a group, generate a new product family.

The program manager translates the strategic and tactical decisions in the product team and portfolio team into operational action in the projects. With a program manager and a program plan, the size of the projects can be restrained so that each project can focus its work and set limits for its results. This reduces the uncertainty that the projects have to deal with, thus enhancing the prospects for focus, collaboration, and knowledge-building in each project, while holding the projects together so they can make up a whole. To be able to support the projects with technical decisions, the program manager needs deep and broad expertise chiefly in technology and production technology. But to be able to develop the right product architecture, the program manager must also understand the importance of different features and how they are used in customers' applications.

So, what is the difference between having a program manager and organizing projects in multiple subprojects? There are several significant differences. The program manager works with the product team to plan in the long run how products, platforms, and modular systems will be developed, reused, and improved to fit into different market segments. Another difference, compared to how many matrix organizations work, is the mandate given to the program manager as an experienced technical manager, which makes the program manager an influential decision maker. Thus a program manager can give the projects actual decision support and backing in the event of a conflict of interest. The line organization owns and cares for resources. The line organization is also the unit that shifts resources to feasibility studies, projects, and the assignment team. Management and control of the work is carried out by means of interlinked pulse meetings, not through a project manager or other manager. Yet another difference from projects with subprojects is that each project in a program can be organized, planned, and staffed based on their specific prerequisites. This means that projects that are part of a single program do not need to run at the same time, as is often the case with subprojects that go on as long as the project is in progress. With projects organized in programs, one gains a greater flexibility and focus on the results that each project will deliver.

Toyota reorganizes for product management

In the early 1990s, Toyota carried out a major reorganization of its development unit. At that time, they had long-term experience with multi-projects, because they had introduced this form of project work back in 1953. The results of the reorganization have been documented by Cusumano and Nobeoka (1998). The rationale for the change was that the development unit had become increasingly hard to manage as Toyota expanded rapidly. The number of projects and features had become too large for communication and management to work. Since the project approach had been introduced, each independent project had been responsible for developing its own new car model. Now the projects had become increasingly autonomous and started to compete with one another for resources. Even worse, the various projects also competed for market share, because the various car models trespassed on one another's customer segments. As long as market and sales growth were strong, this was not a big problem. But when growth stalled in the early 1990s as a result of the faltering Japanese economy, the situation became pressing.

The solution Toyota chose was to split up its organization and create four different development centers: one center for each platform plus one center for common components. The division made it possible to focus on common visions and customer segments at each center. The division also reduced the size of each development center, facilitating communication and enabling staff to sit together in a single building.

They chose to continue with the strong matrix organization from before, in which the management of each project had a mandate to genuinely control the project. The projects were led by a "chief engineer" (a role I have chosen to call "program manager"). In connection with the reorganization, they initiated weekly meetings between line managers, chief engineers, and the head of the unit (equivalent to what I call "program pulse meetings"). Through the weekly meetings, they quickly revealed problems and could make decisions. The chief engineer was no longer alone but was backed up by the development center's most senior decision maker. This made it possible to consider the coordination between projects and the long-term plans when making decisions, which simplified and accelerated the implementation of decisions.

But by far the most important change during the reorganization was establishing a unit for each development center that would work on the strategic design. These strategic units were given overall responsibility for product management. They were to focus on reducing costs and increasing profitability by reusing designs and reducing the number of components. With product management, combined with more explicit portfolio management, they achieved coordination of their multi-project organization, which used to be lacking. The work on strategic design gave Toyota a long-term competitive advantage.

Toyota instilled several features in its product management. They were able to concentrate their efforts on customer needs, modular construction, and continuous improvement. In a classical line organization, line managers are expected to conduct the strategic work but, as research has shown, in practice they have no time to do this (Jacobsen and Thorsvik, 2008:462). At the same time, the division into multiple development units, each with its own platform, gave Toyota a structure that put customer needs at the center. Each platform responded to identified customer needs in its customer segments. With the division of the organization, it became possible to focus and thus get closer to the customer.

The platform would now be common to all projects at the development center. Developed modules would be reused in multiple projects. This ended the freedom that projects previously had to create unique but expensive solutions. Through the reuse of designs, they intended to shorten development cycles as well as reduce production costs, at the same time as product quality would improve.

Once the product was in the market, they had to work for continuous improvement, one of Toyota's strong suits. But it is not enough to make improvements in the production process alone. The design itself needs to be improved continuously to achieve even higher quality in the product. Old modules should be replaced, but only when better performance and lower costs have been demonstrated with a new module. Improving a design is about systematically building knowledge. Every problem always has yet another technical solution. A design is never finished. It can always be made better. Without product management, this constant quest for perfection becomes a problem for the operation. Engineers do not want to release a half-baked design. They want to spend more time refining it. With product management, the creative energy of the engineers can be channeled into areas where it creates the most benefits and can be controlled so the launch is not delayed. The project teams at Toyota were encouraged to work out several alternative solutions early on, among which product management could choose. This rewarded project teams for working more with creative problem-solving, which generated new and more in-depth knowledge of the design.

The lesson to be drawn from this description of Toyota is that enhancing focus by dividing the organization into independent units can create much better conditions for management, communication, and decision-making. By focusing, the complexity in the work is reduced. For example, this makes it possible to get decisions every week or, if necessary, just-in-time, which facilitates the circulation of information and speeds up projects. This focus also means that the number of projects becomes manageable, as does the number of products. Then it is possible at the management level to coordinate projects as well as product components between projects. Along the way, one has also created a situation in which knowledge can be reused, which reduces costs and shortens lead times. The result is much more effective product development that can bring out profitable products quickly.

Summary of product management

This chapter has shown the coordinated tasks that rest on the product team and how important these tasks are for a company to develop profitable products at a fast pace.

The product team's overarching task is to maximize the profitability of the company's products in the long run. They shall act to improve the margins on existing products and initiate the development of new products that may not be profitable until a few years later. The product team prepares background data for decisions that enable the portfolio team to make strategic decisions that lead the development work in the right direction. They prepare business goals for new products and operational goals for existing processes. These goals indicate where to invest resources to develop and strengthen products and what savings or earnings potential the investments may have.

The product team pools information about customers' needs and defines which of these needs can be transformed into profitable products, taking into account the competitive situation and the company's own possibilities and limitations, technological advances, and trends. Together these form a strategic design that will constantly be challenged and remodeled. To communicate their strategy and invite discussion, change, and learning, the product team prepares graphs that show the long-term goals and plans for the products, as well as the driving forces and position in the industry where they operate. These graphs and tables are hung up on the product pulse board.

The product portfolio includes summaries of a few key parameters for products currently in the market and new products under development. The aim is to achieve an analysis and visualization of the products so investments can be directed to the right place.

In the business goals, the product team singles out the potential for increased revenue in the priority market segments as well as the development efforts required to satisfy customer needs there. The program plans manifest the work to achieve business goals through a series of feasibility studies, projects, and other initiatives.

Modular systems and platforms are one way to reuse technical knowledge. It is the task of product management to build up and maintain such a system and to weigh the trade-offs required in individual products. It is also the product team that works out the product architecture and defines which features the products will have.

During the course of the project, the product team provides decision support on questions related to technology and the market. At the weekly program pulse meetings, led by the program manager, the projects highlight the problems that they cannot handle themselves.

5. Building knowledge

Product development is all about learning, which can only occur in cross-functional teams. As discussed in previous chapters, learning is a result of cooperation between different people. In this chapter, I will show how the development process can be shortened by front-loading work, reusing knowledge, and following a set-based, or concurrent, design process. Shortening lead times is an end in itself, because shorter lead times provide faster feedback and thus faster knowledge creation.

Product development is solving problems

When developing products or improving processes, the challenge is to solve a large number of technical problems. The problems can be of different types and differ in difficulty. What they all have in common is that their solutions require access to knowledge that is initially missing. The knowledge must be developed while the product is being developed. New knowledge must be generated, and old knowledge must be placed in a new context. This is about technical and functional knowledge as well as knowledge of customer needs and how the customer will use the product. If you can accelerate knowledge building, you can solve the problems faster and thus also shorten the development cycle, which over time will enable you to better satisfy customer needs.

According to Wheelwright and Clark (1992), solving problems is a learning process. No matter how much knowledge an engineer has about a given problem at the outset, there are always unique aspects that need to be understood before a good design can be developed. Except when solving the simplest problems, a developer cannot immediately produce a good, complete design in one fell swoop. That requires multiple iterations, in which the developers learn at every step a little more about the problem and the alternative solutions available. In the end, the developers produce a final design with complete specifications.

Knowledge building can be seen as the heart of a development operation. The knowledge is used to generate value in the form of solved problems as well as technical specifications and manufacturing documentation for new products. Knowledge building also entails constant adaptation to changes in the market. According to Prokopenko et al. (2009), adaptation requires an ability to take in feedback, in-house creativity to process and analyze the information, and the ability to make decisions. The feedback could come from customers, the market, suppliers, and other stakeholders. Being able to vary feedback channels is a success factor (Grinyer and Norburn, 1975), as it gives a more distinctive picture of the situation.

In-house creativity involves working with impressions and forming a common understanding of the feedback. This is more difficult than it may sound. Information that you do not understand can be misinterpreted or overlooked. In-house creativity emerges in interaction between people, for example at pulse meetings and workshops, in teamwork and other contexts where new information can be combined with existing knowledge and form a fresh view of reality. According to Prokopenko et al. (2008), learning decreases when creativity is at a high level unless it is balanced by an increase in decision-making (ibid). Passing judgment at a crossroads is what is often called decision-making. When we choose which solution we are going to focus on, we simultaneously choose to ignore other options, thereby reducing uncertainty. Thus, building a large store of knowledge in an operation requires a fast pace of decision-making, otherwise uncertainty increases. This uncertainty manifests itself as stress, paralysis, or activities that dissipate stress but do not create value. Because Pulse uses pulse meetings to propel the decision-making process, increased creativity calls for more frequent pulse meetings. In challenging feasibility studies and design-intensive parts of a project, teams can use fast-track studies with pulse meetings every hour or two.

Solving problems and building knowledge cannot be combined with a standardized development process, where the workflow is predetermined. In a standardized development process, the only work carried out is predictable work, which minimizes all the risks and external interruptions. External information and feedback is undesirable and avoided. Creativity and new ways of thinking are perceived as internal opposition, which is resisted (Ismail, Malone, Geest, and Diamandis, 2014).

Building knowledge means daring to take risks. Problems and opportunities cannot be foreseen. A good system for product development must be able to grab hold of problems, opportunities, and unforeseen developments and deal with them. The approach used must allow local initiatives within a strategic design. This is not the same as having personal priorities, that is, individuals going off in their own directions, often for personal advantage, regardless of what the rest of the operation is doing. For the enterprise to operate as an entity, it must be possible to focus efforts in the same direction.

To achieve effective product development, there must be both creativity and structure, according to Rubinstein and Firstenberg (1999). The approach must be sufficiently creative, flexible, and unplanned to allow exploration, innovation, and adaptation. At the same time, it should be sufficiently structured to provide stability for the initiatives conceived. A good real-time system can handle not only anticipated occurrences but also the unexpected. Creativity in a group can be stimulated by people probing ideas, actively seeking problems, and communicating liberally to test thoughts and ideas against each other. Once the group has decided what to move forward with and is ready to execute the ideas, the group needs the stability of a structured approach. The more the group is oriented towards finding problems when initiating and beginning projects, the less problem solving is needed towards the end.

In Pulse, the apparent dilemma between structure, on the one hand, and local initiative, on the other, is resolved by a constitutional structure of pulse meetings. Metaphorically, this might be seen as the company's operating system. It is both the machinery that propels work forward and the protocol that describes how handshaking will occur between different parts. This means management has control over the whole, but they cannot control the parts and therefore do not have detailed control of them. Ralph Stacey, the renowned organizational expert, has described this phenomenon as management being in control and management not being in control (2007:449). In Pulse, creativity and dynamism are generated at the employee level, which increases the enterprise's ability to adapt at the management level. This results in some "disorder" at the employee level, in that many local initiatives will be taken, which creates the conditions for order at the management level.

A non-linear system with too little variation gives rise to chaos in the operation.

By far the biggest problem with standardized processes, Six Sigma, and other quality methodologies is that they create "order" at the employee level. Expressed in a different way, they seek to create a system with little variation. But a development operation is a non-linear system. Research on complexity has found that a non-linear system with unduly low variation can give rise to chaos, a state in which very little value can be generated (Thietart and Forgues, 2011:60). So an orderly system at the employee level can give rise to a disorganized, chaotic system at the management level.

Accelerated problem solving

In product development, one is often faced with problems and challenges that require trade-offs. One example is "the fit problem" versus "the performance problem." A fit problem is about finding room for all the features in a limited space and getting the parts of a complex design to fit together at the end. A performance problem is about reaching defined targets for critical parameters, such as sufficiently low fuel consumption.

Problem solving is an iterative process with ideas, trials, and failures. The work is guided by knowledge of the underlying cause-and-effect relationships. Development work can be seen as a series of problem-solving cycles. Each cycle starts with a description of the problem through comparisons of existing knowledge with target values, after which all possible solutions that are available are identified. Then models are built that can be used to validate the solutions. The models are tested against the existing requirements and restraints. The results are analyzed and evaluated. The new information that is then available reveals aspects and relationships that could not have been anticipated or were not previously identified. If the results from the first round are good enough, the problem is solved. Usually, though, these solutions must be modified, as well as the models, after which new tests can be performed.

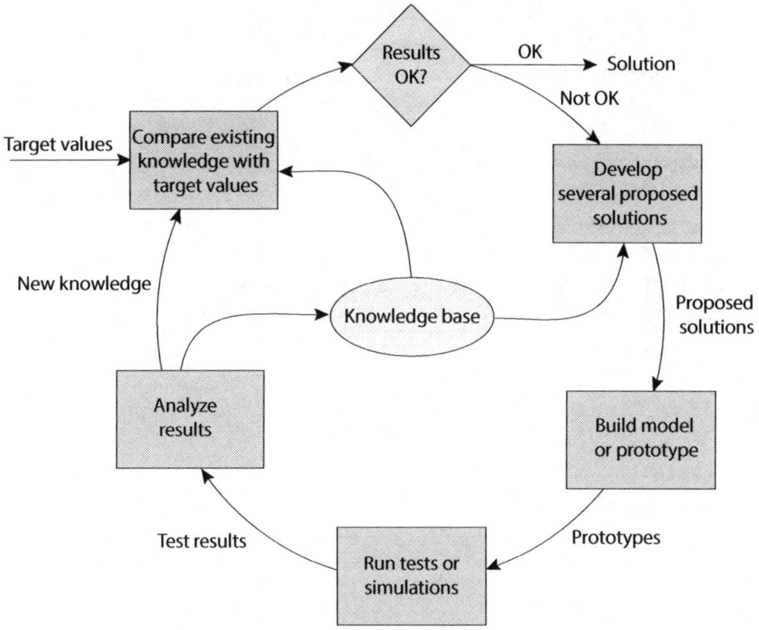

Figure 5-1. Problem-solving cycle. Begin by comparing the target value with existing knowledge. If the results are not satisfactory, identify several proposed solutions and then build prototypes, test them for the requirements, and finally analyze the results and ask whether the solution is good enough.

Each development operation has a certain efficiency that is reflected in the pace at which it solves technical problems. To shorten the development cycle, one can try to speed up the process by increasing the pace in each problem-solving cycle. The development team can increase the pace by shortening loops. This requires faster model building and testing as well as more frequent pulse meetings, maybe every hour or two. The slope of the curve will then be steeper, as shown in Figure 5-2.

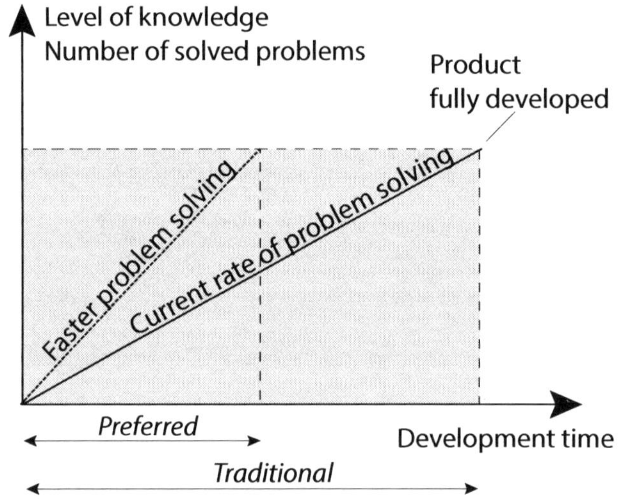

Figure 5-2. Traditional versus faster problem solving. The efficiency of a development operation shown as the pace at which it solves problems. Adapted from Thomke and Fujimoto (2000).

If you can start at a higher level, you will not have to solve as many problems, according to Thomke and Fujimoto (2000). To commence at a higher level, existing knowledge must be reused and communicated. The projects should not reinvent the wheel but build upon the know-how that already exists in the operation. You can also make sure to identify and solve problems quickly at the beginning. Problems that are detected early are relatively simple and cheap to address (ibid).

To start at a higher level, knowledge that is already known must be communicated and applied. For the project's members, it is important to have a common goal scenario around which they can gather to plan and collaborate. The product team has likely worked a long time to define customer needs, prioritize various initiatives in relation to one another, set business goals, establish program plans, and work out architecture. During this process, the product team has built up its knowledge of the new product. That knowledge can be transferred to the project through a joint workshop, in which everyone works together to communicate and visualize the project's goals. The product team can also make sure to involve project members in feasibility studies and, for example, work to figure out different design solutions. This starts the transfer of knowledge to the project earlier. By initiating teamwork even before the project starts, the project can start at a higher level of knowledge, as shown in Figure 5-3.

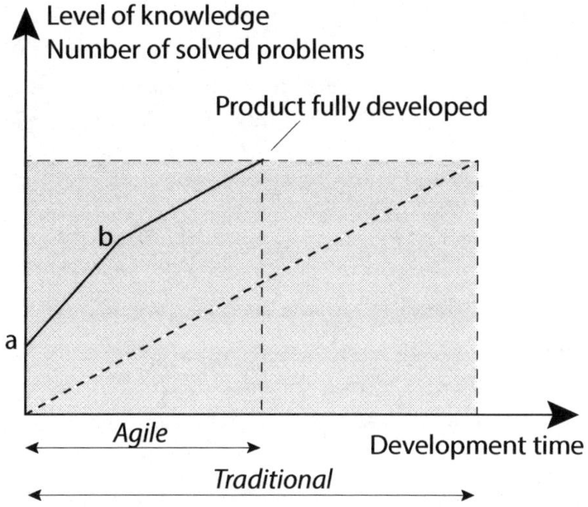

Figure 5-3. Accelerated problem solving. Work starts at a higher level (a), and the pace of problem solving is faster at the outset (a–b). Adapted from Thomke and Fujimoto (2000).

When you reuse previous designs, the knowledge is already built into those parts. If you use a modular system or platform or license outside technology, these become carriers of technical knowledge. The project will then develop certain parts of the product, while other parts will remain intact. At the same time, this will make it possible to easily customize a multitude of products for customers. This strategy is applied by everyone who uses open source code. The popular Android operating system is an example of open-source code based on the Linux kernel. Today it embodies 50 years of accumulated development conducted by tens of thousands of engineers.

Starting with ready-made, off-the-shelf components, design work can be devoted to combining these in a suitable way and developing the parts one wants to improve or the parts that make each product model unique. When modules are improved, all projects can immediately use the new knowledge. Knowledge is transferred between projects quickly, while complexity decreases in individual projects, because so many components and dimensions are predetermined. At the same time, the purpose of development work will shift, from perfecting separate designs, to building up common technical expertise that will fit together into a whole. As a result, development cycles can be shortened, while costs are reduced and quality increased. However, this simultaneously increases the dependencies between the projects, as well as the complexity of coordination between different products, which requires decisions and coordination by an effective product team.

Working faster with problem solving early in the projects means a large number of problems can be solved quickly with relatively little effort. In work on goals and plans at the outset of a project, as well as when the product team previously initiated projects, quite a few problems and misunderstandings are eliminated. In this process, the group's members share their expertise and knowledge from previous projects and from their areas of specialization. During a workshop, the participants can quickly raise one another's level of knowledge much higher. Problems become clearer, as do the possibilities available, at the same time as the group lays a foundation for effective cooperation.

Products being developed today are often technically very complex. It is no longer possible for a single engineer to fully understand all aspects of a product and its production process. That demands several different specialists with expertise in different areas of design, production technology, and procurement. By letting the specialists work together in teams, knowledge will be passed between these areas of expertise. Problems can be detected earlier, ideas can be evaluated critically, and shared knowledge can be built up faster.

Pulse meetings and workshops enable plenty of communication within and between teams and projects, which promotes knowledge transfer between different disciplines. This approach encourages participants to deal with problems and share their knowledge. As a result, creativity rises to a higher level and the structure becomes more fixed, thus increasing the pace of problem solving in the operation.

Many problems are intellectual challenges. Being able to work out a solution not only demands fundamental theoretical knowledge, good methods, and appropriate experience but also uninterrupted time for value-adding work. Project participants must be allowed to work focusing on one project at a time. Splitting up staff on multiple projects or tasks not only dramatically reduces the proportion of hours when they are adding value. It also stresses staff to always do simple things first, so they get at least one thing done. An important prerequisite for effective problem solving, and thus for an effective development process with short lead times, is that employees are not overloaded or fragmented by too many projects or short assignments.

Knowledge can only be communicated by people working together in teams or sharing experience through networks.

Building prototypes and performing reliable tests take a lot of time. But a lot of problems can be solved early on with simple simulations and sketches, mathematical computations, computer support such as computer-aided design (CAD), and statistical design of experiments. Although these methods do not provide an entirely accurate picture of the final product, many simple problems can be eliminated relatively quickly. Simple and fast methods also have the

Paths to accelerated problem solving:

- **Full-time work in teams with complementary expertise.**
- **Frequent Pulse meetings, several times a day at the creative stages.**
- **Planning workshops to communicate the goal scenario between projects and product teams.**
- **Regular demonstrations of subresults.**
- **Employees focusing on one project at a time.**
- **Workshops, fast-track studies, or rapid response workshops convened with different expertise to solve problems or prepare background data.**
- **Modular systems.**
- **Simulations, computations, sketches, CAD, and statistical design of experiments.**
- **"Go and see for yourself," networking, internship, and study visits.**
- **Building and transferring knowledge.**

advantage of allowing many proposed solutions to be tested in a comparatively short time.

Knowledge can also be transferred between projects. Solutions to problems that have previously appeared in one project can be used to solve current problems in another. Some knowledge is suitable for being written down. This is true of formalized knowledge that can be documented in reports, tables, or matrices. The mere fact that information is available rarely guarantees that it actually gets used. Many engineers take pride in coming up with their own solutions. The program manager and project manager must ask for summaries of existing knowledge as key background data for their decisions.

Far from all knowledge can be formalized. On the contrary, most knowledge is tacit; that is, we are not consciously aware of it. Thus, the bulk of all knowledge is communicated only by people working together in teams or sharing experience through networks (Takeuchi and Nonaka, 1986).

"Go and see for yourself" is a maxim at Toyota. To truly understand a problem, you have to see the effects for yourself. Reading a report or having someone describe the problem is not enough. For a design engineer, this might mean that the problems that emerge when a new product's manufacturing process is being tested must be studied carefully on site. Only then can the engineer make the right adjustments to the design to fix the problem. At the same time, the design engineer has acquired a deeper understanding of production conditions, which will be useful the next time a component has to be designed. Similarly, managers and decision-makers also need to go and see for themselves how the systems work so they can understand the problems and make the right decisions.

Build and transfer knowledge

For an operation that works with product development, reusing knowledge is a success factor. The results generated in a development operation, such as knowledge, are plain to see. This is true of knowledge about customer needs, the performance of different technical solutions, and new technologies for more efficient production. The built-up knowledge is formalized in specifications, components, manufacturing and development methods, production processes, and product sheets.

The competence in the operation must be replenished continuously, so that for every new problem the process starts at a higher level. This is the case not only for the knowledge of individuals, but chiefly the shared knowledge that can be used in multiple projects regardless of staffing. New knowledge is generated each time someone is faced with a problem. To solve the problem, a person must combine existing knowledge in a new way while developing new knowledge about previously unknown relationships. The solution to a problem is interesting, but even more so is understanding why the problem occurred. That understanding contains the key to avoiding future problems of the same nature.

Working with demanding customers and solving challenging problems, staff quickly develop knowledge. When the operation is overloaded and the percentage of value-adding hours decreases, it not only reduces efficiency and increases costs. Perhaps even more serious is that knowledge creation comes to a standstill. When workers spend a lot of time looking for information, going to nonproductive meetings, and being pressured to solve urgent but relatively simple cases, they quickly lose their competence (Zika-Viktorsson et al., 2003). These are losses that cannot be offset by individual courses or seminars. Many enterprises try to make up for such losses by hiring new staff or engaging consultants, but unfortunately they too soon adjust to the slow pace of work, and their knowledge is drained. To rapidly build knowledge, staff must have a high proportion of value-adding work hours. This in turn makes demands on how many projects the operation can run simultaneously, so that employees will be able to focus on one task at a time. It also requires a decision-making system that can make decisions so that the work is not held up by obstacles or by coming to a crossroads.

Continuous knowledge creation can be facilitated by different techniques, such as workshops, modular systems, and CAD, as mentioned previously. Many of the techniques are tried and tested and relatively easy to use. Despite this, knowledge transfer between projects has been regarded as one of the major weaknesses of the project as a way of working. This is a result of today's line organization, where power tends to be based on access to information and knowledge, which can be used to gain a higher position, better working conditions, or higher pay. People may be tempted to hoard knowledge so they become valuable and even indispensable. In some companies, there are people who live off their reputation of being irreplaceable. These people do not allow others to work in their realm, which would threaten their exclusive position. At the same time, managers are surprisingly tolerant of and in many cases encourage such behavior by appointing such individuals as critical resources in all projects. No attempts are made to break their monopoly on knowledge. On the contrary, everyone in the operation takes pains to rub these people the right way, even top management.

In organizations where power and influence are based on being active and sharing information and knowledge, knowledge transfer has not become a problem that way (Woodward, 1980).

In fields of technology with rapid development and change, a problem may arise as managers and decision-makers quickly lose competence compared to their employees. The problem can become dire if the operation executes just about all its work as projects. Staff working in the projects solve problems daily, communicate with customers, and learn to use new technologies. But management is barely involved in that work. So it is not uncommon to find the most technically competent staff among the most recently employed, at the "bottom" of the organization, because they are the ones who most often work on solving problems. The inverted distribution of knowledge that this results in leads to difficulties when management is supposed to coordinate operations and designate the vision, goals, and strategies. The credibility of management is quickly eroded, which can lead to the projects and assignment operations becoming even more autonomous. To remedy this problem, managers must get back on track. They must be present in the work being done, such as in the product team, portfolio team, and various strategic analyses.

They must use and continuously broaden their knowledge through daily work on strategy and product architecture.

Front-loaded projects

In many projects, problems are discovered late in the development process, making them what are known as "back-loaded projects." According to classic project management, technical specifications should be put at the beginning of the development process, when the least is known, as they are required for making a detailed plan. At the same time, this locks the development process into a few possible solutions. It is often only when the product undergoes final testing or when manufacturing of the product is to begin that the problems emerge. Because the possibility of influencing the design at that stage is almost nonexistent, the problems often become very serious and difficult to solve in a good way. If it turns out that the chosen solution is not tenable, one is forced to back up and work out a new solution. It is very tempting to pursue a bad solution and just try harder, even knowing there are serious flaws, because so much time and resources have already been invested. As a result, problems are discovered late, causing long delays when the problems have to be corrected, as well as large cost overruns when additional resources are called in. Also, staff get drafted from other projects, making it tougher for those projects to meet their deadlines and work in a focused way from the start. The projects become back-loaded with the biggest share of resources at the end, many of which were not in the initial plan. Back-loaded projects can also be called "chaotic." Are the problems that emerge later completely unforeseeable early on? The answer is that an approach in which projects are front-loaded would in many cases avoid such difficulties at later stages.

A front-loaded project is based on customer needs, the effects to be achieved by the user. On the basis of this goal scenario, staff work actively to anticipate and solve as many technical challenges as possible as early as possible. The key is to be aware of the problems early on. Problems that one is aware of can be solved. Cross-functional teams, dedicated staff, a visual approach, simple prototypes, ample communication, and workshops have a significant impact here. They provide more diverse information and a higher level of creativity. But for the projects to be genuinely front-loaded, the operation must also allocate far more resources at the outset to work out critical architecture and evaluate various possible design solutions. Much of that work will be done by the product team before the project even starts. For this to succeed in practice, the pulse meetings must also be frequent. In the early design phase, teamwork is necessary, as are pulse meetings several times a day. The design work can then be carried out in a few weeks. There is a clear link between, on the one hand, early identification of problems and, on the other, effective product development in terms of the development cycle, productivity, and product quality. The reason is that problem solving becomes more expensive and more difficult the further the project has progressed. Front-loaded projects are a strategy in which the development process is streamlined by moving the identification and problem solving to the initial work on a project (Thomke and Fujimoto, 2000).

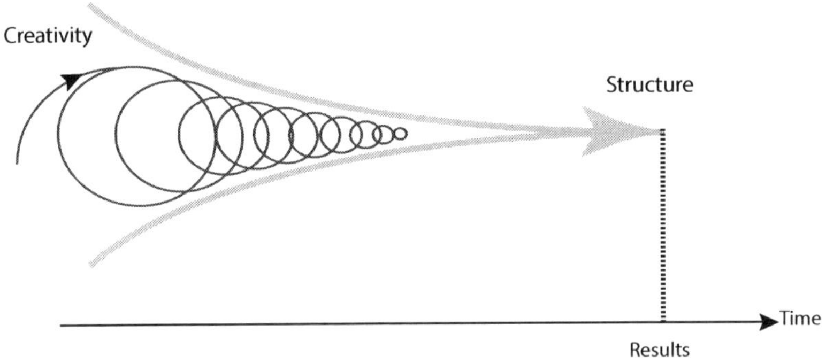

Figure 5-4. Front-loaded projects. In front-loaded projects, a high level of creativity is used at the start to find multiple possible solutions. Little by little, solutions are combined and eliminated, which locks in ever more parameters in the design. The movement is from creativity to structure.

The more parallel solutions one works with, the lower the risk of ending up with difficult technical problems. By working with several solutions, knowledge is also built up faster. You learn what works and what does not. The proposals that do not meet expectations will gradually be eliminated. The final design will be a combination of the best solutions.

Reusing knowledge through modular systems also reduces the risk of severe technical problems, according to Smith and Reinertsen (1998). (See Figure 5-5.) With many ready-made components to start with, design work can be devoted to combining these in a good way and developing the parts one wants to improve. This reduces the risk in an individual project, because so many components and dimensions are already predetermined.

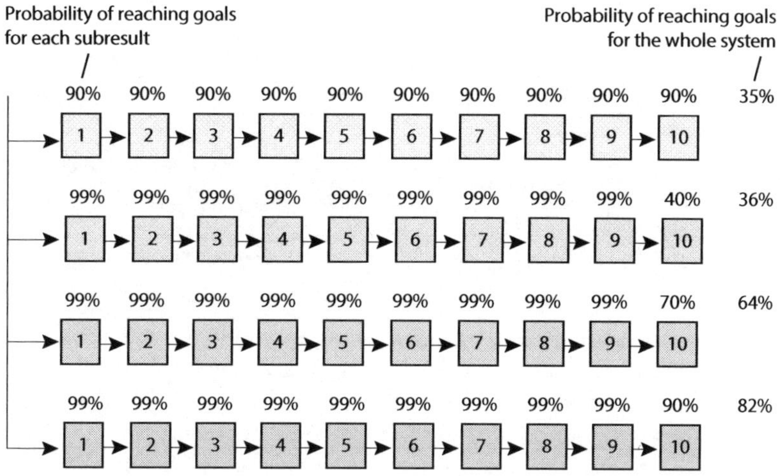

Figure 5-5. Technical risk. If the technical risk is concentrated in a small number of components, it is easier to achieve the system's overall performance requirements. Adapted from Smith and Reinertsen (1998).

Front-loaded projects, in which one works with several solutions in parallel (Kennedy, 2003), follow what is called "set-based design" or "concurrent design," as shown in Figure 5-6. This method of working is based on the problem-solving cycle. Each solution is evaluated and compared with one another as well as the critical parameters set by the project's product goals. The solutions that do not work well enough are weeded out little by little. The number of possible solutions is gradually reduced as they are combined with one another in different ways. The risk of ending up without any workable solution at the final stage is very small. To work with many possible designs at the outset, fast and simple methods should be used for evaluation and screening, such as simulations, sketches, mathematical computation, and computer support using CAD.

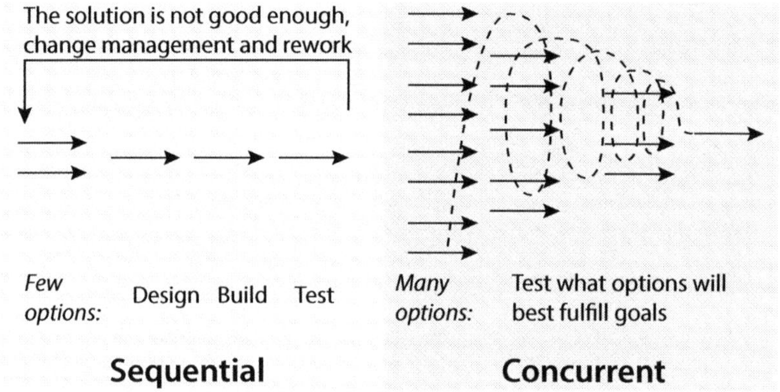

Figure 5-6. Concurrent (Set-based) design process. In the concurrent design process, several alternative solutions are conceived at the start then tested and combined until the one that best fulfills the goals is selected. In the point-based sequential design process, a technical specification is fixed initially, so only one solution is developed. If that solution does not work, the development process has to start from the beginning. Adapted from Kennedy (2003).

The concurrent design process means working with many options and many perspectives, which makes it possible to shorten lead times. The design decisions are aimed at combining solutions and gradually reducing the number of possible solutions. By thinking in subsystems or modules, which can be combined with one another, many alternatives can be found for the final design, thus reducing the risk in development projects. For the operation, this approach continuously generates more knowledge than is needed at any one time. But the knowledge not used at that time is not wasted. Every solution produces data in the tests and evaluations carried out. The results can be compiled in graphs that plot critical parameters against one another. That knowledge can be used in other projects and to foster understanding of underlying relationships.

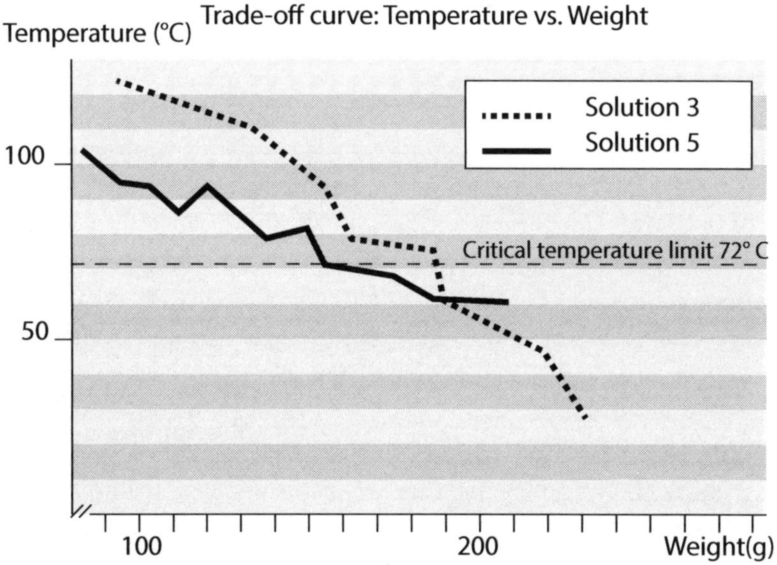

Figure 5-7. Trade-off curve for temperature versus weight. Measurements of two critical parameters of two prototypes. The parameters are used to evaluate two alternative solutions.

Front-loaded product development at Toyota

According to Thomke and Fujimoto (2000), Toyota intensified its efforts to speed up its development process in the early 1990s. They wanted to reduce the time from an approved design to the start of production, to better respond to an accelerating rate of change in customer needs. Among many other initiatives, they chose to speed up prototyping by identifying and resolving design problems earlier. To do this, they streamlined the transfer of problems and solution-specific knowledge between projects and simultaneously introduced an early use of advanced simulation techniques. To measure the effects of these initiatives, they collected data about problem solving in all projects. The effects could be measured not only in shorter lead times and lower costs. Above all, the problem-solving pattern changed over time. Whenever they succeeded in bringing forward problem solving, knowledge transfer between projects also increased, CAD tools were applied even more diligently, and production technology was involved even earlier in the design decisions.

In the late 1980s, half of all problems were still unresolved when pilot production started (decision point S5). In the early 1990s, efforts focused on improving communication and interaction "face-to-face" between different design sections, resulting in more problems being discovered early on. In the mid-1990s, they began using three-dimensional CAD to quickly find fit problems, which made problem identification possible even earlier. Later, various simulation techniques were introduced to also find functional problems while actively transferring knowledge between projects.

At the end of the 1990s, Toyota solved almost 80% of their technical problems by the first prototype stage (decision point S2). During the same period, they were able to decrease lead times and costs by 30%–40%. Multiple simultaneous initiatives may also have helped shorten cycles and reduce costs.

The only way individuals can do their jobs is to solve, in interaction with other individuals, problems that are real for the enterprise and express needs and activities that are understandable to everyone. The less one defines status, roles, and how communication will be done, the more important individuals' activities with real-world tasks become when the individuals view these as instructions and routines.

Solving 80% of technical problems translates into reduced uncertainty, in terms of complexity theory. It is important to remember that uncertainty has been reduced at an overall level, not at the employee level in the work itself. It is through increased communication and interaction between people that the problems have been solved. Real problems are the tasks to be solved, while the work of individuals is not predetermined. Burns and Stalker (1994) have described this as follows. The only way individuals can do their jobs is to solve, in interaction with other individuals, problems that are real for the enterprise and express needs and activities that are understandable to everyone. The less one defines status, roles, and how communication will be done, the more important individuals' activities with real-world tasks become when the individuals view these as instructions and routines (ibid). The challenge is to create a structure in which this is possible.

Summary of knowledge building

This chapter has shown that knowledge building can be regarded as the heart of a development operation.

No matter how much knowledge one has about a given problem at the outset, there are always unique aspects that need to be understood before a sound design can be developed. It is not possible to produce a complete design in one fell swoop. That requires multiple iterations, in which the developers learn at every step a little more about the problem and the alternative solutions available. In the end, the developers have produced a final design with complete specifications.

The development process can be seen as a series of problem-solving cycles. Each cycle starts with a description of the problem, after which the possible solutions available are identified. Then models are built that can be used to validate the solutions. The models are tested against the existing requirements and restraints. The results are analyzed and evaluated. If the results from the first round are good enough, the problem is solved. Usually, however, these solutions have to be modified, as do the models, after which new tests can be performed.

The efficiency of the development process is reflected in the pace at which problems are solved. To speed up problem solving, existing knowledge can be communicated and reused, for example through modular systems. Problems can also be solved faster at the start of projects using simulations, prototypes, and computations. Problem solving is also greatly accelerated by doing work in teams with complementary skills, communicating and making decisions through pulse meetings, using workshops to communicate within projects and with product teams, and allowing staff to focus their work on one project at a time.

Problems detected early are relatively inexpensive and simple to address. Front-loaded projects apply a high level of creativity at the outset to find multiple possible solutions that are gradually combined and eliminated, thus locking in a growing number of parameters in the design. Multiple parallel solutions reduce the risk that a project will be delayed by difficult technical problems.

My most important point in this chapter is that it is through cooperation between people in different constellations that learning occurs. And learning is product development. Comprehensive project models and other bureaucracy obstruct learning or wholly prevent it. Because learning is based on encounters between people, the arenas where encounters can occur are key to successful project development. In the next chapter, I will discuss how an organization based on arenas may be designed.

6. Just-in-time decisions

In this chapter, I will describe how an agile organization can be built up. The problem I want to solve is how to get away from the predominant functional organizational structure in which information and knowledge are power. I also want to establish a structure in which it is possible to make decisions "just in time." An operation that works with development has a variety of tasks, from short assignments and resource allocation, to comprehensive new development and strategy work. An agile organization should be able to handle all these tasks in parallel.

Decision-making in the development process

The development process can be organized in different ways. Each operation is unique in its details, adapted to the constraints set by its environment, culture, and management philosophy. If we strip away all the details to instead study the broad strokes, we find several similarities among different development operations. But we also find dissimilarities in other respects. Such dissimilarities may be the way decisions are made, what types of projects are run, how recurring and unique tasks are organized, and how decision-making has been delegated to various roles.

Product development is intimately associated with uncertainty, knowledge gaps, and risks. When the development of a new product begins, the finished solution is a mirage, its contours vague and content unknown. Even the understanding of customers' needs is often incomplete or dispersed throughout the operation. Little by little, knowledge is generated that reduces uncertainty, and more and more parts of the design are locked in. In the course of such work, we are constantly faced with a variety of trade-offs that, to a greater or lesser extent, will influence the final product and future profitability. Some of the decisions will also influence other products.

A lack of decisions will delay and, in the worst case, halt the work. The absence of coordinated decisions poses a major risk in that different individuals and groups may concentrate their efforts in different directions. When a decision is finally made, it may mean parts of the development work must be augmented or even redone.

The pace at which knowledge is generated influences development time. However, to speed up the development process, information must not be piled up but must be sifted through, and the way forward that will advance the process must be chosen. With each choice, alternative solutions are discarded, and uncertainty about the future design decreases. Every decision of this type sharpens the contours of the as yet unfinished product and guides the next few initiatives in the right direction. A large part of these decisions are made by the developers in their daily work, based on their know-how as design engineers. This is the case for choices concerning how the solution will be engineered, for example. Decisions linked to customer needs and relevant to the effects the operation wants to achieve with customers are made by the product team. I refer to the decisions made and work done by the product team as "strategic product development." It is tough for developers to deal with uncertainty in customer needs, because they rarely have an overall view of the big picture (Adams et al., 1998). Thus, for a project to succeed, the project group and the product team need to work together closely based on their different perspectives.

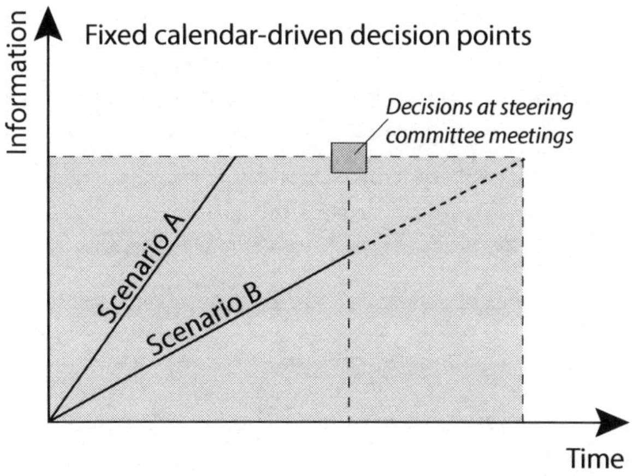

Figure 6-1. Planned decision points. Decision points that are scheduled based on a fixed plan, such as in a Gantt chart or a waterfall model with gates. Adapted from Holman et al. (2003).

Many project models recommend setting fixed decision points for projects, often at quite long intervals, as shown in Figure 6-1. The decision points usually mark transitions between different phases of a project and are sometimes called "gates." There are too few of these decision points to satisfy the needs of the project for decisions at a strategic level. To achieve agile product development, it is necessary to create a way of working that enables decisions to be made when needed (Holman et al., 2003). In Pulse, we recommend projects have pulse meetings at least every day. In addition, there are program pulse meetings, held weekly, which are a forum for escalating issues and problems from the projects to the program manager and product team. The projects also have regular demonstrations of subresults and handover points. Program managers are expected to spend most of their time on-site, so projects can get help with the strategic decisions when they need them, just in time. Strategic decision making goes much faster in Pulse than in a traditionally structured project operation.

It is not reasonable to expect that a few decision points between the strategic level and the project level, as recommended in stage-gate models, will be sufficient. Either the work of the project has flowed smoothly, so it should have been possible to make decisions earlier, or else the project is behind schedule, and the decision will be based on incomplete information. The biggest problem with stage-gate models, though, is that they concentrate on the projects' horizons. That results in a lack of cohesive strategic thinking. Customers and their needs are forgotten, and the project ends up focusing only on resource optimization and cost control.

Some organizations strictly adhere to the decision points, so a project is forced to wait there for its decisions, and as a result the time savings that could have been gained by an individual project cannot be exploited. In the case of delays, a project could be forced to wait on a decision until the next planned decision point, resulting in even more time lost. Delays pile up, while the benefits of time gains are never exploited. This leads to recurring delays, increased costs, and poorer quality, because the projects can never get the decisions when they really need them.

Product development can be seen as decision-intensive work. Efforts to shorten the development cycle must ensure that decision-making becomes more flexible and much more frequent. Decision makers must become involved in the daily work without getting absorbed in details. Projects and assignments need support and guidance so that their work fits into the strategic design through decisions made at the right time, just in time. Likewise, uncertainty also needs to be reduced in strategic work by a fast pace of decision-making. To achieve real-time decision-making at all levels, I organize the operation in a network of pulse meetings.

Just-in-time decisions

To achieve just-in-time decisions, I have designed a network of pulse meetings, a "pulse network," capable of real-time management, as shown in Figure 6-2. Unlike the projects, which are temporary nodes in the network, the hubs in the pulse network are fixed. To make decisions rapidly when necessary and to simultaneously handle shifting needs, the pulse network must have adaptability built-in.

The pulse network should balance structure with creativity. According to Rubinstein and Firstenberg (1999), a good system should be sufficiently flexible and unplanned to allow exploration and creativity. At the same time, it should be controlled and planned so as to provide stability and order for the initiatives taken without arresting all actions with rigid rules and regulations. The decisions to be handled vary in character. Some decisions involve trade-offs in a design and affect whether a design can satisfy customer needs and meet cost restraints, while other decisions deal with prioritizing resources between projects. Questions of detail are best solved by the developers in projects and assignments, while questions that require an overall view are handled by multi-project management.

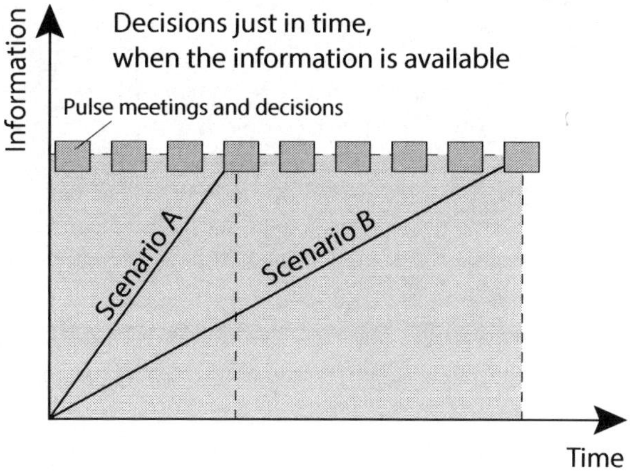

Figure 6-2. Just-in-time decisions at frequent pulse meetings. With pulse meetings, decisions are made as soon as the background data is ready, just in time. Adapted from Holman et al. (2003).

Having a single steering committee for all ongoing projects and having the committee handle all decisions would make things unmanageable. The questions are too diverse in nature and vary too widely in importance. The steering committee would be in a never-ending meeting. In practice, it is just as difficult to delegate more and to have the project manager make more numerous and more important decisions. One project manager cannot coordinate multiple projects. The risk is that the projects would become autonomous and compete with one another for customers, resources, and technical solutions. Neither can a single project manager have the knowledge and overview needed to make economically correct decisions in the trade-offs between, for example, production costs and launch dates.

There must be decision-makers to back up the projects with decisions in the various areas where decisions are needed, when they are needed.

A fundamental structure for decisions

An agile structure for decision-making must consist of multiple decision-making units that make different types of decisions. Dividing the decisions into different categories, handled by different decision-making groups, reduces the complexity. As a result, each decision is easier to make.

The generic foundation described here needs to be adapted to each individual company. For example, large corporations might need multiple hubs in their pulse network to be able to handle more cases and higher complexity. Companies that have different business areas might need to adapt the structure to fit these areas. To build the best pulse network possible, an enterprise can analyze how decisions fit together at the management level. For example, one company might drive the development of new products and markets, and these tend to fit closely together. They might also drive the development of their production system. There are some links and dependencies between product and market development and the development of production systems, but you may choose to keep the pulse networks for those separate with only a few overlapping persons (such as the CEO). Another example is companies that drive product development projects in parallel with customer projects for unique customer solutions. You may choose to use two partly separate pulse networks (one for development and one for customer solutions), with shared portfolio management and resource management but separate product management teams, program pulse meetings, and projects.

At the operational level, projects act within the strategic design by applying rules and structures that they have designed themselves, such as goal scenarios, synchronization plans, risks, and rules for social interaction. The projects make decisions affecting their own daily work, backed up by their rich knowledge of the details. This works in technical coordination between different components as well as the allocation of resources to different tasks.

At the strategic level, the program manager resolves issues that affect multiple projects within one program. The program manager decides which technical solutions to move forward on and provides assistance on technical issues that the projects are not capable of solving on their own. The program manager is a critical resource for successfully speeding up decision-making in a development operation. Deficiencies in this position will lead to the product team being overloaded with cases and the projects not getting their decisions in time. A program manager must also be physically present to lead the operation during most of the working hours. Cusumano and Nobeoka (1998) have called this position "chief engineer," which emphasizes the importance of engineering know-how.

The product team works out business goals and program plans for priority areas, with the aim of initiating projects based on solid background data. Satisfying all customer needs is not profitable. The product team will also work strategically with a product portfolio and long-term plans for technology and the market.

While the product team is developing strategies to be executed through projects, assignments, and analyses, the portfolio team works out a strategic direction. In which markets should the enterprise operate and which business models should it use? How should the enterprise position itself? Which technologies should it develop itself, and which should it buy externally? What should it manufacture itself, and what should be bought? These are some of the questions that the portfolio team formulates answers to in a strategic direction. The portfolio team prioritizes the results that the product team should produce in the coming period. After each period, the product team also demonstrates their results for the portfolio team. The portfolio team starts projects and closes finished projects or closes projects prematurely. Once a project has been started, been assigned a priority, and thus been allocated resources, the portfolio team must be steadfast. They must resist the temptation to casually change priorities or shift resources, because that would interrupt ongoing work and create a messy situation in the projects.

The weekly allocation of resources is managed by the resource team, which also ensures the development over time of their employees based on changing needs. The resource team is aided by the priorities and allocations set by the portfolio team.

Different types of projects

When an enterprise wants to create a more effective structure for product development, a good starting point is to try to identify what different types of projects are run. Nowadays all kinds of initiatives are often called "projects," from one-person assignments lasting a few days, to multi-million-dollar investments with a development cycle lasting several years. However, decision-making cannot be effective if all initiatives are handled the same way. Thus it is necessary to create a structure in which the various initiatives are assigned to categories. As with all models for categorizing, there will be borderline cases, with subsequent discussions about where the initiative actually belongs. But a model helps place the vast majority of cases quickly in their proper category, thereby creating flexibility in work.

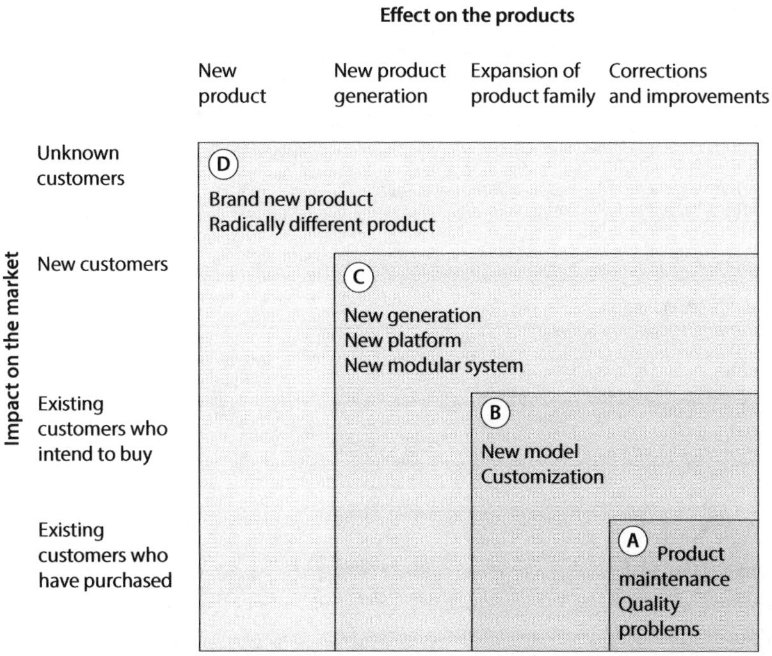

Figure 6-3. Project types. Four different types of projects in a multi-project organization and the extent to which these project types affect the product and market. Adapted from Wheelwright and Clark (1992).

The model described in Figure 6-3 should be seen as an example. In many cases, it can be used straight off, but each enterprise must evaluate the model in their own context and adapt it as needed.

Box A, the lower right-hand corner of Figure 6-3, contains short initiatives to address urgent quality problems and carry out minor improvements, sometimes called "product maintenance." I have chosen to call these short initiatives "assignments." Boxes B, C, and D contain bigger initiatives, which I have chosen to call "projects." B projects include the development of new models and customization. In C projects, new products, product families, modular systems, and platforms are developed. D projects develop new technologies. An example of the results of a D project might be a prototype that represents how the technology can be used by the customer. Sometimes there are also E projects, feasibility studies and other initiatives run by the product team. These studies often involve analyzing and defining customer needs, developing the business model to better match the customer needs, and developing the architecture and key features of the product.

A: Assignments

Most development operations have a continuous inflow of issues and questions concerning existing products and their production processes. These are cases that relate to product maintenance in various ways and, in many enterprises, cause major interruptions in operations. It is also common for these cases to attract a lot of attention at all levels of the operation, because they are perceived as urgent. Because there are so many cases, shorter or longer interruptions constantly occur in the project work. These interruptions are expensive. There is a risk that the operation will devote a significant share of its resources to issues perceived as urgent, leaving too few resources to work on more long-term development. The solution is to introduce assignment management with established resource restraints for all cases relating to existing products and production processes.

In many companies I have worked with, two-thirds of working hours have been devoted to recurring short interruptions. Is taking care of product maintenance worth that high of a cost? Probably not. The alternative is to create a system and a few simple rules that will provide order and reduce the impact of urgent interruptions. Product maintenance cases as such are not sufficiently important for the portfolio team or product team to address their decisions. Treating these cases as work done and coordinated in different departments is not useful either, because the separate departments in a functional organization cannot get a coordinated view of priorities and actions. In Pulse, I have set up separate channels for assignments and projects. The projects are started by the portfolio team. They have calculated how many projects the operation can run simultaneously without getting overloaded, say, five projects. When a project is concluded, a new project is allowed to start. The same applies for assignments. Pulse includes an assignment manager who queues, prioritizes, and starts assignments at the same pace as other assignments are completed. This allows a limited number of assignments to access the system at the same time, thus enabling control over throughput and lead times. The resources working on assignments meet daily at the assignment pulse meetings. The concept of assignment management is one example of how I have implemented just-in-time decision-making in Pulse. The advantage is that the enterprise can handle the urgent cases that it is truly important to do something about. This frees up substantial resources for working with product and market development.

The enterprises that use Pulse have chosen two different ways to staff their assignment group. Some have a dedicated team that works solely on assignments. But it is more common for the assignment manager to apply for resources from the resource pool in the same way that projects do. The major advantage of the latter is job rotation. Many different kinds of cases are brought to the assignment pulse that the participants must tackle. A case is not merely given to "expert A" but is put up on the assignment pulse board. The participants at the pulse meeting choose—usually on their own, sometimes with the help of the assignment manager—which assignments they will carry out. Then they have to find the knowledge necessary to carry out the assignment. All enterprises that have embraced rotating assignment teams report a substantial boost in competence within the enterprise.

B: New product variant within the framework for an existing design

The pressure on short lead times is greatest in projects in the category of adaptations, new product variants, models, and customer-specific solutions. In these projects, customers have often been promised a delivery date. The technical complexity is usually not that high, which makes the project risks relatively low. Revenue from a single B project is also low, but by working with model upgrades, the lifecycle of products can be extended and the investments made already can be better exploited.

Management's influence on project work is crucial for success. The product team must always be present for the strategic trade-offs. Weekly program pulse meetings of the project managers and the program manager and demonstrations of subresults are key ingredients in the recipe for success.

C: New product generation

The development of a new product generation is a long-term investment that requires major resources. This makes the projects large, too. Considerably more staff and resources are spent on these projects than on the development of a new model. The business risks (and business opportunities) are significant because of the huge costs and the big changes being sought. However, by using Pulse the problems and obstacles that inevitably exist can emerge sooner and get fixed faster, so lead times can be kept short.

Projects to develop a new modular system or a new platform build basic functionalities to fulfill the fundamental needs of customers in the future, and those functionalities will later generate a product family of different models. Thus the demands on designs are tougher in these projects. A design must be adaptable and flexible and should link to previous product generations and even future ones, so that customers are familiar with and continue to buy the products but get added value in each new generation (Wheelwright and Clark, 1992).

As long as the operation does not invest in production equipment, the biggest risk in a new development project is tying up staff for a long time. Some companies choose to strengthen the organization with additional resources during periods when a new product generation is in progress. This can be done by using consultants, external engineering firms, or partnerships with suppliers. The portfolio team plays a key role in determining how these projects will be assigned resources.

D: Brand new product or technology

This category also includes projects that work on research and technology shifts. Brand new technology is rarely developed. A good product with a good manufacturing process can survive for many years, through updates of its modular system and extensions of new models. Projects that actually manage to radically change the technical building blocks are few. Many more projects never find an effective solution. This means that an operation needs to continuously run multiple D projects over an extended period to produce any technological breakthrough.

Developing brand new technology can take a long time. It is also associated with great uncertainty, as success is never assured. No one has yet seen the solution to be produced. Few people can even imagine it. The projects are also difficult to plan because of their great uncertainty. At the same time, these projects will provide the major breakthroughs that will radically change conditions in the market. Missing out on a crucial technology shift may mean the end of the enterprise.

Guidance as to which new technologies the operation should try to develop comes from the strategic direction. To avoid inhibiting creativity in these long-term projects, control should not be strict. Instead, one should largely rely on the skilled engineers and scientists to come up with pioneering ideas, given the right conditions. In developing brand new technologies, focused teamwork is essential for success, as is close cooperation with customers who are willing to evaluate prototypes.

Some common forms of organization

Among companies engaged in product development, there are two main types of organizational structure: the functional and the matrix. To these I would add a third, the pulse organizational structure, which has a different starting point.

The form of organization should support and control the work performed within its domain and with respect to its operating environment. In practice, a number of trade-offs are necessary: between coordination and delegation, continuity and temporary solutions, structure and flexibility—to name a few. Some forms of organization will promote communication, knowledge creation, and rapid decision-making to a greater extent than others. I argue that a multi-project organization based on Pulse is better suited to meet the increasing complexity in the world at large.

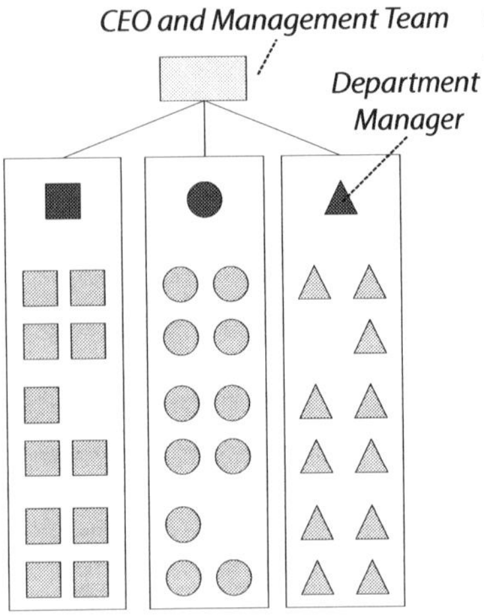

Figure 6-4. Functional organizational structure. For simplicity's sake, only three departments are shown here.

Functional organizational structure

When tasks are broken down into smaller parts to enable specialization and efficiency, one must simultaneously create a structure enabling coordination of the work of the various parts. In a functional organization, similar tasks are brought together in departments, as shown in Figure 6-4. At the overall level, the organization is divided so that production, product development, marketing, purchasing, and accounting end up in different departments. Within each department, further segmentation is possible. For example, the product development department can be divided into different sections for developing hardware and software. At the lowest level, software development could be divided into architecture, interfaces, and testing.

In a functional organization, the manager for each department makes all its important decisions. The managers are responsible for planning, organization, leadership, and control in their respective departments. This applies, for example, to the development of new products, a responsibility that falls on the R&D manager, though it is often initiated by a product manager in the marketing department. Control and planning are based on annual budgets. Collaboration between the different departments is poor, resulting in long development cycles. If a person in a functional organization uses the term "project," they are probably referring to a task rather than the method of working. If there are project managers, they are assistants that support the department managers in planning and coordinating specific tasks.

Matrix organizational structure

Many functional organizations that want to use the project as a way of working choose to reorganize themselves as a matrix organization. The transition to a matrix organization is a relatively small step. Employees remain in their departments under their department managers. Budgetary control, in which costs are allocated annually to different types of account and cost centers, is augmented by project management. Project managers are appointed to plan, organize, and control the work in each project. The relationship between departments and projects is regulated by the projects requesting results from the departments. It is customary to speak of a boundary between "what and when" and "how and who." The projects determine what results should be produced and when they should be completed. The departments determine how the work will be carried out and who will do it.

In practice, either the department managers will be the stronger party and make all important decisions, or the project managers will. This is why researchers such as Ulrich and Eppinger (2003) divide matrix organizations into two different types based on where the power to make decisions resides. When the power lies with the department managers, it is called a "lightweight project matrix organization." When the power lies with the project managers, it is called a "heavyweight project matrix organization" (ibid). (See Figure 6-5.)

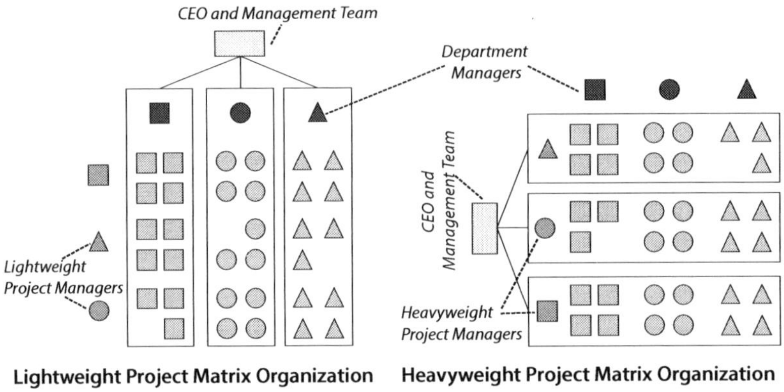

Figure 6-5. Lightweight vs. heavyweight project matrix organizations. Three departments and three projects are shown. Real-world companies usually have many more.

Japanese automakers have used heavyweight project matrix organizations since introducing the project as a way of working in the mid-1950s. In contrast, American and European companies have used lightweight project matrix organizations. This has given the Japanese automotive industry a clear competitive advantage (Womack, Jones, and Roos, 1990). In many organizations, management has worried about creating project teams that are granted too much authority. A team can easily become autonomous and start developing its own goals, which are not necessarily related to the operation's goals (Wheelwright and Clark, 1992). This phenomenon became known as early as the 1970s, when experiments began with self-managing groups in production (Stjernberg, 1993). If delegation is to succeed, the strategic work and communication must at the same time be strengthened to hold the parts together.

To work efficiently on a project, most participants must be engaged on a full-time basis (Adams et al., 1998). Various studies have shown that if employees are divided among different projects or different assignments, efficiency drops fast. As soon as we participate in more than two projects, our efficiency drops sharply (Wheelwright and Clark, 1992; McDonough and Spital, 2003).

Working in projects in functional and matrix organizations quickly becomes messy. The "chimney organization" structure will make innovation more difficult or prevent it altogether (Adams et al, 1998). And the strategic work gets lost when the projects are the center of attention (Cusumano and Nobeoka, 1998). These are a few of the reasons why I decided to develop a completely new form of organization: the multi-project organization based on Pulse.

Provide projects with resources

Before we go into how an effective multi-project organization based on Pulse is structured, it is important to understand how the functional and matrix organizations organize resources and generate results. Work in a project can be carried out in two ways. Either the work is distributed to the different departments or kept together in the project team. If the work is performed in different departments, the operation loses the potential for dynamic action that teamwork offers. A team made up of people with different skills can solve much more demanding tasks than the individuals can on their own (Alberts, 2011; Adams et al., 1998). If the work is done in the project, department managers lose control over the work (Cusumano and Nobeoka, 1998).

Multi-project organization using Pulse

What I want to achieve with a multi-project organization is to be able, on the one hand, to pursue continuous strategic development work that initiates the projects and sets the framework for the operation's direction and, on the other hand, to work in various teams composed of different skills. I also want to use visual just-in-time control and be able to deal with problems at their source. Traditional organizations have been built up around titles or rank. In my view, this creates many limitations, because information and knowledge become power. To explain how agile multi-project management using Pulse works, I will describe a typical Pulse organization.

Pulse is based on an organization of pulse meetings arranged in a network. Such an approach provides new degrees of freedom when work needs to be organized. Pulse meetings are arenas where information and knowledge are shared. Power in Pulse is always associated with pitching in and working and thus sharing information and knowledge. Pulse meetings are also arenas where teams can make decisions and deal with problems that have arisen. To be able to work strategically and operationally at the same time, several kinds of pulse meeting are needed for different pulse teams. Finally, we also need some fixed roles: product manager, program manager, assignment manager, and resource manager. Pulse includes project managers, but they have slightly different tasks than in traditional project management.

Product managers work with the product lifecycle and are expected to be well-acquainted with customers and the market through contacts and analyses. Program managers work internally within the enterprise, to create a technical architecture and run programs of projects. The product manager contributes knowledge about what customers want, while the program manager contributes knowledge of what the enterprise can develop and manufacture. The assignment manager has the operational role to prioritize and queue assignments as well as to hold the daily assignment pulse meetings. The product managers, program manager, and assignment manager together form a product team (as shown in Figure 6-6) that holds frequent product pulse meetings. Their joint task is to prepare the background information that enables them to launch the right projects with good potential and to initiate actions that can increase the profitability of the existing product portfolio.

Each project forms a project team whose participants can be changed during the course of the project to fit the need for expertise and resources. Each project holds frequent project pulse meetings. The project manager's task is to safeguard the technological integrity of the project, represent the project externally, form the project group into a team, and handle conflicts that arise.

Parts of the company's management team form a portfolio team that holds frequent portfolio pulse meetings. They decide where resources will be invested, which possibilities will be explored, and which risks they are therefore prepared to take. They also manage the constitutional structure, which means they make changes to the network of pulse meetings and roles when necessary and develop the organization to be able to operate in new markets.

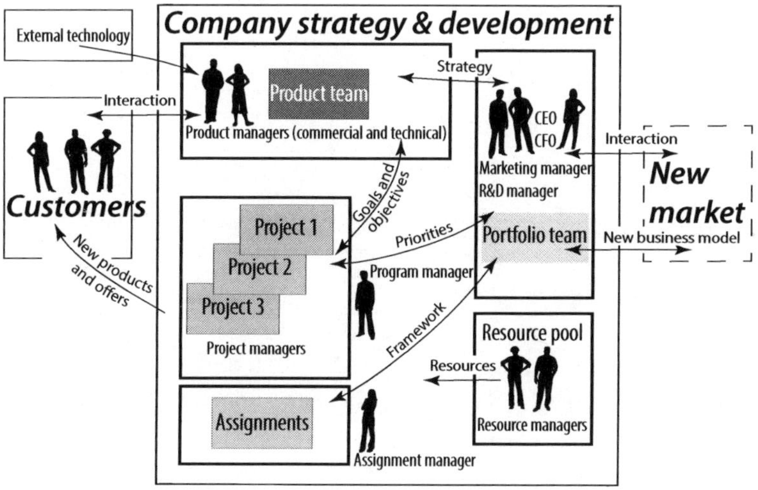

Figure 6-6. Roles and teams in Pulse.

Resource managers have staff responsibility and sometimes also responsibility for equipment and methods used in the work. Each week, resource managers allocate resources to projects and the assignment team at the resource pulse meetings. They also make sure that resources and working methods are developed in the long run.

Project pulse meeting

Projects in Pulse can be planned with a scrum-like method based on periods of a fixed length. For each period, the project team plans as

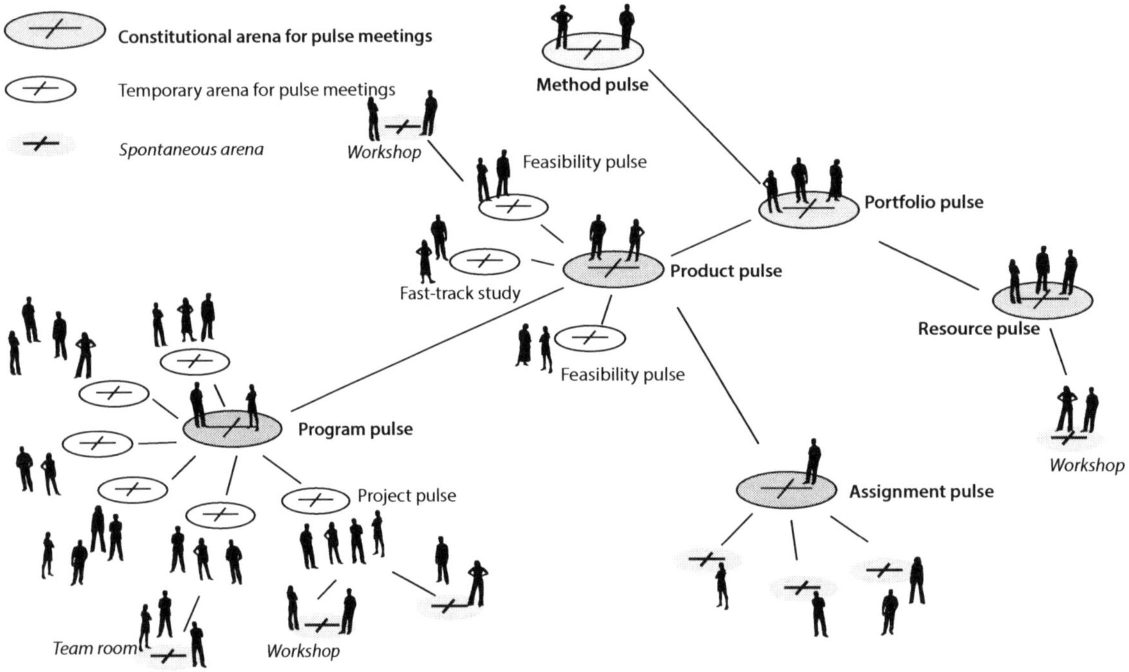

Figure 6-7. Example of a small pulse organization. The shaded circles represent fixed, coordinating pulse meetings that make up the skeleton of the multi-project organization. The unshaded circles represent temporary pulse meetings held to drive a temporary initiative.

many subresults as they deem reasonable to complete. The alternative to this is to use synch planning, in which the length of each period is adapted to work packages of subresults that belong together within the workflow. (The name "synch" comes from the synchronization between teams.) Scrum planning works best if there is great uncertainty and a work flow cannot be defined, while synch planning is used when work flows can be defined. In synch planning, several teams can work in parallel. A synchronization plan specifies the work packages for each team, what is to be handed over between teams, and when that will happen. The handover points in a synchronization plan set time limits. Synch planning allows dynamic project teams whose composition can be modified as work progresses and changes. It is also possible to have fixed teams or a combination of the two. Major projects are generally carried out by several different teams, whether dynamic or fixed.

The projects typically hold pulse meetings daily. But among the enterprises using pulse are examples of intensive projects that hold pulse meetings every two hours. During periods of low activity, longer intervals between pulse meetings are chosen. It is the meetings between people that create movement and transformation (Karrbom Gustavsson, 2005:215). The frequency of pulse meetings determines the pace and is crucial for how long the project will take.

Project teams can sit in the same room or same building or be geographically spread out. Sometimes a project is spread over several continents and time zones. When teams cannot meet physically, they use videoconferencing equipment for the pulse meetings. Some use special equipment and a leased line for communication. Others use Skype, Hangouts, or similar tools via the Internet. The best learning—that is, the fastest and best product development—occurs when the participants work in the same room with interrelated tasks.

The number of projects in Pulse is limited based on the operation's capacity and the desired lead time, according to Little's law. The lead time is the ratio of the number of projects in progress to the throughput. If you have 10 projects in progress and conclude five projects per year, the lead time will be about two years. If you want to cut lead times in half, you can halve the number of ongoing projects. The alternative is to increase the number of resources so that throughput increases. When Pulse is introduced, much of the waste in the operation is eliminated, so throughput can increase. As a result of controlling the number of on-going projects and assignments, it is often possible to cut lead times by at least half. In Pulse, the portfolio team starts projects at the same rate as they are concluded and thus largely determines the lead times in the projects.

Assignment pulse meeting

Within the framework for strategy and development, major projects are not the only efforts carried out. Shorter tasks are also carried out. These can relate to many things, from product maintenance and quality problems, to customer support and minor adaptations. A simple rule might be that anything over a certain size (such as 200 working hours) is a project and everything less than that is an assignment. The number of ongoing projects is determined by the portfolio team, which queues and starts projects as spare resources become available. Assignments must also be queued and limited, otherwise there is a risk that the operation will be overloaded by work that has not been prioritized. Often it is said that assignments are carried out "in the departments." This means that department managers and employees each set their own priorities. To take control over the flow of assignments, Pulse uses assignment pulse meetings that are led by an assignment manager. The assignment manager receives all assignment requests and sets priorities. The assignment team is staffed in the same way as the projects. To maintain control of the workload and avoid suboptimization, no development work is performed in the departments. The reason is easy to understand. If an enterprise has 10 managers in its design, production technology, and marketing departments, each of which sets his or her own priorities for the tasks, it is highly unlikely that they will pull in the same direction (Simon, 1997). This is true regardless of how many overall goals and plans one has.

Program pulse meeting

Each week, the operational projects touch base with the strategic level at the program pulse meeting. This pulse meeting does not have its own pulse board so it uses the projects' pulse boards. Each project manager brings up any problems or questions that the project needs help with. The program manager makes a decision immediately or takes the problem on to the resource pulse, product pulse, or portfolio pulse meeting.

The program pulse meeting is one of several methods for getting the operational and strategic levels to interact. As I see it, it is not a one-way flow from top to bottom, as it is sometimes portrayed. A lot of things happen at the operational level that affect the strategies. An adjustment often needs to be made immediately to maintain the enterprise's initiative in the market.

Resource pulse meeting

In Pulse, resource planning is done at two levels: overall planning and weekly allocation.

The overall planning looks at the whole, never single individuals. The calculation of the number of projects based on Little's law is one such example. The portfolio team, which starts the projects, must take into account critical resources so that they do not start multiple projects that need these resources at the same time. The overall prioritization and planning uses simple methods and tools, so there is usually enough time for analyses and decisions at one portfolio pulse meeting.

Allocation of resources is done week by week, as individuals, teams, and equipment are divided among the projects based on the priorities set by the portfolio team. The allocation is assisted by a resource pulse board that ensures that individuals are not overburdened or fragmented. One person can only work full-time on one project at a time. The methods are so simple that planning for the coming week can be done during one resource pulse meeting. Recurring conflicts over resources must be resolved by the resource managers together with the portfolio team.

The project managers and assignment manager who need resources and the resource managers who can allocate resources participate in the resource pulse meetings. Resource managers are responsible for human resources, so they move people to various projects or to the assignment team. At the resource pulse meeting, resource managers can see where the operation has its bottlenecks and remedy them, to increase the throughput and shorten lead times. Resource managers also allocate critical equipment.

Product pulse meeting

In Pulse, there is always at least one product team responsible for working with strategic product development in priority segments. For each segment, they make an overall plan with business goals and a program plan. A program plan can extend two to three years down the road. The plan specifies which development efforts are needed to achieve the business goals. Typical initiatives might be feasibility studies or market analyses that the product team will do itself. There might also be larger initiatives that, if approved by the portfolio team, will be carried out as a project. Some smaller initiatives can be carried out as assignments. The program plan can also contain marketing campaigns and launch activities. The program plan is executed via the program pulse and product pulse meetings, while initiatives are carried out as projects, assignments, or feasibility studies or by the product team itself.

Internal development of production, logistics, and administration, for example, is planned in a similar way through operational goals and program plans.

The work in the product team is driven forward using a scrum-like approach. The team creates a queue (backlog) for all the work that they need to do. The program plans are one starting point, but more cases need to be dealt with. Unexpected things are constantly popping up in the business environment and demanding attention, while a steady stream of questions and concerns that should be investigated come from the projects. Urgent matters are dealt with immediately, while everything else goes into the backlog. The team works in a four-week cycle. A period begins with a demonstration of the prior period's results for the portfolio team. Together with the portfolio team, priorities are assigned to the backlog, and an appropriate number of tasks are picked out to be accomplished by the product team during the upcoming period. The product team uses daily to weekly product pulse meetings to coordinate their work to complete the tasks that will shape a strategic design and execute the programs.

Portfolio pulse meeting

The portfolio team starts with the enterprise's goals and direction. They make overall decisions about where the resources will be invested, as well as the risks and opportunities that they are prepared to expose themselves to as a result of these decisions.

It is the portfolio team that starts and concludes projects. To become a candidate for starting, the project must have sufficiently high financial and strategic attractiveness and reasonable business risk relative to the economic potential. The background data that the product team prepares is intended to convince the portfolio team that such is the case.

The product team works predominantly within existing business models. If the company wants to develop new business models and achieve innovations in the market, such initiatives should be driven by the portfolio team.

The portfolio team owns and manages the constitutional structure. Thus they are responsible for changing the structure when needed. They use a backlog and work in periods in the same way the product team does. The portfolio team's backlog is prioritized by the CEO (or equivalent) in dialogue with the rest of the team and sometimes with the board of directors. The portfolio team conducts portfolio pulse meetings once or twice a week to coordinate their work and take care of decisions needed.

Method pulse meeting

The rules jointly established for interaction within and between the various teams in Pulse must be managed. That task is given to the method team, staffed with a cross-section from the pulse organization. In addition to changing and improving the joint rules, the team should also monitor how well the rules are followed.

Coordinating pulse meetings

The coordinating pulse meetings consist of program pulse, resource pulse, product pulse, and portfolio pulse meetings. These should be in sequence, one after the other, on one day each week, so that needs and problems discovered in the projects can be dealt with quickly. These meetings are usually scheduled on Fridays or Mondays, so participants can travel on other days of the week. A typical coordination day begins with the program pulse meeting (coordination of projects with a strategic design), followed by the resource pulse meeting. These are followed by pulse meetings for the product team and the portfolio team. This totals four pulse meetings, all of which can be held in 20–30 minutes each. In less than two hours, any and all obstacles to forward motion in the projects and assignments have been discussed and dealt with. The worst thing that can happen in a project is that nothing happens (Karrbom Gustavsson, 2005). What sets a successful enterprise apart is that management—in Pulse, the portfolio team—does not accept that projects get blocked (McDonough and Spital, 2003). This is also what I can observe in those enterprises that use Pulse. The companies that succeed best have compelling managers active in the daily work. Thanks to the coordinating pulse meetings and visualization in the pulse room, the portfolio team has the capability to be in control of the situation and can quickly take action when necessary.

Summary of just-in-time decisions

In this chapter, I have shown the need for decisions at the right time, just in time. The problem with making decisions according to a predetermined schedule is that either you lack information or you have to wait for a decision. To shorten development cycles, work in the projects must be supported and guided by more frequent and flexible technical, commercial, and strategic decision-making. It should be possible to make a decision as soon as the background data is ready. This requires a network of frequent pulse meetings linking the entire operation.

There are various types of project. The short product maintenance initiatives that I call assignments address urgent quality problems and make minor improvements to existing products. The longer tasks can be described as projects. These include the slightly smaller projects that develop new models and adapt products for customers, as well as the far more comprehensive projects that work with new product generations, modular systems, and platforms. In addition, there are projects that develop brand new technologies or are engaged in research.

Enterprises engaged in product development usually have one of two main types of organization: the functional or the matrix. Neither is suitable for rapidly developing new products, because they either lack the capacity for interaction within projects or lack the prerequisites for long-term, coordinated strategic development work. That is why I propose a new organizational form based on the network of pulse meetings in which people meet and make decisions: a pulse organization.

A pulse organization consists of a variety of pulse meetings where information and knowledge are shared for decision-making. There are weekly portfolio pulse meetings to decide on project starts, project priorities, and market development, to address shortcomings in the constitutional structure, and to take actions that will shape a strategic direction. The product team sets the operation's strategic design and coordinates their work at the product pulse meetings, held daily or weekly. The resource pulse meetings take place weekly, where the resource managers together with the project managers and the assignment manager allocate resources for the upcoming week. The daily assignment pulse meetings manage and execute all short tasks. The program pulse meetings take place weekly and are a way for projects to raise issues to the program manager that they need help with. The projects have daily, or sometimes more frequent, project pulse meetings that will move the work forward.

7. Portfolio management

Every operation's resources are limited—whether time, labor, or financial resources. Economy and prudence are required if the resources are to be converted into high and sustainable profits. To avoid overloading and fragmentation, it is necessary to limit the number of projects. And it is the portfolio team's task to determine which projects will be allowed to start and when. In this chapter, I will describe how that work might be done.

The portfolio team sets the operation's strategic direction, which helps them to assess the projects' strategic significance as well as prioritize the product team's work.

The portfolio team owns and manages the constitutional structure. They can use key performance indicators to monitor how well the enterprise is managing to achieve its overall strategic goals.

Prioritize resources

There are always limits to the human, material, and financial resources that determine how many projects and assignments the operation can carry out during a certain period of time. The ultimate responsibility for how the resources are utilized lies with the portfolio team. They decide which projects will get permission to start and at what time. And they set the limits on resources for assignment management. The basis for these decisions is a project portfolio that obtains data from the product team's candidate projects and product portfolio as well as from ongoing and planned projects. The project portfolio is a compilation of key parameters that provide an analysis of each project's profitability and resource needs from different perspectives.

The portfolio team makes sure the operation's resources are not overloaded by determining which projects will be carried out, the order in which they will be carried out, and at what time they will start. The portfolio team also decides whether to prematurely terminate a project that does not reach its set goals.

The project portfolio is a compilation of proposed, ongoing, and recently completed projects. This compilation provides the portfolio team with the overview needed so they can manage a multi-project operation. The project portfolio shows the mix of projects that the enterprise is running and will run in the future as well as the outcomes of projects concluded in recent years. With the help of the project portfolio, the portfolio team can balance resource needs and ensure that the projects are reasonably planned over time in relation to one another.

The project portfolio gathers a few important parameters that form the basis for determining which projects will be carried out. The portfolio also shows the current status of projects in progress, the projects' relative priorities, and profitability. The parameters should be selected to illuminate the operation based on various criteria and to reflect the many often conflicting demands.

Each operation has a maximum throughput for work that it is capable of completing during a given unit of time. The throughput can be measured in the number of projects completed each year, although the size of projects varies in practice. If management starts fewer projects than the operation can handle, the result will be lower productivity than is possible. In Pulse, however, staff need not be underutilized, because assignment management is intended to serve as a resource buffer. Anyone with time left over is supposed to go to the assignment pulse meeting and pick up an assignment. Thus the portfolio team can see if there are spare resources for starting more projects by studying the number of participants in the assignment pulse meeting. They can also see if too many projects have been started by studying the resource pulse board. If a low-priority project has a hard time getting resources, then too many projects are in progress at the same time, which also results in lower productivity.

The portfolio team's pulse board and pulse meetings

The members of the portfolio team should continuously ask themselves what is preventing the operation from becoming more productive and profitable. The members of the portfolio team must find the answer to that question by going and seeing for themselves the root causes of problems and interruptions that occur, which actions, decisions, and background data are needed to get to grips with these and implement corrective actions and decisions. For example, a possible cause of poor margins and lack of profitability could be too few new products and the products not being genuinely relevant to customer needs.

The portfolio team should not only be able to work with long-term strategies but also be involved in the operation to influence the outcome of completed, ongoing, and upcoming projects and other investments. With the portfolio pulse meetings, the portfolio team can coordinate their decisions and efforts so that they have an impact on the multi-project process. At the same time, frequent portfolio pulse meetings are a direct channel to information providing valuable insight into where interruptions appear and how well corrective actions work.

The portfolio team works like the product team in a four-week cycle, as shown in Figure 7-1. Each period begins with demonstrations, of the product team's results as well as the portfolio team's results. Then the portfolio team prioritizes both their own and the product team's backlog, so that everyone can jointly plan the next period.

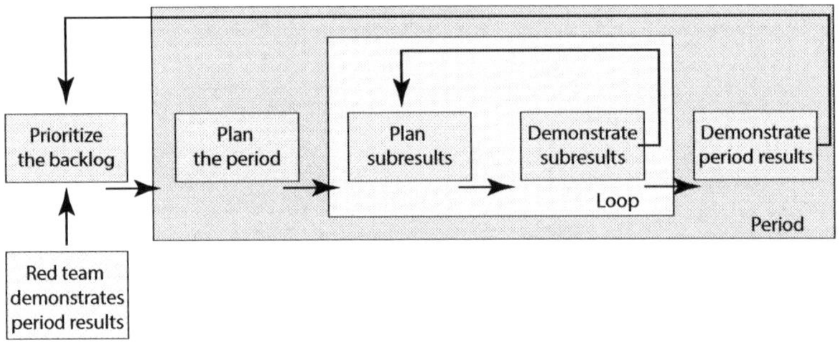

Figure 7-1. The portfolio team's work cycle.

I recommend that the portfolio team hold pulse meetings at least twice a week to drive the strategy and development in their enterprise. In practice, many portfolio teams in today's Pulse enterprises hold one pulse meeting a week. My understanding is that this is sufficient if the operation only conducts incremental development within an existing business model. In such cases, the number of strategic decisions is limited, as almost everything is already fixed by existing structures and products. However, if the ambition is to develop new markets, business models, and innovations so as to be stronger when the new day dawns, pulse meetings once a week are much too infrequent. Nowadays when I ask what pulse enterprises perceive as their bottleneck, everyone says that it is the pace of the product and portfolio teams. And the product team's forward motion strongly depends on the portfolio team keeping the same pace in their internal discussions, decisions, and actions that enable them to shape and constantly reshape the strategic direction. Opening new markets means that the structures are not yet set and the possibilities are unlimited while the risks are high. The portfolio team's continued presence is necessary for the team to be able to link up with partners, select a path that reduces uncertainty, and pool their efforts in order to have an impact.

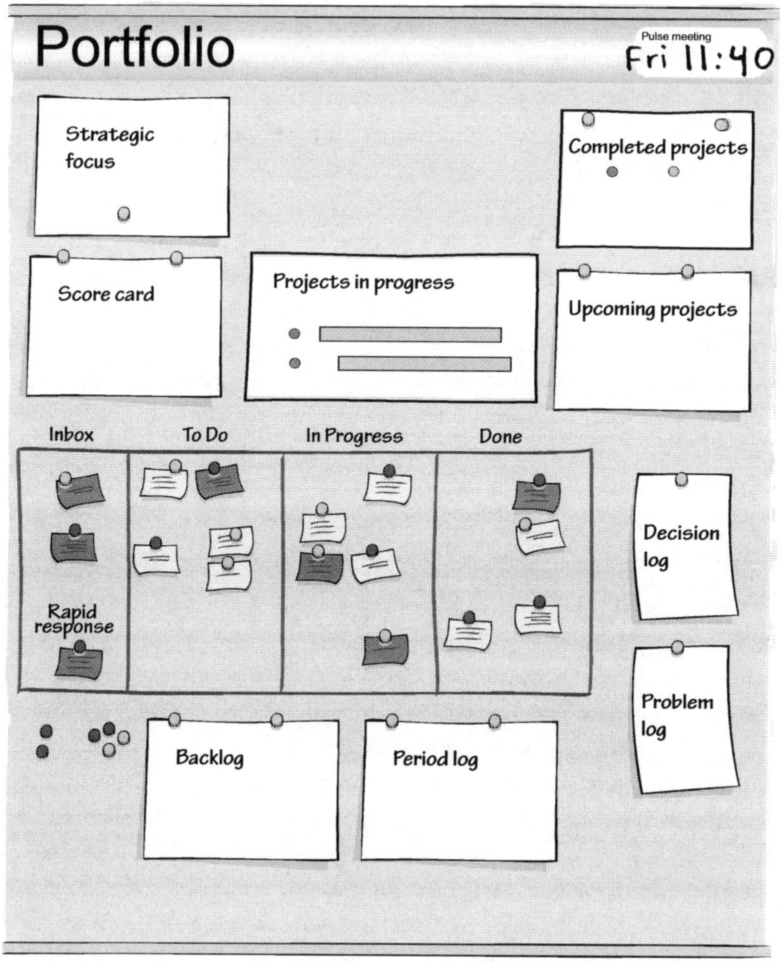

Figure 7-2. Portfolio pulse board.

To arrive at consensus, the portfolio team must work together on issues at the pulse meetings and in workshops with other agents. Also, the impetus of the portfolio team is necessary for getting new products into the market. If a project has problems of some kind, and the product team or resource pulse are unable to solve them, then the portfolio team must act. And those who are successful at managing their portfolios do exactly this, according to McDonough and Spital (2003), through daily management of the project portfolio.

What is difficult for the portfolio team, however, is to continue working with strategic and structural issues and decisions even when the pace of decision-making accelerates. There is a risk that the top executives will take operational control and start making decisions and taking initiatives that should actually be handled by the projects or product teams, thus sabotaging the self-organizing work throughout the pulse network. In my experience, many managers avoid acting or speaking out so as to give their subordinates room to grow and to become more independent. Naturally, this is a delicate balancing act. But with a strategic direction and continuous dialogue, managers can express their expectations and provide the support needed to individuals and groups without risking "micromanagement."

The contents of a portfolio pulse board varies with each enterprise and its needs. The most commonly occurring elements are shown in Figure 7-2. The enterprise's strategic focus, drawn as a goal scenario, is in the upper left-hand corner. Under the goal scenario is a scorecard with the key performance indicators used to monitor how well the operation is achieving its strategic goals. In the middle of the board is an overview showing projects in progress. This visualizes when the projects were started, when the product will be launched, and when the projects should be completed, and shows the unique priority each project has. On the right side of the board are tables showing completed projects and pending candidate projects. The number of candidate projects in the queue should be about the same as the number of completed projects each year (McDonough and Spital, 2003). In the middle of the board is the activity window where the portfolio team visualizes its own activities and problems they need to handle using sticky notes. New cases in the inbox come primarily from other teams that need help with problems that have arisen.

At the bottom of the board is the portfolio team's own plan (backlog), a list of issues the portfolio team must work on to fulfill the strategic goals. These might include contacts, investigations, background data, summaries and reports, campaigns for support, and changes in the organization and conceptual structure. The portfolio team will fill in their backlog little by little with more corrective actions, tasks, ideas, and problems they need to deal with.

Some portfolio teams augment their backlog with an annual plan, including items such as the product team's scheduled demonstrations. It also has other important recurring events, such as final accounts, trade fairs, and seasonal releases that affect the rhythm of the enterprise.

The project portfolio as a control instrument

The project portfolio summarizes important data for all the projects in one place. That gives the portfolio team an overview and potential for coordination. Properly composed, the project portfolio can serve as a dashboard that the portfolio team uses to channel money, time, and labor where they will have the greatest benefit. The management get a snapshot of pending, ongoing, and completed projects. With the project portfolio, the portfolio team focuses their attention on profitability. At the same time, they can easily check that the operation is not overloaded with too many projects or running under capacity. Also, the project portfolio makes it possible to eliminate interruptions so that staff can concentrate on one project at a time. That shortens lead times and lowers costs, while priority can be given to the projects expected to earn lots of revenue or make significant savings.

The portfolio team uses the project portfolio to prioritize the order in which projects will start, opt out of or downgrade the priority of unprofitable projects, and stop and shut down projects that for some reason should not run to completion. There are four important decision-making situations when the project portfolio is used. These are when starting a new project, following up on a project in progress, evaluating a completed project, and evaluating a new candidate project.

To obtain a serviceable project portfolio, a few key parameters must be selected and used to prioritize the projects, and a limited amount of important information must be compiled about ongoing, upcoming, and completed projects. Too many parameters and too much information obscure the picture, which ruins the whole point of the portfolio, that is, overview and coordination. Which parameters to choose and what information is important differ from operation to operation. Three parameters that are usually included are financial significance, strategic significance, and business risk.

Type	Name	Description	Scope
A	Assignments	Product maintenance that corrects errors and shortcomings in existing products. Urgent interruptions in existing processes that need to be addressed quickly.	Very short
B	New model	Short development projects that develop new product models. Delivery project that installs the product in the customer's facility. Customer projects that customize products. Quality projects that improve production processes, work environment, or product design. Capacity projects that increase production volumes and secure future supply.	Short
C	New generation	Long-term development projects that develop new product families, production technologies, and modular systems.	Long
D	Brand new technology	Pre-development projects researching new technologies.	Short to long

Figure 7-3. Example of a checklist for classifying projects and assignments.

In most cases, a development operation performs several different kinds of task. In many cases, all the tasks are referred to as projects, even if each task is different in nature, has a different scope, is initiated in different ways, and delivers its results to different recipients. That is why I recommend dividing projects into different types. Each project type fulfills its task to give the enterprise competitive advantage. The projects generate different results, have different prerequisites, and need different amounts of resources and background data. A breakdown into different project types will facilitate portfolio management and resource allocation, at the same time as it simplifies the overview and makes it possible to balance the portfolio with different types of project. (See Figures 6-3 and 7-3.) A large operation that can assign separate staff to different project types might then need to define several different portfolios, one project portfolio for each main category.

Assignment portfolio for smaller tasks

Smaller tasks seldom involve more than one or two people for a few days or weeks. I call these "assignments." The number of assignments can be very large in some enterprises. Assignments are often urgent, so they are like interruptions to developers, because they always steal time from the priority projects. This decreases the time left over for project work and, above all, the time left for undisturbed and focused work.

An assignment might consist of making corrections or adjustments to existing products, making minor adaptations to meet specific customer needs, overcoming interruptions and assisting with problems in ramping up production, or preparing production documentation for special orders. To some extent, such assignments will be the result of previous shortcuts or mistakes made during the development process. But some deficiencies and gaps that appear later in products and processes are impossible to foresee or uneconomical to address earlier. It is better to address them when they pop up. Thus, after the launch of a new product or implementation of a new process the number of assignments may rise, and they can easily multiply to an unmanageable number. Faulty or nonexistent control of short-term cases will overload resources and cripple the work of the entire development operation. In many enterprises, creating systems that successfully manage assignments becomes crucial to being able to minimize lead times for projects and bring out more innovative products.

To control the amount of resources set aside for product maintenance and incremental improvements, as well as to minimize interruptions to the projects, dedicated staff can be appointed to work exclusively with assignments. Such a solution has its advantages and disadvantages. One advantage is that a permanent team quickly becomes accustomed to solving such tasks. But there are several disadvantages. First, a dynamic assignment team can vary in number and composition and thus serve as a resource buffer. Second, work on assignments is an opportunity for professional development, because the developers will be able to solve a wide variety of tasks. That is why the majority of enterprises using Pulse today have chosen a dynamic resource pool where the staff alternate between projects and assignments, as this provides faster and broader professional development for the developers.

Dynamic assignment management is based on an assignment budget, which is part of the total development budget. The budget may need to be adjusted over time, as a result of the number of new products to be launched. The assignment budget is set by the portfolio team and specifies how many resources, as a proportion of the total resource pool, should be dedicated to assignments. Just as the number of projects is limited depending on the capacity of the operation, the number of assignments allowed to run simultaneously must also be limited. A new assignment can only be started when another has concluded.

If the assignment portfolio is to serve as a management tool, all assignments must pass through the assignment manager, who prioritizes and ensures that the proper number of assignments are open. This requires discipline. Perhaps the production manager has had a habit of going straight to the first, best engineer when production problems arise. By claiming "production always comes first," that manager has been able to simply poach staff from the development operation. Similarly, salespeople might have had a habit of involving development engineers in work on quotations or as experts in customer relations. By claiming "customers and sales always come first," they have also been able to obtain resources. Surprisingly often, such resources are borrowed free-of-charge by the production manager or sales manager. To some degree, it becomes a bad habit to ask for help with tasks that one should handle oneself just because it is easy to ask and does not cost anything.

On the other hand, the developers have been happy to help. In a chaotic situation, where the priorities of different assignments and projects are unclear and the individual ends up choosing between different tasks, tasks perceived as urgent will always take precedence over long-term tasks. This is partly because the arguments about the importance of production, customers, and sales sound reasonable, partly because short assignments give faster feedback. Individuals can quickly see the results of their efforts. In contrast, long-term development work can often be strenuous, intellectually exhausting, and just plain hard. It may take a long time before any breakthrough is made in a development project. Work done is not always visible, either, and it is easy to get bogged down. If the individual has multiple assignments and projects that are waiting to be done but have not been prioritized in relation to one another, it is easy for that individual to switch to a task that is easier and faster when the current task gets difficult or boring.

Assignment number	Significance for customer	Significance for throughput	Significance for personal safety	Status	Priority
1524	high	low	low	open	
1358	high	high	medium	open	
1878	low	low	high	in queue	2
1457	low	high	high	in queue	1
1733	medium	low	low	in queue	4
1696	low	medium	low	in queue	3
1514	high	high	low	closed	

Figure 7-4. Example of an assignment portfolio with open assignments, prioritized assignments in the queue, and recently closed assignments.

If the salespeople more or less constantly need technical support, one possible solution is to set up a sales and quotation pulse meeting. The cases that cannot be resolved at that pulse meeting can be handed up to the product team or initiated as assignments. If production has an urgent need for support when problems occur, assignment management can organize a help desk.

With an assignment portfolio, the assignment manager can take control of how many short assignments are in progress at the same time and make sure not to start more than can be handled by the resources available. (See Figure 7-4.) All ongoing and pending assignments are compiled in the assignment portfolio, and the assignment manager prioritizes them based on a handful of selected parameters. A decision must then be made on how many assignments can be run at the same time. The number that is appropriate is determined by the size of the operation and the assignments' share of resources. In small enterprises, the limit is one to three assignments at the same time, in larger companies 5–20. Remember that setting a limit on the number of assignments is intended to prevent resources from being overloaded. All assignments benefit from some assignments being postponed. By queuing the assignments, they will be completed faster than if done simultaneously. The assignment portfolio will be a way to eliminate interruptions and instead stay focused in the development process. As soon as a case is finished, the next one can start.

To set up an assignment portfolio, first list the current assignments, both ongoing and those that have not yet started. After that, determine the number of assignments that will be open at the same time. To be able to prioritize among the pending assignments, the assignment manager sets a few parameters. For example, it might be the importance to the customer, importance to throughput in production, and importance to personal safety. The pending tasks are assessed, and values are set for the parameters, so the relative priority of each assignment can be decided by the assignment manager.

Project portfolio for larger tasks

The larger tasks are different types of "real" projects. They require work by cross-functional teams and therefore involve many different functions in the enterprise. With the project portfolio, the portfolio team can be certain to get a good mix of different projects, including less comprehensive new models or extending existing products into new markets that provide secure revenue in the near future, as well as longer and riskier development programs for new product generations or markets that have greater potential. In addition, the portfolio can include analyses and studies of new technologies or business models that the enterprise will live on in the future. In the short term, prioritizing short customer projects can increase revenues. In the long run, the same priority can exhaust the enterprise's chances for survival. The trade-off between quick revenue and long-term sustainable profitability is not simple. With the project portfolio, these decisions can be made by the portfolio team and not be left to the individual employees, which would happen if priorities were vague.

The balance between different project types in the project portfolio will partly depend on the maturity of the market where the enterprise operates. A new market demands brand new products. In contrast, a mature market provides fewer technological breakthroughs and tougher competition, so more of the work will focus on producing multiple product variants and initiatives that cut costs.

The project portfolio is used to set priorities for new projects when they start, to follow up projects in progress, and to evaluate completed and upcoming projects. Thus the project portfolio can be regarded as four different parts: one for setting priorities among ongoing projects, one for monitoring the progress of ongoing projects, one to queue and evaluate the projects that are waiting for free resources, and one to compile the effects of completed projects.

The aim of the project portfolio is to create an overview, prevent projects that lack resources from starting, and assign each project a unique priority. Assigning each project a unique priority facilitates resource planning, because the project with the highest priority will be scheduled first. For individuals, too, this makes it clear which tasks should be carried out first. If the workflow gets clogged, everyone knows which of the ongoing projects has priority. Expanding and coordinating the efforts invested in the highest priority projects will result in increased throughput and increased profitability.

Use the project portfolio for decision-making

The project portfolio is used by the portfolio team in four key decision-making situations: first, to determine which projects will start; second, to follow up ongoing projects; third, to evaluate completed projects; and finally, fourth, to assess the potential of new candidate projects.

Start a project

With more ideas for profitable projects than the operation can run at the same time, the portfolio team must decide which candidate projects will get the go-ahead and when they will start. The portfolio team will also set relative priorities on the projects started. The priority ranking is one way to direct resources to the right project, with the highest priority getting resources first, followed by the project with priority two and so on. This does not mean that a project with higher priority can take resources from other projects. Staff are allocated at the resource pulse meeting by the resource managers by priority and based on the projects' resource plans. If a project requires significantly more resources than planned, this will signal the portfolio team that the project is deviating from its budget. When a project has completed the subresults that a person has contributed to, the project manager will return that person to the resource pool. The person can then be assigned to another project.

If the proper number of projects are running, all projects will get resources. If too many projects are in progress, primarily those with the highest priority will get the resources they need to do a good job. If projects were not prioritized in relation to one another, the resources might get spread thin among too many projects, so that very little value-adding work would get done.

	Parameters				Information					
Project	Financial significance	Business risk	Strategic significance	Priority	Status	Start date	Completion date	Project type	Description	Included in the program
Sinus	High	Medium	High	1	In progress	Nov. 2015	Sep. 2016	B	Increased capacity	Asia 2010
Novart	Medium	Medium	High	2	In progress	Apr. 2016	Oct. 2016	C	Developing new product generation	Heavy duty
T60	Medium	Low	Low	3	In progress	Feb. 2016	Dec. 2016	B	Customer project	Biotech
Diod 6	Low	Medium	Medium	4	Planning in progress	Feb. 2017	Jan. 2018	B	Development of a new model	800 series

Figure 7-5. Project portfolio for projects in progress. The parameters chosen here to determine priority are financial significance, strategic significance, and business risk. In addition, overall information on the projects has been added.

To be able to prioritize the projects, a few key parameters are compiled for all the projects, as shown in Figure 7-5. Based on these parameters, each project is then assigned a unique priority. The project portfolio can also be augmented with other important information. This might be project type, providing a quick overview of where the project portfolio has its main focus, or which program each project is linked to.

Which basic parameters the portfolio team will use to prioritize its project portfolio depends on the conditions for the operation, projects, and products. Common parameters used to set priorities are financial significance, strategic significance, and business risk. Another parameter that can be used to prioritize a project portfolio is the projects' delivery dates, that is, how much time remains until revenue starts flowing in. Three to four is an appropriate number of parameters to make the project portfolio easy to survey. The more parameters there are, the harder it gets to set priorities, as it becomes impossible to get a snapshot of the projects. In other words, the project portfolio is not supposed to compile all the information available on the projects. Rather, emphasize the data that is vital for making decisions. Each parameter in turn can be based on a weighted combination of several aspects or criteria.

By far the easiest approach is to set priorities based on the time remaining until delivery. The shortest time to completion gets the highest priority. The advantage of this approach is that the focus is placed on those projects that will soon be completed and generate value. New projects automatically end up last in priority.

Assigning a value to business risk, strategic significance, or any other selected parameter is largely a judgment call. The portfolio team must discuss and argue as a group to arrive at a decision. In these discussions, various aspects will be taken into account from the areas represented by the participants in the portfolio team, such as technology, marketing, production, and finance. The discussions ensure that the group achieves consensus, which reduces the risk of decisions being undermined by personal priorities. By starting with composite parameters that describe the projects' conditions and opportunities from different perspectives, the portfolio team will have a broad basis for decisions that, at least in part, is derived from facts, which improves the quality of the decisions. The same parameters are used to weight all the projects, promoting predictability in the decisions. Over time, the value of the parameters for new projects will be assigned in comparison with other projects already assessed.

How often new projects start will depend on how long the projects are, how much resources they take, and how big the operation is. The portfolio team needs to organize their work based on how often projects are completed and new ones start. It is common for an enterprise to finish one project a month or every other month. Then they can also start one new project every month or every other month. Of course, this requires analyzing and preparing the next project at the same time as the portfolio team may need to put time and effort into getting the new product from the concluded project delivered to the market.

Once the priorities are set and the projects started, the portfolio team must resist the temptation to casually change priorities. Constantly changing priorities has the same effect as not having any priorities at all; it prolongs the time it takes to implement all projects and reduces profitability. Even if the portfolio team does not always make completely correct decisions when they prioritize projects, decisions made are far better than no decisions at all.

Project	Prio.	Status	Start date	Completion date	Project type
Sinus	1	In progress	Nov. 2015	Sep. 2016	B: Capacity
Novart	2	In progress	Apr. 2016	Oct. 2016	C: Development
T60	3	In progress	Feb. 2016	Dec. 2016	B: Customer project
Diod 6	4	Planning in progress	Feb. 2017	Jan. 2018	B: Development

Figure 7-6. Visualized project portfolio. Example of a project portfolio put up on the portfolio pulse board so that everyone in the operation can find the information.

The project portfolio is one way to communicate information about the projects that the operation is running. (See Figure 7-6.) The priority of each project must be communicated to everyone working on or affected by the projects so other priorities are not given preference locally. That is why the project portfolio is put up on the portfolio pulse board. Sensitive information can be removed or coded so that outside visitors do not understand.

Follow up projects in progress

In the project portfolio, the portfolio team compiles the parameters used to follow up on the projects. For example, planned expenses, revenues, and delivery times can be compared with the most recent projections for the same parameters. The purpose of the follow-up is to identify if any of the project priorities should be changed, if actions or decisions are needed to handle situations that have arisen, or if any project needs to be shut down prematurely as a result of weak profitability. The profitability of the projects changes continuously, as the project budget is replaced by actual costs and delivery dates, and manufacturing costs are adjusted based on updated forecasts. There are multiple economic parameters that the portfolio team can monitor in a project portfolio to analyze the profitability of projects in progress. These include forecast revenue, projected delivery date, sunk development costs and projected development costs, and estimated production costs.

The expected revenue from the project's results is affected if market conditions change or if the delivery date is delayed. The projected delivery date can be compared to the original delivery date to see if the project will be delayed. A delay of the project could mean the loss of major revenue.

Sunk development costs refer to the resources that have been consumed in the project up to the current time. The final development costs can be forecast based on the sunk development costs and the pace of work in the project. The product's production cost is determined by the design, the purchase of components, the production process chosen, and volume. For products intended to be produced in large volumes, a low cost of production is significantly more interesting than a low cost of development.

Changes in revenues or expenses cause changes in profitability. A previously profitable project can become unprofitable if it is postponed. The difference between revenues and expenses provides a continuous snapshot of the project's financial situation. If the trend is towards ever-higher costs at the same time as revenue declines, the project will eventually become unprofitable. Then it might be better to shut down the project than let it run its course. At the same time, the investments already made must be monitored. If the operation is going to lose money, it should be as little money as possible. If a project is shut down after big investments have already been made, the upshot could be bigger losses than if the project runs to completion. This means that the further a project has advanced and the more resources it has already consumed, the more likely it is that it is more profitable to run the project to completion. At the same time, this decision must be weighed against the fact that resources will be commandeered by a relatively low-priority project if the decision is made to continue.

Computing the sunk development costs and forecasting the final costs of projects requires following up the sunk costs, such as working hours already expended and other costs of travel, supplies, and equipment. Some companies use a time-reporting system. Others simply base their estimates on the project's time budget that comes from the synchronization plan. If the project has met its delivery deadlines and used the resources as planned, then the working hours in the project budget are a good gauge of the final working hours. If the project has missed its delivery date, then that has to be adjusted for. This gives a reasonable estimate of costs with minimal effort. A time-reporting system requires administrative resources in the operation. There is also the risk that staff will focus on the wrong thing, that is, reporting time instead of producing results. Remember that the lead time in many projects is far more costly than the project's labor costs.

Evaluate completed projects

When projects are completed, it is time to evaluate whether the effects were achieved. (See Figure 7-7.) The purpose of an evaluation is to learn to make better investment decisions, to learn lessons that can foster the success of other projects, and to take action to address cost or revenue issues. It should be possible to figure out actions that increase profitability and multiply the impact of already completed projects and sunk investments. To obtain data on sales revenue and cost savings, the evaluation cannot be done until some time after the project has been completed and the product has been launched in the market or the process improvements have been deployed.

The portfolio team is mainly interested in the economic impact of the projects, in the form of increased revenues or reduced costs. Did the product achieve the profitability initially planned? Of course, it is also interesting to look at a project's effect goals, which describe the customer needs that a project should satisfy or process improvements that a project should achieve in the operation. With the division that I use in Pulse, between the portfolio team and the product team, the evaluation of the effect goals will primarily be the responsibility of the product team.

Project	Budgeted development cost (€ mn)	Final development cost (€ mn)	Initial delivery date	Final delivery date	Current revenue (€ mn)	Forecast Revenue 3 years (€ mn)	Volume per month (units)	Margin
Titus	0.6	0.57	Dec. 2014	Nov. 24, 2014	1.1	5	650	35%
SP52	2.5	2.8	Sep. 2015	Jan. 5, 2016	0.8	15	45	45%

Figure 7-7. Project portfolio for evaluating completed projects.

Some of the information compiled in the project portfolio can be used to calculate key performance indicators (KPIs), such as throughput and delivery precision. Additional parameters that are not compiled at follow up of projects in the project portfolio can also be chosen , such as goal achievement.

If KPIs such as throughput, lead times, and delivery precision are monitored, then the evaluation of the projects will be a good opportunity to summarize, present, and discuss data. It might also be appropriate at that time to analyze and discuss how the operation's capability has developed recently and to agree on the actions that the portfolio team should take in the future. A good KPI might be the proportion of sales or profit coming from products launched in the previous 3–5 years. This provides an indication of how effective the operation is. There is a risk of focusing narrowly on lead times and delivery precision. An enterprise must dare to take reasonable risks in new development to achieve an impact in the market. Enterprises using Pulse usually have the capability of executing complex development projects in 3–9 months, which is much faster than the competition can. This capability can be used to "shake out" as many competitors as possible from the market.

Evaluate new candidate projects

New projects that have not yet been started or been assigned a priority can be collected in a list of upcoming projects (short list). The number of new projects in the list is adjusted to how often the operation completes a project and thus can start a new one. The projects in the short list are picked by the product team, which subsequently also works to provide candidates with thoroughly prepared business plans, effect goals, and profitability calculations. The portfolio team uses the list of upcoming projects to discuss the candidates with the product team. Are they focusing on the right candidates? Is it a good mix of different project types, different market segments, and different initiatives? Through discussions, a common understanding is reached concerning the results and effects that the projects are expected to deliver and how well they fit into the strategic direction, which can later be transmitted to the project teams when the projects start.

When it comes time to start projects, the portfolio team uses the short list to select a project. Then, this project should suit the resources available and also fit into the mix of projects already in progress.

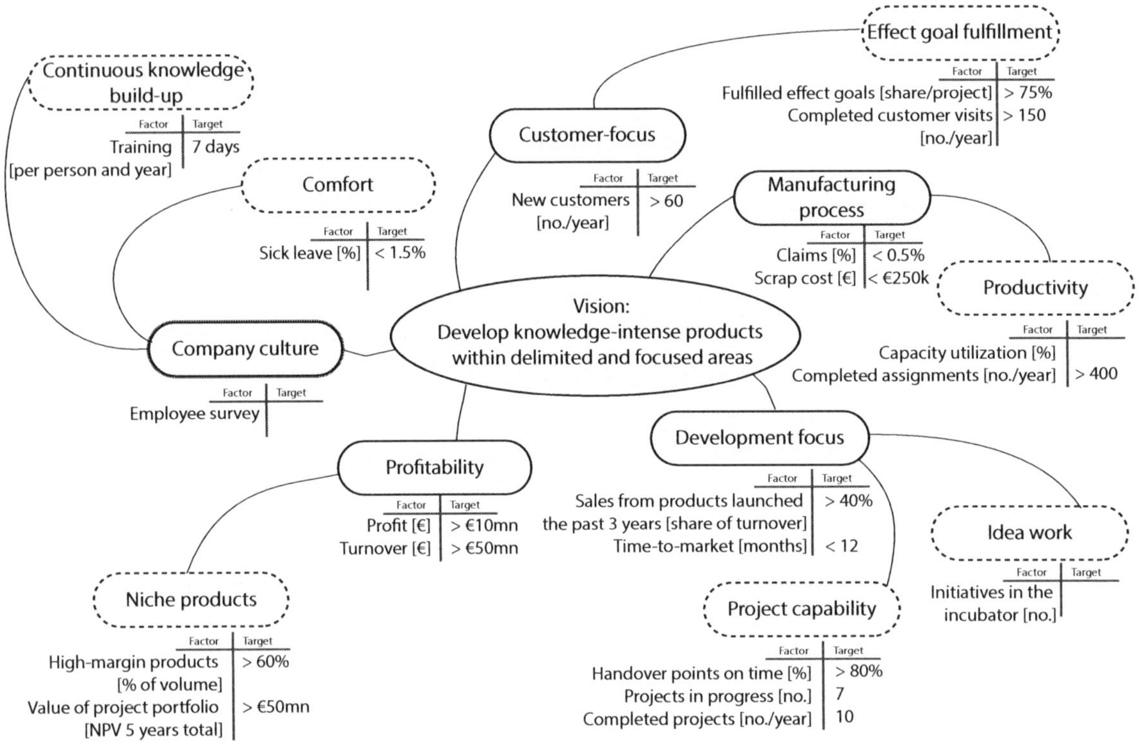

Figure 7-8. Strategic direction. Vision, focus areas, and success factors.

Key performance indicators

All systems have natural variation. This means that a distribution of outcomes around a mean value must be accepted. There is an upper and a lower limit within which the system should be allowed to adjust on its own without corrective action. Reacting to and trying to control the natural variation is not only useless but also reduces the system's performance. The wrong action could nudge the entire system into uncontrollable and self-reinforcing instability.

Continuously taking measurements provides KPIs, which can be used by the portfolio team to gauge the operation's performance and potential for improvement. KPIs are chosen to complement one another, because no single parameter tells the whole truth about the operation. With several different indicators, multiple aspects can be covered that together contribute to high and sustainable profit.

Good KPIs are derived from the operation's strategic direction expressed as a vision, focus area, and success factors. Based on these, appropriate indicators can be identified. To avoid a one-sided focus on economic factors, it is a good idea to strike a balance between different types of indicator. In addition to a financial perspective (represented by revenue or profitability), one might include a customer perspective (such as customer satisfaction or market share), a learning or development perspective (such as the number of new ideas or new products' share of sales), or productivity of internal processes (such as lead times or throughput).

The following are a few examples of key performance indicators that are appropriate to monitor in a multi-project organization striving to become more agile in the market. Note that it should be possible to derive the indicators from the strategic direction. (See Figure 7-8.)

Throughput shows the number of projects delivered during the period. High throughput indicates high efficiency and short lead times.

Work in progress (WIP) shows the average number of projects in progress during the period. A high value or a rising trend indicates that the operation is overloaded with too many projects, which will reduce throughput. Alternatively, the projects might all be small model upgrades that will not provide long-term profitability.

In the same way as for the parameters in the project portfolio, the KPIs should not become so numerous that they obscure the overview. The portfolio team must agree on which KPIs they will follow up and determine how each indicator will be calculated and presented. How often should indicators be compiled? Monthly or quarterly is usually appropriate.

The purpose of the indicators is to articulate the operation's performance, to identify system errors that can be corrected, and to assess improvements achieved through the actions taken. If any of the KPIs selected has a mechanism that encourages competition within the operation, then it must be removed. Key performance indicators are a powerful form of feedback. What gets measured, proliferates. Thus, it is important that the indicators truly encourage behavior among employees that increases the operation's long-term profitability.

Remember that results from every system are distributed around a mean value, even the success of projects. It is just as unproductive to proclaim heroes in individual projects that have done well as it is to name scapegoats in projects that have failed. Instead, figure out which of the conditions contributed to success, and apply that knowledge in other projects.

What characterizes a successful portfolio team

The portfolio team uses the project portfolio to ensure the operation's resources do not get overloaded. The portfolio team decides which projects the operation should run, which ones are worthwhile candidates on the short list, and which are not interesting. According to a major study carried out by McDonough and Spital (2003), there are a few things the portfolio team needs to think about. There are behaviors that reduce the success of a project portfolio. First, to overutilize individuals' expertise by assigning them to many projects at the same time. This should definitely be avoided so as not to sabotage short lead times and high profitability. Second, to spread the financial resources among many projects. In both cases, the lack of concentrated resources becomes an Achilles heel for the success of the projects. Third, to replace staff on the project teams against the wishes of the project team while work is in progress. The projects not only lose knowledge in the changeover, but the group dynamic is also disturbed, which can take a long time to repair. According to research, the most devastating change is to switch project managers.

So what actions are associated with successful portfolio management? Success can be defined in at least two different ways. One way is to look at how well the projects satisfy the strategic goals. Another way is to show how financially successful the projects are on average. The recipe for success will differ to some extent depending on which of these approaches is taken. In the following, I discuss the difference.

Reaching strategic goals

Effective portfolio management means that a portfolio team must deal with the uncertainty and risks inherent in all development operations. One way to reduce risks is to promote only projects that target existing markets and take advantage of existing technologies. The assumption made here is that focusing on the familiar not only reduces risks but also results in more successful projects. But that assumption is false, according to McDonough and Spital (2003). On the contrary, enterprises with a small proportion of safe projects, in terms of technologies and markets, are more successful. The reason is that high uncertainty and risk are also related to high revenue. Avoiding risk is not a success strategy, because the consequence is a low return. Instead, the risks should be managed, through the staffing of the projects (ibid) and a multi-project management who can make decisions when needed.

To achieve the strategic goals, the following are needed

- **A small proportion of projects with low risk in terms of technology and markets.**
- **A larger proportion of staff dedicated to projects with higher technological risk.**
- **A high throughput rate, projects being completed quickly, resulting in a shorter planning horizon.**
- **Resource buffers that can be used in the event of unforeseen problems.**

Some companies have spread their developers thin across a variety of projects, according to McDonough and Spital (2003). The guiding principle seems to be maximum load on all personnel. This gives rise to what the researchers call "seagulls, who fly in, make their contribution and fly off." According to McDonough and Spital, there is a fundamental problem with this. It prevents learning in the operation, because learning is something that occurs in interaction between people who are exploring a new problem. Researchers Jean Lave and Etienne Wenger have coined the term "situated learning" (Södergren, 2005). Situated learning refers to the fact that when we study a phenomenon, we learn about the phenomenon and its context at the same time (ibid: 78). If staffing is done using "seagulls," no situated learning occurs, because developers who are just stopping by a project never have time to immerse themselves in the context. As Södergren puts it, they never have a "close encounter" with the problem. McDonough and Spital arrive at the recommendation that the project should have a core team who are not replaced during the course of the project. This is particularly the case for projects with high uncertainty. Most of the knowledge generated through situated learning is not written down but exists only in the individuals and can be shared through teamwork.

To be a successful enterprise, it is therefore necessary to allocate a larger proportion of full-time resources to projects with high technical risks. This makes it easier for the employees to understand the difficulties they must master. Then they can more quickly build and communicate knowledge within the group. When the project's challenges get bigger, the members have to learn more and solve problems faster.

Most projects that I have seen have a mix of people working full-time on the project during an interval and others contributing part-time. Many projects change character during the course of the work. In the beginning, the project may focus on design, while the latter part of the project is dominated by adjustments in production. This will gradually change the staffing, something that is built into the synchronization plan in Pulse. But it is still possible to keep a core team intact throughout the project.

Successful portfolios have high throughput. The operation has not been overloaded, so that the projects can be completed quickly. No projects get left on a back burner. Employees work in cross-functional teams. These teams have been assembled to solve a specific task and may exist for a few hours or several months. A high proportion of teamwork gives rise to greater organization, providing more ideas and more creativity. But increased creativity leads to more hard choices, which give rise to uncertainty unless decision-making accelerates. That is why it is necessary to hold pulse meetings frequently at all levels, in order to manage uncertainty. Increased uncertainty makes it harder to make predictions, which increases the importance of a fast and flexible response. It is through high-frequency decision-making that uncertainty can be handled. A portfolio team capable of leaving its mark on the operation through daily control is a significant success factor for an enterprise, according to

McDonough and Spital (2003). To that I would add the need for a package of methods that enable feedback, variation, and decisions.

Financial success

To achieve financial success, the following are needed

- **A limited number of projects in progress, resulting in better focus.**
- **Resources being scheduled before a project starts.**
- **Multi-project management that makes decisions just in time.**
- **Frequent evaluation of the projects in the portfolio.**
- **The portfolio team closing down projects that are not up to scratch.**
- **The same criteria being used to assess all projects.**
- **The portfolio team not accepting delays. Resources being added when problems arise.**

A financially successful portfolio gives rise to many products that are successful in the market. The success factors here differ slightly from the strategically successful portfolio.

Starting lots of projects will overload the operation. In contrast, starting few projects can lead to an insufficient number of new products in the market. Successful enterprises start projects at the same pace as they complete projects. When a project is completed, a pulse board will be freed up, and a new project can start. It is common for a medium-sized operation to complete six to 12 projects each year. Thus, the same number should be started. The number of projects in progress is then around five to seven, sometimes as many as 10. Having a limited number of projects in progress means that the portfolio team and the product team have time to perform their share of the work, which improves the potential for the development projects.

Successful enterprises evaluate their portfolio at least every month. More frequent reviews of the projects in the portfolio can lead to faster feedback, reduced uncertainty, and faster fixes. Sometimes the portfolio team has to decide to close down a project or change its direction.

The portfolio team uses the same criteria for all projects in order to select, prioritize, and possibly close down projects in successful portfolios. Decisions should be made in context and with consistency.

When a project signals it has problems it cannot solve, and these problems cannot be solved by the product team or resource management, either, the problem will land in the portfolio team's inbox on the pulse board. Successful enterprises have the ability to find a solution to every problem. This does not mean that all problems have a solution, but all problems get a decision. It might mean the project

It is the portfolio team that sets the pace in the operation through its actions.

may continue working with increased risk. That is when the portfolio team, through its decision, has assumed the risk. It is by continuously dealing with the situations that arise that the portfolio team signals the importance of acting now. It is the portfolio team that sets the pace in the operation through its actions.

Summary of portfolio management

This chapter has shown how a project portfolio provides an overview of the proposed, ongoing, and completed projects. Using the project portfolio, the portfolio team can make sure not to start more projects than the operation is capable of running, can give each project a priority to balance the need for resources as well as coordinate the projects so that there is a good mix of different project types, and can ensure that they are properly scheduled in relation to one another.

The project portfolio is a compilation of a few important parameters that form the basis for determining which projects the operation will carry out. It also shows the current status of projects in progress, the relative priorities of the projects, and their profitability. The parameters should describe from various perspectives the projects' profitability and risks.

So that the assignments do not disrupt the development projects, an assignment manager is needed to ensure that there are not too many cases being dealt with at the same time, and an assignment portfolio is needed where assignments can be prioritized and queued.

The project portfolio is used by the portfolio team in four key decision-making situations: to determine which projects to start and assign each project a unique priority, to follow up projects in progress, to evaluate completed projects, and to evaluate new candidate projects.

Common parameters used to prioritize projects are delivery time, financial significance, strategic significance, and business risk. Three to four is an appropriate number of parameters to make the project portfolio easy to survey.

The purpose of following up projects is to identify if any project's priority should be changed, if other efforts are needed, or if any project should be shut down prematurely as a result of weak profitability.

The purpose of evaluating completed projects is partly to learn from mistakes and successes so that, over time, better investment decisions can be made that further the success of other projects, and partly to take actions that can increase revenues from investments already made.

Continuously taking measurements provides key performance indicators, which can be used by the portfolio team to gauge the operation's performance and potential for improvement. A few suitable key performance indicators are throughput, number of projects in process, delivery precision, time to market, payback period, and goal achievement.

Projects will wait to get started based on the order of priority determined by the portfolio team. Planning critical resources provides a smooth workflow near the operation's peak capacity. Without that planning, there is a risk of overload and self-reinforcing instability in the system. I will discuss resource planning in more detail in the next chapter.

8. Resource management

Strategic resource management is done by the portfolio team when they decide which projects will be carried out and how much capacity to set aside for assignment management. The operational tasks of allocating staff and other resources to projects and assignments are handled by resource management. At the core of their work is the resource pulse meeting. In this chapter, I will describe the work of resource management. A prerequisite for being able to manage resources is that the operation has at its disposal the resources necessary for the development process, which can be a challenge. I will therefore discuss this and the consequences of fragmented control of resources.

What resources are available in strategy and development?

If an operation is viewed as a "functional organization," one of the departments will be named "design department" or "R&D department" and will be expected to work on product development. This is correct, of course, but far from the whole truth. Developing a product is much more than just designing it. A new product must also be manufactured, assembled, distributed, sold, and serviced in a rational and profitable way, which requires the involvement of many different skills from many different departments.

Comprehending the magnitude of the resources involved in work on strategy and development is often the first stumbling block when introducing Pulse. Working cross-functionally means that projects and teams are composed of people with different skills from different departments that together work out a solution. If no resources are available from purchasing or production engineering, for example, it is often impossible to run the projects in a meaningful way. This means that the resource pool that the development operation needs access to and control over should embrace all the skills and departments necessary to achieve new products, and many of these resources must also spend some of their working hours in the manufacturing operations. The challenge for the development operation is to gain access to these resources so that they can contribute to the process at an early stage and thus set the proper prerequisites for the products to be developed.

The Pulse organization

A pulse organization is based on a network of pulse meetings. To administer resources, though, all companies with Pulse have chosen to retain their departmental structure. Thus, behind the pulse organization there is still the functional organization with its hierarchical structure of employees and executives.

In Pulse, a manager in the functional organization is called a "resource manager." That person is responsible for recruiting and developing staff, setting salaries, safeguarding health and safety at work, and promoting working methods as well as allocating resources to projects, the assignment team, and other teams based on priorities decided by the portfolio team. However, resource managers do not really control their employees' work. Employees' activities are directed by visual management at the pulse meetings within each project and team. In smaller companies, there may be one or two resource managers in the engineering department with staff responsibility for 10–30 people each. I refer to all the resource managers together from all the departments that are involved in strategy and development work as "the resource management."

I recommend that product and program managers who work on a product team do not simultaneously serve as resource managers, as resource management takes a lot of time and energy. However, a resource manager may well participate in various strategic initiatives, such as feasibility studies, workshops, and analyses.

Preventing overload and fragmentation

There are two fundamental success factors to think about when it comes to staffing projects and teams. First, it is absolutely necessary to have a sufficiently large proportion of the people in projects assigned on a full-time basis so that they can develop innovative products. Second, no individual should ever be spread thin among a large number of projects and other tasks, because that reduces efficiency and hampers cooperation on teams. Participating in as few as three projects can sharply reduce productivity (Wheelwright and Clark, 1992). Based on these two success factors, my recommendation is that each person works on only one or two projects or assignments at the same time.

To exercise daily management with low uncertainty in planning, I use a weekly allocation of resources in Pulse. This means that a person is allocated to one or two projects each week. However, to keep creativity and efficiency high, resource managers should avoid moving people around each week to cover resource gaps. Individuals should have completed their subresults before they are moved to a new task. Otherwise, the work will be interrupted midway, causing substantial losses, because some work will have to be redone when somebody finally gets time to deal with it. If resources are continuously in short supply, there are likely too many projects and assignments going on at the same time. That is, the operation is overloaded, causing turbulence, with low resource utilization and high stress. The solution is to temporarily close some projects and assignments or to recruit more employees.

Little's law states that the lead time equals the ratio of the number of projects in progress to the throughput.

$$\text{Lead time} = \frac{\text{Work in Progress}}{\text{Throughput}}$$

If the business has the capacity to carry out and complete 12 projects each year and currently has six projects in progress, the lead time for the projects will be six months, according to Little's law. Because a majority of all development work is manual, the throughput depends on the total number of work hours available throughout the operation to implement projects during one year, as well as the size of the projects. In addition, bottlenecks will further limit throughput, because all resources cannot be used for all development work, and many tasks require special skills or equipment.

But Little's law applies only as long as the system does not have a shortage of or excess capacity. One factor to take into consideration is what lead time the projects can plan on and, from their point of view, will be the shortest possible lead time. There are often fixed lead times that cannot be shortened with more resources. For example, the lead times for trial runs or the procurement of tools and materials in effect put a limit on how fast the projects can be accomplished. If the shortest possible execution time is four months for a typical project, then in the example above a reduction from six ongoing projects to four will shorten the lead time to four months. But a reduction to two projects will not shorten lead time any further. In contrast, the throughput will fall to six projects per year, while a large proportion of the resources will be underutilized or work on product maintenance.

A corresponding collapse will occur if the system is overloaded. If the number of projects in progress is increased to 24 (which is not that unusual of a scenario in enterprises not using Pulse), Little's law states that the lead time for the projects will increase to two years. However, what I have observed is that lead time increases significantly more than that, at the same time as throughput decreases. The reason is that the long lead time increases the number of late changes and reworks in the projects, which further delays completion. Fragmentation also leads to many projects running out of steam, that is, they never pass the finish line. The products that get launched are often half-finished and, for the most part, pretty mediocre. The result is poor profitability on the new products.

Having an appropriate number of projects in the pipeline leads to the enterprise over time getting many more new products into the market. And by marshaling its strength for every project, the operation can accomplish pioneering initiatives despite great uncertainty, because only projects with technical and commercial risks lead to new and profitable products (McDonough and Spital, 2003).

The portfolio team selects which projects will be carried out and when they will start. The job of resource management is to allocate resources to these projects. If there are insufficient resources, resource management should signal the portfolio team that this problem exists, so they can take action. The portfolio team either makes sure more staff are hired, extends the planned execution time for the projects so they correspond to the availability of resources (which increases the risk of small and fragmented project teams with low efficiency), or closes down one or more projects.

When the portfolio team is faced with the decision to start a project, in addition to the number of projects that are already under way they should take into account which resources are available. If the projects in progress consume virtually all the resources with a specific expertise while resources with other expertise are free, the portfolio team needs to take this into account. In other words, they cannot merely follow the order of priority on the short list of candidate projects. It is particularly important to pay attention to the critical resource and the current utilization of its capacity.

Critical resource

In every system, according to Goldratt (1997), there is a limiting factor that determines the speed of the entire system. Bolstering other factors will not have a positive impact on the system. An operation can be regarded as a system where there is one type of resource that sets the pace for the work, the "critical resource." All other resources will be available in surplus, to some extent. Following this line of reasoning, controlling the workload on the critical resource is sufficient to avoid overloading the operation as a whole. By focusing on the bottleneck resource, the complexity in resource planning significantly decreases (ibid). (See Figure 8-1.)

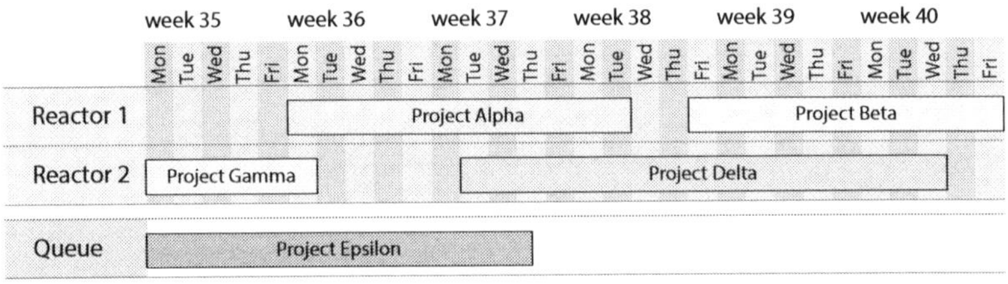

Figure 8-1. Planning the critical resource. In this example, the critical resource consists of two reactors used for development trials.

Overall planning provides control of the workload on the critical resource as well as a smooth work flow near the operation's peak capacity. Without that limitation, the enterprise risks overloading capacity and triggering self-reinforcing instability in the system, which causes all employees to feel overloaded with work. A general feeling of stress and a heavy workload is a sure sign that the operation as a whole is performing far below its peak capacity. After checking the status of the critical resource, new projects and assignments can be started where capacity is available. This means that some projects will lie around waiting to get started based on the order of priority determined by the portfolio team.

The critical resource determines the pace of work and the throughput of the entire operation. To produce as much as possible, the bottleneck resource must never be idle. The solution is to create a backlog of work. That backlog should not be so short that the critical resource might suddenly have no tasks. But the backlog should not be too large, either, so that capital gets tied up unnecessarily, lead times get longer, and subresults become out-of-date. Every operation must adapt the backlog to find its optimum length. When the critical resource has completed one assignment, it begins work on the next task in the backlog. The backlog is arranged by order of priority for the projects waiting, so the bottleneck resource always works on the highest priority projects first. If a project encounters a problem, its planned deliveries to the critical resource could be delayed. The critical resource would then begin working on another assignment in the backlog, even if the delayed project has a higher priority. The critical resource should neither wait for subresults nor interrupt an assignment it has already started.

To identify where the critical resource is located in the operation, the resource management can study where projects usually suffer from a lack of resources. The critical resource could be some expertise in the operation that is always overloaded, such as the system architects or test engineers. But it could also be an apparatus, such as test equipment or a pilot plant. Because the identification and management of the critical resource will lead to projects being postponed so as not to overload the operation as a whole, this practice will eliminate most resource conflicts and speed up throughput for all projects. If the operation runs many similar projects, a bottleneck that is constant over time can usually be identified. However, the more varied the projects that the operation runs and the fewer they are, the greater the risk that the critical resource will shift over time at pace with the projects' progress and their changing resource needs. The system then becomes more dynamic and much more difficult to manage. With a critical resource that is shifting, backlogs are no longer worth setting up. Instead, the operation must rely on the dynamic management that resource management introduces through the weekly resource pulse meetings.

A resource other than the critical one may get overloaded temporarily as a result of fluctuations in the workload. That is why the operation cannot cut back on resources that are "noncritical." These resources must be able to handle the natural variations that occur in the workload without jeopardizing throughput. The backlog for the critical resource must always be maintained. The farther away from the critical resource an individual works, the greater the fluctuations are and the greater the excess capacity that is required. Noncritical resources have some excess capacity, at least in terms of their mean value over an extended time. Overcapacity leads to individuals having periods when they are not fully occupied. In Pulse, assignment management plays the vital role of providing priority tasks for these individuals when gaps occur.

I want to emphasize that no detailed work plan is made for the critical resource. Instead, the portfolio team makes sure to start projects at a pace at which the bottleneck resource has the capacity to carry them out. The backlog of tasks drawn up for the critical resource shows what they should start working on when a task is completed. Depending on the length of the tasks, daily or weekly pulse meetings are used to plan the next day or next week based on the current situation. If the critical resources work in projects, the daily project pulse meetings will guide them in their work. The critical resources, as well as all other resources, are then allocated weekly at the resource pulse meeting to the projects that need them.

Because projects in Pulse are planned using synchronization plans that in turn produce resource plans, among other things, it is tempting to compile all the resource plans into one spreadsheet that shows the resource needs forward in time so as to identify overload points ahead of time. My firm opinion is that this work is pointless. No coordinated long-term planning of all the resources of the operation is needed. It will still be impossible to know in advance exactly when various resources will be needed. The projects' resource needs will fluctuate, and alongside these needs other urgent tasks will arise that must be resolved. When all these fluctuations stack up, the operation's total resource plan will quickly become outdated. At the same time, daily management of tasks and weekly allocation of resources at the resource pulse meeting are necessary. Resources that are not used in the projects will be allocated to the assignment team.

However, individual resource managers might benefit from planning the work load for their staff approximately so they can see how extended periods of intense and focused project work can be interspersed with other tasks, recovery time, and professional development in other areas.

The resource pulse board and resource pulse meetings

The operational allocation of resources takes place at the weekly resource pulse meetings in conjunction with the other coordinating pulse meetings. The resource managers responsible for personnel and equipment participate in the resource pulse meeting. Project managers, assignment managers, and team leaders who need resources also participate. The basic rule is that the resource managers allocate resources to projects, the assignment team, and other teams. This movement of resources is a work directive, so it can only be done by a manager with such authority. A resource is moved from a project, the assignment team, or some other team to the resource pool by a project manager, assignment manager, or team leader when the person completes his/her tasks. The allocation also follows the priority that the portfolio team has set on the projects. This means that the project with priority No. 1 receives its allocation first. Resources are usually allocated to the assignment team last, which means that all resources not used in the projects will work with assignments. Assignment management works like a rubber band, stretching or contracting depending on the projects' resource needs at any given time. However, over time the assignment manager must ensure that the amount of resources actually allocated to the assignment team is within the overall framework set by the portfolio team.

The resource pulse board (shown in Figure 8-2) has boxes for all ongoing projects and feasibility studies, a box for the assignment team, and a box for the resources that are not available. Every person who works with strategy and development has resource magnets. In Figure 8-2, each person has two magnets. One magnet indicates part-time, two magnets indicate full-time. Thus each individual can work with a maximum of two projects at the same time, or on a project and the assignment team. Even critical equipment may be allocated on a resource pulse board using magnets.

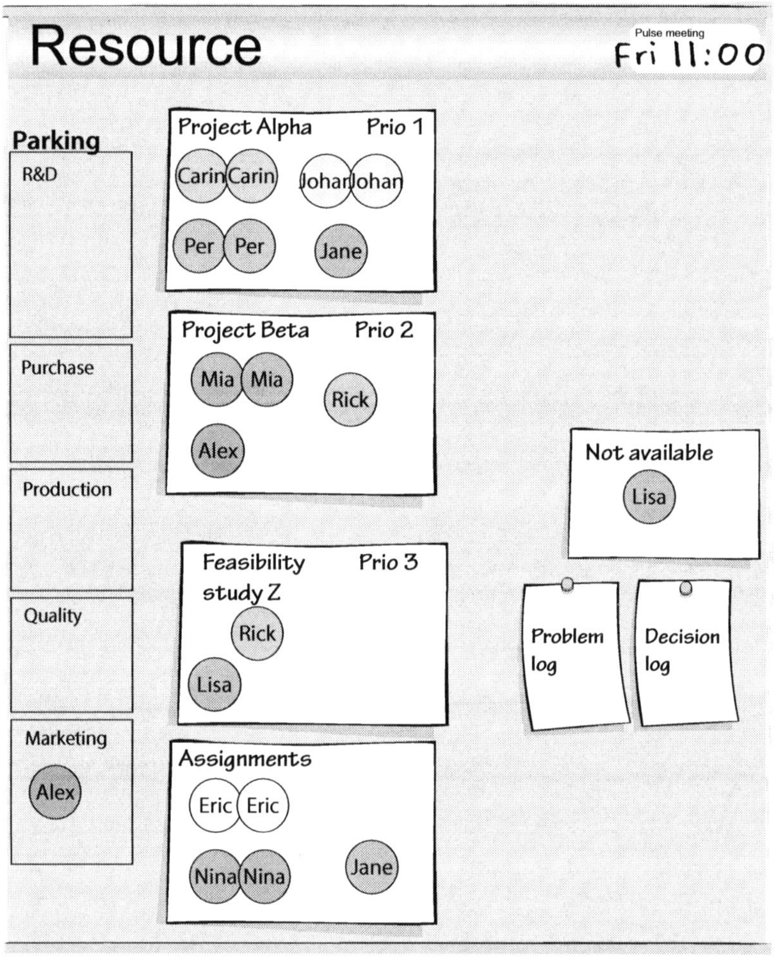

Figure 8-2. Resource pulse board. A simplified example with 10 people divided into two projects, one feasibility study, and the assignment team. Jane and Rick divide their time between two different commitments. Lisa is not available part of this week. Alex is only needed half-time for development work this week. Others work full-time, as shown by their double magnets. The magnets are different colors, which represent different expertise: design engineer, purchaser, production engineer.

Should the managers also have resource magnets? Some companies have chosen to also show what the managers' time is used for and have augmented the board with spaces for the product team, HR management, and the portfolio team.

Some preparation is necessary for the resource pulse meeting to work. The projects must estimate the resources they need and when they are needed, which is done in planning before the project starts. This is a rough estimate that gives an approximate indication of the skills needed and the number of people. The method is called synchronization planning. In classic project management, it is common for plans to constantly change. In Pulse, the main rule is not to change the synchronization plan. Problems, deviations, and unexpected events are handled by priority in the project or handed off to a pulse team where decisions and actions can be taken. The approximate resource parameters that the project estimated from the beginning should be fixed, and changes in these must be approved by the portfolio team. This means that the project with priority No. 1 cannot demand all resources unless it is provided for in the resource plan adopted for the project.

Before the resource pulse meeting each week, the project managers discuss any resource changes with the resource managers. The resource managers in turn plan the changes and discuss them with the people concerned. For this to be possible, the project team must have jointly discussed the following week's resource needs beforehand at a project pulse meeting.

When problems occur in allocating resources based on existing needs, this should be documented as a problem. Over time, that documentation can provide background data making it possible to pinpoint the operation's critical resource.

When resources are scarce, that is, when not all projects receive the resources they ask for, the resource managers may be tempted to split the resources into smaller parts. By adding more magnets, they solve the problem: suddenly there are sufficient resources. But their solution is an illusion. The resources are spread thin, and teamwork is shattered, resulting in lower efficiency and less creativity. The task of resource management is to allocate and concentrate the resources based on the priorities set. When resource scarcity arises, it must be visualized so that more long-term actions can be taken, such as initiatives to develop and broaden skills so that the operation becomes less dependent on individual experts.

Access to resources outside the development department

The resource pulse works fine as long as the resource management has control over the resources, that is, they can marshal the resources needed for work on strategy and development. Problems often arise when the development operation shares resources, such as purchasers and production engineers, with production. The reason is that problems in the sales and manufacturing operations tend to take precedence over development work, resulting in large and costly interruptions in the projects. My advice is to avoid sharing resources as far as is practicable. (See Figure 8-3.) If the development operation needs the equivalent of two full-time positions in purchasing, then there should be two strategic buyers who work in projects to choose suppliers and draw up contracts with them. Other buyers work with operational purchasing for production. Over time, purchasing staff can rotate through different tasks to broaden their knowledge. The need for technical production expertise can be solved in a similar way.

If the operation is small, it is not possible to split up people for production and development. But it is still possible to focus the resources by setting aside time for each kind of work. For example, a purchaser could work with development projects on one specific day each week.

When a new product is introduced in production, many production resources are often involved. This work can be seen as part of a development project, in which case the resources needed are allocated there. Or it can be seen as work scaling and fine-tuning production, that is, regarded as a production project, run by the production or production engineering departments. Whatever the enterprise chooses, all projects are included in the product team's program plan and in the project portfolio managed by the portfolio team, and any problems that arise must be quickly flagged in the pulse system if corrective action is to be taken.

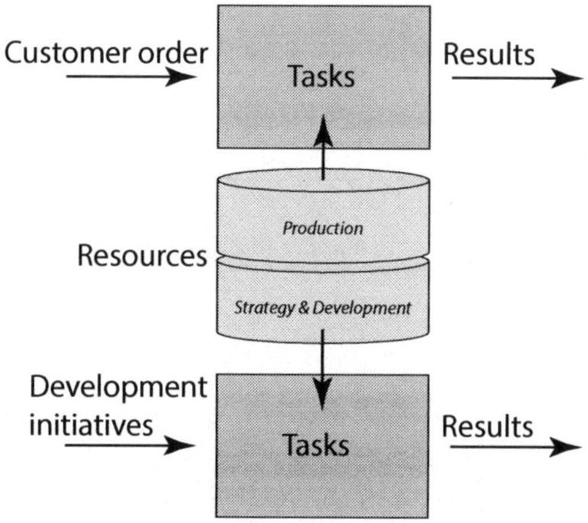

Figure 8-3. Diagram showing how resources are split between production (sales to delivery) and strategy and development.

Summary of resource management

In this chapter, I have shown how the resource management provide the assignment team, projects, and feasibility studies with staff resources. A resource pulse board creates transparency, showing which projects are in progress, where resources are currently in use, and any resource conflicts. The resource management consists of all managers who have staff responsibility for the employees working with strategy and development.

Resource management plays a key role in preventing individual employees from becoming overloaded or spread thin. They are also responsible for ensuring expertise in the long run. An effective way to develop an individual's expertise is to let the individual participate full-time in a project team. It is alongside others in a specific context that people learn.

In the next chapter, I will sum up the book.

9. Agile multi-project management

In this chapter, I will summarize the conclusions in this book.

This book began with me pointing out seven wastes and four basic problems. The wastes are: developing the wrong products, fragmentation that causes unnecessary mental shifts, long distances in time and space, waiting time, faulty practices, overengineering and overdocumentation, and unnecessary inventory and lead time. Each of the seven wastes has multiple concurrent causes. The basic problems, as I see them, are overload and fragmentation, relay race thinking that results in a lack of cooperation, strategic work that is too weak and fragmented to handle the complexity of the development process, and an organizational structure that puts obstacles in the way of new products to be developed. Considering these basic problems, I have defined four principles for agile multi-project management using Pulse (shown in Figure 9-1).

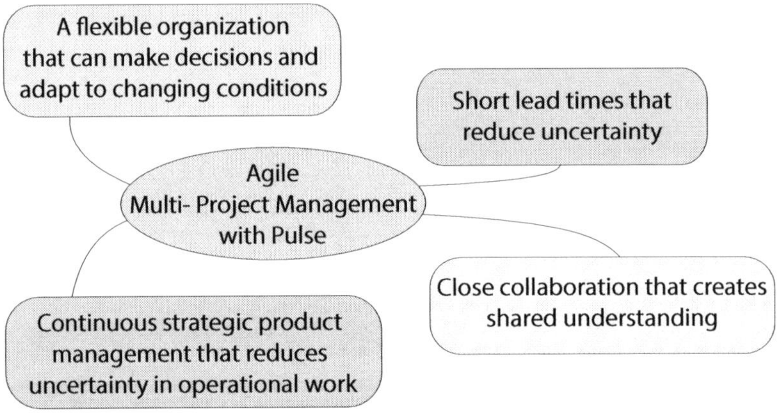

Figure 9-1. Principles for agile multi-project management using Pulse.

Short lead times that reduce uncertainty

When the time between idea and realization is short, developers can quickly verify whether an idea works. If the results do not meet their expectations, they can choose to modify the solution. With each iteration, they learn what works and what does not work, at the same time as they learn the development process. The faster they can test solutions, the faster knowledge is accumulated and the faster product development moves forward. Over time, this can build up knowledge, giving an insurmountable advantage over competitors. These iterations will partly be done in interaction with customers, who will then also develop at the same pace.

To achieve short lead times at all stages and in all the work that is done, it is important to first and foremost prevent overloading and fragmentation of resources. This will require company management (which I call the "portfolio team") to act as gatekeepers and not start more projects than the operation is capable of running. It also requires that they take control of all short assignments that otherwise have a tendency to interfere with the work in long-term projects.

Even if the portfolio team adjusts the number of projects to their desired lead times, the resource management must also make sure to allocate resources on a weekly basis and handle the resource conflicts that will arise as a result of natural variations in the system. By visualizing the current allocation of resources, the resource managers and portfolio team can see which resource problems the operation has, where the bottlenecks are, what resources are available, and thus which solutions are available in the short and long run. Through unified assignment management, the resource managers can also make sure to take advantage of the resources in surplus for high-priority product improvements and at the same time relatively quickly make individuals more versatile.

Unfortunately, waiting times are all too common in projects—waiting for results, materials, information, resources, and decisions. Within the operation, everyone should strive to shorten all waiting times for priority tasks. The external waiting times are often difficult to influence and must be dealt with using active strategic planning to manage the risks.

Close cooperation that creates shared understanding

Successful product development is all about assembling a group of people with different skills who are given the time and opportunity to explore a challenging area together. The number of people working together has to reach a critical mass and be kept stable over a long enough time for this to happen, which, again, is related to actions taken to prevent overloading and fragmentation.

A bureaucratic way of working with complicated project models and divisions into narrow roles creates distance between people and impedes cooperation. Instead, the actual situation and the overall strategic design should guide the team to the results required. It is in the dialogue between team participants that the work is formulated and delegated. With visual management, it is easier for the members to see and discuss where they are in their work, where they are going, and what obstacles stand in the way. But in order for there to be shared understanding that can lead the team forward, the goals and plans visualized on the pulse board must be worked out by the team members together. Teams that meet daily or even more often will develop close teamwork. At the pulse meetings, the team can coordinate their efforts and the members can share their experiences, which moves the work forward. The more frequently the team makes decisions together, the faster the work proceeds.

Continuous strategic product management that reduces uncertainty in operational work

The design and cultivation of strategies is a task without interruption or end. The more the product team can prepare and investigate at the strategic level, the simpler and shorter the projects will be. But that does not mean that project work is merely shifted onto the product team. The idea is to work continuously with overall models and snapshots of the market, customers, needs, opportunities, and problems to be able to draw joint conclusions from them. The visualization helps the enterprise's employees share knowledge and compare their experiences at the same time as they help decision-makers make coordinated and consistent decisions even under time pressure.

Innovative products are rarely based on entirely new technology but are usually the result of existing technologies combined in a new way. Thus, the ability to harness and build on previous knowledge is crucial. This is done partly through close cooperation and short lead times and partly through components, modules, and platforms that are reused.

Overengineering and uncertainty about requirements easily arise if the project team does not understand the purpose of the project or if their comprehension of the goal is not consistent with the product team's. The work initiating the project will develop shared understanding in the product team, which must be transferred to the project team, as they jointly work out the goal scenario for the project.

Then the key is to keep this shared understanding alive as the work progresses, new knowledge is added, and circumstances change. By checking in weekly through program pulse meetings, the projects can flag problems that they need help with. With frequent scheduled demonstrations of subresults, the product team can ensure that the results still fit into the strategic design.

A flexible organization that can make decisions and adapt to changing conditions

A fundamental problem with today's organizational models is that they are based on a feudal structure where power is inherited and knowledge strengthens the individual's position. This makes it more difficult to develop, learn, and spread knowledge, which requires that information be shared, of course.

In Pulse, the constitutional structure of a network consists of pulse meetings. Some of these pulse meetings are permanent and serve as the backbone of the operation's multi-project management. Other pulse meetings are temporary, to carry out projects or feasibility studies. At the pulse meetings, all the decisions are made that lead the operation forward. To support the decisions, information is made visual on pulse boards. This information is shared and builds up a collective understanding of the conditions and goals. But this picture is constantly changing. New knowledge is added, the operating environment is changing, old truths are challenged, and the information on the pulse boards must be changed. The only way to influence the decisions is to share information and knowledge that shapes and reshapes the shared views.

With a visualization of the operation's various aspects, both strategically and operationally, management can create transparency. They will then gain control of the operation at an overall macro level. But to gain that control, they must have delegated assignments and mandates to self-managing working groups, groups who are also given the prerequisites to solve their tasks. How these groups will work and what actions they will take is impossible to predict.

Their actions will arise from each particular situation and be shaped by the group's members. In other words, management control at the macro level depends on their having no control at the micro level.

Agile multi-project management

Uncertainty about the future is increasing as markets, companies and people become more interconnected. Dramatic changes will happen more often, and businesses will have to adapt faster to survive in tough competition.

Agility is the ability to successfully create, cope with and exploit changes in circumstances. When working with product development, that will include the ability to shift direction when markets and customers change their behavior. But it also means introducing new techniques that could potentially change the whole business.

Pulse is an organizational model for agile multi-project management. After 10 years of using Pulse, we can confidently say it works! Companies that have been using the Pulse concept for many years report that they continue to achieve short lead times, high project throughput, and fast change when circumstances change. That all adds up to significantly higher and more sustainable profitability.

Glossary

Term	Explanation
Adaptation	The behavior of a system changes through an increase in mutual information between the system and a potentially complex and changing environment. Adaptation presumes different alternative actions (variability), acknowledged feedback, and decision-making capacity.
Agent	Individual or group acting inside a system, such as a project group consisting of people who jointly decide what tasks have to be done by the next day or a project member who takes on some of those tasks.
Agile	The ability to successfully create effects in the market and take advantage of opportunities that arise. How agile an operation needs to be depends on the complexity of its environment and the cost of errors that occur when the operation does not act on signals.
Architecture	1. Overall technical structure of a system. The architecture defines the prerequisites for the product's functionality and puts restrictions on the design of the product. 2. Flows and meeting points that have been built into the work site. These could be, for example, open-plan offices, pulse rooms, meeting rooms, hallways, or individual offices. The architecture sets the stage for how the agents working at the work site can collaborate and organize themselves.
Arena	In this book, this word is used to describe a formal meeting at a certain place where information, problems, needs, and knowledge are shared by people. In Pulse, the pulse meetings are arenas for permanent or temporary teams, where they can make decisions, deal with problems that have arisen, and form a common view. Pulse meetings take place in the pulse room.
Assignment	All tasks in a development operation that are not already included in projects. For example, questions from production or salespeople that may take a few minutes to answer, minor modifications and adaptations, and product maintenance. By only having two ways of working, projects and assignments, it is possible to organize two channels that analyze, prioritize, and start tasks taking into account the operation's available resources. See also *project*.
Assignment manager	Manages the assignment operation and is responsible for building up a system that handles and prioritizes assignments. Member of the product team.
Assignment portfolio	A compilation of all ongoing and pending assignments and their relative priorities based on a handful of select parameters.
Assignment pulse meeting	Permanent pulse meeting to coordinate the accomplishment of short assignments.
Bottleneck	Critical resource that is finite and limits the total throughput.

Business goals	Estimate the economic growth that a customer segment can achieve within a limited period of a few years based on existing robust customer needs. To define how the company intends to achieve its business goals, break down the customer needs into development goals, which will later lead to the initiation of one or more projects that will be kept together in one program.
Business risk	The risk that factors in the business environment (such as changes in market conditions, customer behavior, or technology trends) will have a negative impact on volumes and margins and thereby reduce revenue.
Capacity	The rate at which information can be reliably transmitted. In a multi-project organization, the capacity is related to the amount of resources available and how well those resources interact. See also *throughput*.
Complex system	See *nonlinear system*.
Complexity	Can be described statistically as the minimum amount of information needed to be able to reproduce a system. The complexity of a system increases with the number of agents, the number of interactions between the agents, the complexity of the agents, and the complexity of the interactions.
Concurrent (Set-based) design process	In a concurrent (set-based) design process, several alternative solutions are conceived at the start, and those that best fulfill the goals are successively selected and combined. Compare to *sequential design process*.
Constitutional structure	Formal rules that specify how the operation's organization is structured, for example through positions, roles, authority, decision-making units, and permanent pulse meetings.
Contract-driven projects	A few customers with different unique requirements place orders in the form of contracts that the supplier then fulfills by carrying out contract-driven projects.
Coordinating pulse meetings	The coordinating pulse meetings consist of program pulse meetings, resource pulse meetings, product pulse meetings, and portfolio pulse meetings. These should be in sequence, one after the other, on one day each week, so that needs and problems discovered in the projects can be escalated quickly.
Cross-functional work	Working together across functional boundaries to produce good solutions to complex problems by applying broad expertise in many different areas (such as production, design, logistics, and marketing).
Decision process	The flow of information, problems, and people that over time transform feedback and alternative actions into decisions.
Efficiency	The degree of goal achievement in relation to use of resources, that is, how well the goals set for the operation are fulfilled and the amount of resources consumed in their fulfillment. The term includes productivity and goal achievement, both of which are high in an efficient organization.

Emergence	In emergence, a complex pattern is formed based on the interaction of simple structures or behaviors. Often a system that is extremely simple at the micro level can result in great complexity at the macro level, so it may be said that the macro properties emerge from the micro properties.
Escalate	An issue that is escalated is taken over by a more qualified global authority with broader powers. In Pulse, this means a problem that cannot be solved at the operational level (such as in a project) is handed to a strategic level (such as the product team).
Feedback	When information about the outcome of an event or phenomenon in the past affects an event or phenomenon in the present or future. Feedback is part of a system's mechanism for checking itself. Feedback can be self-reinforcing (positive) or limiting (negative).
Financial significance	A weighted combination of multiple financial parameters, such as revenue, cost of investment, and payback period, which can be used, among other things, to prioritize projects.
Functional organization	Sometimes also called "hierarchical line organization." Similar tasks are pooled in functions. At the overall level, a division is created so that, for example, production, product development, marketing, and accounting and finance end up in different departments. In each department, further divisions may be made; for example, the department for product development can be divided into separate functions for hardware and software. In a functional organization, the managers for each function make all important decisions. They are also responsible for planning, organization, and management.
Hub	Connection point in a network. May also be called a node.
Iterative work	Work during short periods for which one receives feedback for that period that influences what to work on during the next period and how.
Just-in-time decision	A decision is made when there is a need and the requisite information is available, so that decision-making units must meet often and communicate generously to ensure everyone has a common view enabling decisions to be made more often. Implemented in Pulse through pulse meetings.
Kanban	A kanban is an information carrier in lean production that signals material requirements based on actual needs. Using kanban, one can create automatic interactive ordering (pull) between different parts of a system. In manufacturing, a kanban may refer to a bin or a pallet that can accommodate a limited number of items or a certain type of an information card that specifies the item number and quantity. The number of kanban is limited to provide a level workload in the operation.

Key performance indicators	Measurements taken continually to gauge the operation's performance and potential for improvement. In product development, other forms of information carriers are used in limited numbers to similarly restrict the load on the system. For example, the number of projects and assignments that the operation can have in progress at the same time is limited. Similarly the number of activities on which one individual can work at the same time is limited, as is the number of projects in which an individual can participate.
Lead time	The time it takes from processing input data and raw materials to delivering the desired results. Lead time is the length of time the customer has to wait before its needs are fulfilled. In product development, for example, lead time may refer to the time that passes from a customer need being acknowledged until a product fulfilling that need is available in the market. Lead time may also refer to the time that passes from the discovery of a problem until a decision has been made on how to deal with it.
Lean	Originally the Toyota Production System. Short lead times, pull planning, level workloads, dealing with problems, customer focus, eliminating waste, optimizing the system, and working in teams.
Linear system	In a linear system, the results increase in proportion to the inputs, and the whole is the sum of its parts. See also *nonlinear system*.
Little's law	John Little has proved that the amount of work is equal to the throughput multiplied by the lead time.
Matrix organization	An organization in which the participants report to more than one manager. For example, a project manager may set a goal for some work and a function manager may evaluate the quality of that work and decide which methods should be used. The relationship between functions and projects is regulated by projects demanding results from functions. The projects determine which results will be produced and when they will be ready. The functions determine how the work will be done and who will do it. See also *functional organization*.
Method pulse meeting	Permanent pulse meeting whose task is to administrate the common rules, serve as a forum for conflict resolution, and act as supervisory body.
Modular system	A modular system contains several possible articles for each component, which can be combined with one another into a finished product. This makes the number of possible product variants extremely large. The modular approach enables a wide variety of products to be quickly customized for customers.
Multi-project	In an operation, this refers to running in parallel several technically and commercially interdependent projects that also depend on the same resources.
Multi-project management	Team and individual decision-makers who work on coordinating the technical, commercial, and resource aspects of all the operation's projects.

Network	A structure of units that are linked to one another by relationships and connection points (hubs) and that together form a network. Networks of people are made up of teams or individuals (agents) that are linked to each other through relationships, information flows, or having members in common.
Node	See *hub*.
Nominal group technique	A method used to involve all participants in the work of the group. First, all participants write their own sticky notes. Then the notes are presented and arranged in different structures depending on the task.
Nonlinear system	A nonlinear system arises when three or more agents interact. In nonlinear systems, the interaction between agents can emerge as disproportionately large or small outcomes that consequently result in the whole not corresponding to the sum of its parts. There may be feedback loops, delays, trigger limits, and qualitative changes that give rise to abrupt changes.
Operation	A group of people who together perform something and strive for common goals. The way they interact is called organization.
Operational goals	These define how much margins on existing products could be improved by shortening lead times, reducing costs, and increasing capacity. Operational goals are aimed inwards at the organization itself. Streamlining processes and improving products make it possible to save money and satisfy customer needs for fast delivery and reliable products. This differentiates operational goals from business goals, which strive to increase revenue through new products or new markets.
Organization	A system of continuously coordinated activities and efforts.
Organizing	Interaction between individuals that results in internal limitations on participants in order to increase the probability of synchronized action and value-added work.
Overload	When a system has too much work in progress in relation to its available resources, its throughput suffers negatively. This extends lead time dramatically, resulting in major energy loss.
Position	A position that has been filled for the time being. Compare to *role*.
Process	A chain of linked activities or steps that use information and resources to provide a product or a result. Repetitive processes can be described by how the various activities or steps should be performed and in what order.
Process development	Extends from an analysis of opportunities, ideas, and problems to the new process being in operation. Includes all the work required to be able to develop new or modified processes.
Product	Good or service.
Product development	Extends from an analysis of opportunities, ideas, and customer needs to the launch of a new product. Includes all the work required to be able to offer new or modified products in the market.

Product generation plan	A plan that shows how long-term technology development, development of new production technologies and new modular systems, generational shifts, launches, and model introductions fit together for one product family.
Product line	A group of products with similar characteristics and technology or that all target the same group of customers. This allows them to be brought together in strategic planning, development, production, or marketing.
Product maintenance	Minor improvements, modifications, and adaptations made to the existing designs in order to remedy deficiencies, reduce costs, and secure the supply of components.
Product manager	Member of the product team. A product manager must understand customers' needs today and several years into the future, see which of these needs can be converted into profitable products, understand the possibilities and limitations of his/her own enterprise, and, based on this, draft goals and long-term plans that communicate the direction to the rest of the organization. So the product manager can be seen as the customer's advocate in the organization and vis-à-vis the projects.
Product pulse meeting	Permanent pulse meeting to coordinate the efforts of the product team.
Product team	A cross-functional team of commercial and technical product managers. They drive the work to translate customers' needs and the operation's possibilities into business goals and program plans that describe development efforts into the future. The product team initiates projects and is the recipient of the projects' results. They will ensure that the technologies in the results of the projects harmonize in the long term, build up the operation's long-term expertise, and ensure that the operation's products are profitable in the short and long run.
Production	Using repetitive processes for sales, manufacturing, and delivery of products to customers, users, or resellers.
Productivity	A measure of the value produced per unit of resources input. Productivity can be measured as the proportion of the energy added that is converted into value-added work.
Program	Shows the analyses, studies, projects, and assignments required to realize an overall long-term business goal. Thus a new product can be developed through successive or parallel projects and assignments.
Program manager	Member of the product team. Maintains communication between the product team and the projects, responsible for technical aspects of a group of projects whose technologies are interdependent, defines the technical architecture of the products, leads the weekly program pulse meetings, and has the authority to make technical decisions.
Program plan	Describes in general the steps that must be taken to achieve the business goals, in the form of market studies, feasibility studies, projects, launch activities, and the like. Each program plan is linked to one business goal (or one operational goal). Program plans make it easier to see the context of the work done in the organization and how the various projects jointly contribute to the organization's profitability.

Program pulse meeting	Permanent pulse meeting for coordinating all projects in progress. Led by the program manager. Allows projects to escalate problems they cannot handle on their own.
Project	A way of working in which a clearly defined task is solved by moving resources with different expertise to the task so that they can solve the task together. See also *assignment*.
Project pulse meeting	Temporary pulse meeting for the project team that is held as long as a project is in progress, intended to coordinate work within the project.
Pull	A system of automatic ordering ("pull planning"). An example from production is when a unit orders materials based on their actual needs when their buffer stock has reached its lowest level. In product development, pull is achieved by projects and teams being self-organizing and using a distinctly iterative approach. The opposite is when an external agent orders, plans, or schedules interaction, which is called push. A pull-based system has lower costs for interaction than a push-based system does. See also *push* and *kanban*.
Pulse	An organizational structure built as a network of pulse meetings where people meet frequently and make decisions together at pulse boards. Suitable for running multi-project operations.
Pulse board	A board that shows visual and up-to-date information on the goals, plans, situation, problems, activities, and decisions. Used by the operation's different self-organizing teams to drive their work forward. The visual information on the pulse board is prepared by team members together to create a common view to support their work and decision-making.
Pulse goal scenario	A visual representation of a goal. For example, a project goal scenario could display the vision, effect goals, and product goals in a mind map.
Pulse meeting	Short (5–30 minutes), frequent (daily or weekly) decision-making meetings in a self-organizing group. A pulse meeting is an arena and takes place at a pulse board where visual information is presented that the group needs to see the current status, get feedback, and make decisions. Pulse meetings are the hubs of the pulse network.
Pulse network	A network of pulse meetings that allows real-time management. While the projects are temporary nodes in the pulse network, the coordinating pulse meetings are permanent hubs. A functional organization includes, on the one hand, a formal organization including positions, posts, rules, and mechanisms for interaction that provide legitimacy and, on the other hand, an informal organization in the form of spontaneous networks of people. A pulse network incorporates the informal organization into the formal structure.
Pulse room	A common room where all pulse meetings are held. In this room, information that the operation's various self-organizing teams use for their own and joint work is made visual on pulse boards.

Push	A system in which an external agent orders, schedules, or plans how interaction will be carried out. For example, in production a central unit may use forecasts to plan how materials will be sent out to different units. In product development, push occurs when a project manager or project model plans how and when work will be carried out and who will do it. Compare *pull*.
Real-time management	Planning and management done in real time, as one looks a few hours into the future, so that uncertainty can be kept at a low level. In lean practice, this is called pull or visual management. The current situation with its immediate needs governs what needs to be done next. In production, kanban is used to achieve real-time management. In Pulse, regular and frequent pulse meetings are used.
Role	Temporarily appointed person who gets specific authority and responsibilities, such as a project manager. Compare *position*.
Rules	Limit the scope for action and thus channel the agents' energy and resources into joint efforts. Used within a group to enable cooperation and by several groups together to facilitate interaction among the groups. Also used to compose the organization's constitutional structure. Cooperation relies on trust that all parties concerned will comply with the rules, which requires some possibility of monitoring. See also *method pulse meeting*.
Scrum	A method for software development in which a self-organizing team works in fixed time periods. The team selects and adjusts the number of results to be completed for one period at a time. A product owner prioritizes a backlog of functions from which the team picks results for each period. The method is used in Pulse, for example to plan work in the product and portfolio teams.
Self-organizing	When no central unit or external agent has controlled the organizing, the system is said to be self-organizing. The participants have jointly devised how they want to work and who will do what. They can also adapt to changing conditions over time. See also *organizing*.
Sequential design process	The technical specification is set initially, so only one solution is developed. If that solution does not work, the development process must start over from the beginning. Compare to *concurrent (set-based) design process*.
Simple rules	Minimalist rules that avoid developing a complexity incapable of adaptation.
Sitting	Several people gather for a few hours seated around a conference table to discuss and possibly make decisions on various cases.
Speed	A measure of how well a project in its planning has successfully used resources to shorten development time. Speed indicates how many full-time resources work in the project on average. The more resources that work, the greater the possibility of teamwork and the quicker the project is finished.

Steady flow, Level workload	A steady flow or a level workload occurs when the number of ongoing cases in a system is adapted to the capacity of the system. Often requires a queuing mechanism to level out the flow over time and prevent overload. See also *kanban*.
Strategic design	Prepared by the product team, who work continuously to describe the commercial and technical strategic design, which furnishes information that backs up the portfolio team's decisions whether to start selected projects. For example, a strategic design might describe what needs and opportunities there are in the market, which customer segments to focus on, which products should be developed, as well as in what steps, how the products should fit together in terms of technology, components, and architecture, which product variants to offer in which price segments, which projects to start and with what priorities.
Strategic focus	Prepared by the portfolio team. A strategic design shows what business models the enterprise has, in which markets and market segments they should be active, how to position themselves in the market, and what technology to develop and produce themselves.
Strategic product management	The work led by the product team of selecting which products to develop for which customers and then preparing defined projects.
Strategy	A snapshot of the overall goals and plans at that precise moment, based on the current interpretation of existing internal and external information.
Synchronization plan	An overall network plan with the project's subresults, work packages, scheduled handover points, workload, and resource needs. Drawn up jointly by the project team at the start of the project.
Team	A self-organized group that collaborates on a given task, with the group's members having a common understanding that success can only be achieved with the participation of everyone.
Throughput	The number of units that can be completed in a specified time interval, such as how many projects can be completed in one year by a development operation. The throughput of a product development operation depends on the amount of resources available in the form of development staff, test equipment, and spare production capacity. Throughput is limited by bottlenecks.
Uncertainty	The difference between the information one has and what one would need to make the right decision. With many equally probable events, uncertainty increases as the number of possible outcomes increases, so that a process with many possible outcomes has high uncertainty.
Visual flow	When the tasks that are planned, ready to begin, in progress, and accomplished are put in full view of all agents. In production, this makes it possible to see how a product is refined through the processing and assembly of substances and components. In product development, it is possible to see how activities and tasks flow on the pulse boards.

Visual management	A pull system in which patterns emerge from the information that the team has in front of them and help agents understand the system's status. In production, this may be implemented using a visual information carrier such as a kanban. Product development uses pulse boards, on which symbols and summaries condense and visualize information, as well as pulse meetings, where teams use these pulse boards for decisions.
Waste	This term is used in lean practice to refer to the difference between the value-added work and the resources added, that is, losses in the system. See also *productivity*.
Work in progress	The amount of work in terms of the number of articles, products, components, activities, projects, or assignments being processed simultaneously in an operation.
Workshop	A visual working meeting in which a cross-functional team prepares, for an hour or so, information for decisions in an individual case. Visual working methods such as nominal group technique are used.

References

Adams, M. E., Day, G. S. and Dougherty, D. (1998) Enhancing New Product Development Performance: An Organizational Learning Perspective. *Journal of Product Innovation Management*, 15: 403–422. doi: 10.1111/1540-5885.1550403

Alberts, David (2011) *The Agility Advantage: a survival guide for complex enterprises and endeavors.* Washington, DC: CCRP

Archibald, Russell D. (1992) *Managing high-technology programs and projects.* 2. ed. New York: Wiley & Sons

Atkinson, Simon; Moffat, James (2005) *The Agile Organization: From Informal Networks to Complex Effects and Agility.* CCRP. Washington DC

Blomberg, Jesper (2013) *Myter om projekt.* 2. uppl. Lund: Studentlitteratur

Burns, Tom; Stalker, Georg (1994) *The management of innovation.* Oxford Univ. Press. Oxford.

Cagan, Jonathan & Vogel, Craig M. (2002) *Creating breakthrough products: innovation from product planning to program approval.* Upper Saddle River, N.J.: Financial Times/Prentice Hall

Christensen, Clayton M. (1997) *The innovator's dilemma: when new technologies cause great firms to fail.* Boston, Mass.: Harvard Business School

Cusumano, Michael A. & Nobeoka, Kentaro (1998) *Thinking beyond lean: how multi-project management is transforming product development at Toyota and other companies.* New York: Free Press

Czarniawska, Barbara (2005) *En teori om organisering.* Lund: Studentlitteratur

De Maio, A, Verganti, R, & Corso, M (1994) A multi-project management framework for new product development. *European Journal Of Operational Research*, 78, 2, pp. 178-191, Business Source Premier.

Eriksson-Zetterquist, Ulla, Kalling, Thomas & Styhre, Alexander (2006) *Organisation och organisering.* 2. [utök.] uppl. Malmö: Liber

Gleick, James, (1998) *Chaos: making a new science.* Vintage, London

Goldratt, E M. (1997) *Critical Chain.* Aldershot

Gorchels, Linda (2006) *The product manager's handbook.* 3. ed. New York: McGraw-Hill

Grinyer, P, & Norburn, D (1975) Planning for Existing Markets: Perceptions of Executives and Financial Performance. *Journal Of The Royal Statistical Society.* Series A (General), 1, p. 70, JSTOR Arts & Sciences I, EBSCOhost, viewed 8 January 2014

Hendriks, M, Voeten, B, & Kroep, L (1999) Human resource allocation in a multi-project R&D environment. Resource capacity allocation and project portfolio planning in practice. *International Journal Of Project Management*, 17, pp. 181-188

Holman, R. Kaas, H-W. Keeling D. (2003) The future of product development. *McKinsey Quarterly paper,* 2003 number 3, pages 28-39

Ismail, Salim; Malone, Michael S.; van Geest, Yuri & Diamandis, Peter H. (2014) *Exponential organizations: why new organizations are ten times better, faster, and cheaper than yours (and what to do about it).*

Jerbrant, Anna (2009) *Organisering av projektbaserade företag: Ledning, styrning och genomförande av projektbaserad industriell verksamhet.*

Kahn, K (1996) Interdepartmental integration: a definition with implications for product development performance. *Journal Of Product Innovation Management*, 13, 2, pp. 137-151, Inspec, EBSCOhost, viewed 24 June 2015.

Kennedy, Michael N. (2003) *Product development for the lean enterprise: why Toyota's system is four times more productive and how you can implement it.* Richmond, Va.: Oaklea Press

Klofsten, Magnus (2005) Från idé till marknad En diskussion om entreprenörskapets villkor. I: Mats Benner (red). *Innovationer: dynamik och förnyelse i ekonomi och samhällsliv.* Lund: Studentlitteratur

McDonough III, E, & Spital, F (2003) Managing project portfolios. *Research Technology Management*, 46, 3, p. 40, Business Source Premier.

McKenna, Regis (1991) *Relationship marketing: successful strategies for the age of the customer*. Reading, Mass.: Addison-Wesley

McManus, H. Haggerty A. Murman E. (2005) *Lean Engineering: Doing the Right Thing Right.* CEIAT, Queen´s University Belfast.

Millard, Richard L. (2001) *Value Stream Analysis and Mapping for Product Development.* MIT Lean Aerospace Initiativ Master Thesis.

Mitchell, Melanie (2009) *Complexity: a guided tour.* Oxford: Oxford University Press

Moore, Geoffrey A. (1998) *Inside the tornado: marketing strategies from Silicon Valley's cutting edge*. Oxford: Capstone

Ohno, Taiichi (1988) *Toyota production system: Beyond large-scale production*. Productivity Press. Cambridge.

Ostrom, Elinor (2009) *Allmänningen som samhällsinstitution.* Arkiv moderna klassiker. Lund.

Packendorff, J (1993) *Projektorganisation och projektorganisering: Projektet som plan och temporär organisation*, n.p.: Umeå : Handelshögsk. i Umeå, Inst för företagsekonomi, Umeå univ., 1993 (Umeå : Solfjädern).

Phelps, Edmund S. (2015) *What Is Wrong with the West's Economies?* The New York Review of Books. AUGUST 13, 2015 • VOLUME 62, NUMBER 13.

PMBOK guide (2004) *A guide to the project management body of knowledge*. Project Management Institute.

Prokopenko, M, Boschetti, F, & Ryan, A (2009) An information-theoretic primer on complexity, self-organization, and emergence. *Complexity*, 15, 1, p. 11, Publisher Provided Full Text Searching File, EBSCOhost, viewed 29 January 2014.

Rubinstein, Moshe F. & Firstenberg, Iris R. (1999) *The minding organization: bring the future to the present and turn creative ideas into business solutions.* New York: Wiley

Simon, Herbert (1997) *Administrative behavior: a study of decision-making processes in administrative organisations.* Free Press. New York.

Sjöö, Karolin (2014) *Innovation and transformation in the Swedish manufacturing sector*, 1970-2007. Diss. Lund : Lunds universitet, 2014

Smith, P. Reinertsen, D. (1998) *Developing products in half the time: new rules, new tools.* Wiley.

Stacey, Ralph D. (2007) *Strategic management and organisational dynamics: the challenge of complexity to ways of thinking about organisations.* 5. ed. Harlow: Financial Times

Stjernberg, Torbjörn (1993) *Organisationsideal livskraft och spridning: dialog, humanitet, inflytande, konkurrens, livskvalitet, produktivitet, samarbete – ett 20-årigt perspektiv.* Norstedts juridik. Stockholm.

Södergren, Birgitta (2005) Om lärandets roll i komplexa innovationssystem. I: Mats Benner (red). *Innovationer: dynamik och förnyelse i ekonomi och samhällsliv.* Lund: Studentlitteratur

Takeuchi, Hirotaka; Nonaka, Ikujiro (1986) The New New Product Development Game. *Harvard Business Review*, Jan-Feb 1986.

Teresko, J (2006) Learning From Toyota-Again. *Industry Week/IW*, 255, 2, pp. 34-41, Business Source Premier.

Thietart, Raymond-Alain & Forgues, Bérnard (2011) Complexity Science and Organization. *The SAGE handbook of complexity and management.* London: SAGE.

Thomke, S, & Fujimoto, T (2000) The Effect of "Front-Loading" Problem-Solving on Product Development Performance. *Journal Of Product Innovation Management*, 17, 2, pp. 128-142, Business Source Premier.

Thompson, James D. (1967) *Organizations in action: social science bases of administrative theory.* New York: Mc Graw-Hill

Ulrich, Karl T. & Eppinger, Steven D. (2004) *Product design and development.* 3. ed. Boston: McGraw-Hill

Wallander, Jan (2003) *Decentralisation - why and how to make it work: the Handelsbanken way.* 1. ed. Stockholm: SNS förl.

Wheelwright, Steven C. & Clark, Kim B. (1992) *Revolutionizing product development: quantum leaps in speed, efficiency and quality.* New York: Free Press

Womack, James P., Jones, Daniel T. & Roos, Daniel (1991) *The machine that changed the world: the story of lean production.* New York: HarperPerennial

Woodward, Joan (1980) *Industrial organization: theory and practice.* 2. ed. Oxford: Oxford U.P.

Zika-Viktorsson, A, Sundström, P, & Engwall, M (2006) Project overload: An exploratory study of work and management in multi-project settings. *International Journal Of Project Management*, 24, pp. 385-394.

68594629R00144

Made in the USA
Lexington, KY
14 October 2017